MAKE IT COUNT

MAKE IT COUNT

My Fight to Become the First Transgender Olympic Runner

CECÉ TELFER

GRAND
CENTRAL

NEW YORK BOSTON

Grand Central Publishing
Hachette Book Group
1290 Avenue of the Americas, New York, NY 10104
grandcentralpublishing.com
@grandcentralpub

First edition: June 2024

Grand Central Publishing is a division of Hachette Book Group, Inc. The Grand Central Publishing name and logo is a registered trademark of Hachette Book Group, Inc.

The publisher is not responsible for websites (or their content) that are not owned by the publisher.

Some names and identifying characteristics have been changed.

Grand Central Publishing books may be purchased in bulk for business, educational, or promotional use. For information, please contact your local bookseller or the Hachette Book Group Special Markets Department at special.markets@hbgusa.com.

Print book interior design by Marie Mundaca

Library of Congress Control Number: 2024930624

ISBNs: 9781538756249 (hardcover), 9781538756263 (ebook)

Printed in Canada

MRQ

Printing 1, 2024

For Cecelia

2019

I stare at the ceiling, unable to fall asleep. My pulse pounds. The race is tomorrow. I close my eyes. Visualize the track. The starting blocks. The hurdles ahead. I hear the blast of the gun. I see myself flying down my lane. My body moves with precision, just like I've been trained. *Execute, execute, execute.* That one word repeats in my mind. *Execute, execute, execute.* I wish I could quiet my thoughts; I wish I could drift off. I wish the adrenaline would stop coursing through my system. But the scene repeats, the word repeats. *Execute, execute, execute.* I take a breath. Try to calm myself. Say a prayer of gratitude. I'm so thankful to be here, in this hotel, on the night before the 2019 National NCAA Outdoor Track & Field Championships. I'm so grateful for the opportunity to stand up in front of the entire country and compete as my authentic self, the female athlete that I am.

It feels like I've been fighting my whole life to get to this moment.

Where did the battle begin? Maybe it started when I was a child, a young girl in Jamaica, longing for a love my mother refused to supply, all because she couldn't see me as her daughter, she couldn't embrace the fullness of my being. Maybe it started on the red clay of the dirt tracks in my homeland, when I first felt that passion for running, when I understood that this was my calling. Maybe it started when I was first forced to run on the boys' track team, even though I was a girl. Maybe it started the day I realized that there were small, petty people out there who hated me, simply because I had the courage to love myself.

But regardless of its beginnings, the battle continued in the months and weeks leading up to this competition. I'm at the center of a controversy I never asked for. I am a Black trans female athlete who refuses to hide who she is, who dares to fight for greatness, to stand strong in her power and say yes, I deserve the dream that burns so strong in my body, mind, and heart. But because of this, I've had to face unbelievable obstacles. This year—after the intense pain of being forced to run with male athletes all my life—I finally got to compete with the females for the first time. I've never felt happier—I am no longer hiding; I am free to be my authentic self in the sport that I love.

Yet I've also never felt more vulnerable, or more afraid for my safety.

Parents have circulated a petition to have me banned from the NCAA. People shoot me dirty looks at every competition. Yell slurs. Boo me from the stands. I've deleted my social media accounts—I can't look at the steady stream of hate and threats. The biggest threat came from President Donald Trump himself. And his son. They've both tweeted about me. Tweets I refuse to read. My coaches and teammates are deeply concerned. The NCAA has hired extra security to ensure my safety at this competition. I flew into Texas for the championships two days later than the rest of the athletes, into a different airport, hours away from our hotel, all to ensure that no one would be waiting at the airport to attack me. A part of me is grateful for the concern, grateful that my supporters are taking extra precautions. But another part of me is resentful of all the additional hoops I've been forced to jump through to get here, angry that I have to deal with so much that no other female athlete at this competition is forced to endure.

But you know what I call that anger?

Fuel.

That night in my hotel room, I barely sleep. But it doesn't matter. Adrenaline takes over in the morning. I'm in competition mode. My coaches knock on my door. They say it's time for breakfast. I ask if they can bring me some oatmeal and green tea—the only things I want on the morning of a competition. They bring breakfast to my room, and I start getting ready.

My ritual begins. I put on my headphones. Start playing Fall Out Boy. I play the same song before every competition: "My Songs Know What You Did in the Dark." I sit in front of the mirror. The music gets my heart racing, the driving guitar, the repetition of the lyrics. *Light 'em up, up, up. Light 'em up, up, up. I'm on fire.*

First, it's makeup. I beat my face. *Look good, feel good, run fast, win championships.* That's my mantra. I've got a fresh set of nails. They're stiletto sharp. Claws. I finish with my face. Then, the final step. Lashes. I put them on. I look in the mirror. Face—beat. Nails—fresh set. Lashes—on. And there she is: CeCé Telfer. A champion.

I always use percentages to take stock of how my body feels before I compete. Right now, I'm eighty percent ready to dominate my event.

I leave my hotel room. Eighty-five percent.

I meet my coaches in the lobby. Ninety percent.

We walk to the Javelina Stadium. Enter the massive arena. Bleachers rise on either side of the field. People crowd the stands. The red track encircles a bright green field. We make our way to the warm-up area. I can feel the dirty looks aimed my way. I can hear the whispers. I know some people are talking trash. My heart beats faster. I feel my anger rise. I try to keep my temper in check. I feel the impulse to cuss them out, to tell them to mind their business, that they don't know my life, they don't know all the shit I've gone through to get to this stadium today. But I don't. I take a breath. Regain my focus. And convert my anger to fuel.

I'm at ninety-five percent.

It's time for my warm-up. I hit the field. Get my body moving. I feel high on adrenaline. Soaring. I'm surrounded by elite athletes, Olympic hopefuls. And I'm one of them. My pulse races. I sprint over a few hurdles. Just to get the jitters out. To feel my speed coming out of the blocks. My coach watches. He tells me I look good. His only advice: *Come out of the blocks hard.*

Ninety-eight percent.

I go to the tents where the athletes wait for their events. I look to the stands. I see all my supporters in the bleachers, my coaches, my teammates, the athletic director from my school, her two young sons. They're in the stands right above the final 100-meter stretch of the race. They're there to cheer me on as I push to the finish line. I can see the love in their eyes. And that makes me feel grateful, supported, centered. Other people may hate me, but they don't matter. What matters is this chosen family, and the fact that they see me for exactly who I am. I know, in this moment, I am right where I need to be. Right where I deserve to be.

I wish my mother was here. I wish she could see this moment; I wish she could see all that her daughter has achieved, I wish she would invest in me, dream my dream with me. But she never has. Which is why I didn't tell her about today. We aren't speaking. I knew she wouldn't come. There's too much history and hurt between us.

But I can't think about this now. I push my mother from my mind. It's time for the 400-meter hurdles. My event.

I walk to my lane. My hair is slicked back. I'm looking fierce. Feeling fierce.

I'm at one hundred percent.

I walk to lane five. My lane. There's a big yellow block. I stand and wait. Some of the girls are doing attempts over hurdles. To pump themselves up. But I'm not wasting my energy. I don't need to. My warm-ups went well. All I have to do now is stay focused.

Runners to your marks!

I'm in the blocks.

Get set!

I've been training my whole life for this exact moment. I breathe out. Let the nerves go.

Boom! The gun goes off. I'm gone. Out of the blocks. Hard. I'm in warrior mode. Hyperfocused. The only thing on my mind is the finish line. My spikes fly over the track. I say a prayer. *God, please help me through this race. Without shedding blood. God, please protect me from all the danger of this day and night. Please help me finish this race, Lord.*

I pass all the girls in the first hundred meters.

But I still have three hundred meters to go. I tell myself to keep pushing. *You got out of the blocks hard. Keep riding that hardness. You know how to run the race, so run your fucking race. Don't let these girls catch you.*

I know I have to give it my all in the last two hundred meters. But that's what everyone does. So I go harder, earlier. I book it in the last two hundred fifty. Going around the last curve. I'm eating up the track. I'm coming up on hurdle seven. I'm in the lead. Hurdle eight. I'm carrying the race. I'm lifting my legs. *Just lift, lift, lift. Keep going, girl.*

I'm over hurdle nine.

I stumble.

But there's no time to panic. I can't feel my legs. But I'm okay. I don't fall. I stay focused. Get it together. Correct my form. There's only one more hurdle to go. I push harder. *Just keep going*, I tell myself. *The finish line is right there, girl. And if you don't cross that finish line dying, then you did not run that race.*

I leap over the last hurdle.

I cross the finish line.

And I win. I win an NCAA National Championship in the 400-meter hurdles.

The first time for a woman like me.

The joy I feel is immense. All my supporters scream from the stands. I did what my coach asked of me. I made my teammates proud, my school proud. And I made myself proud. Ever since I was a child, I knew that I was meant to be an elite athlete. I've been working my whole life for this one glorious moment. And now it's here. Confirmation that I've been on the right path this whole time. That this is what I was born to do. That this is what I will keep doing, until I have that Olympic gold medal in my hands.

You did it kid, my coach says to me later that day. *Let's go all the way to the top.* He means the Olympics. It's the natural next step. My time today has qualified me for Olympic Trials. Any female athlete in my position should be on a rocket ship toward Team USA. That's what I want. That's the next dream. It's just within reach. So close I can feel it.

But at this moment, I didn't know all that would unfold in the coming weeks, months, and years. I never imagined the forces that would try to stop me from realizing the one dream I've had ever since I was a young girl. I never imagined the fight to get a coach would be so hard, that multiple coaches would take me on, seeing my incredible potential, only to drop me when they learned my story because they worried that taking on such a "controversial" athlete would end their careers. I never imagined that because I am a transgender woman, World Athletics, the international governing body for track and field, would place what seemed to me to be so many roadblocks in my path as I attempted to qualify for the Olympics. I never imagined how they would invade my privacy, police my body, and subject me to treatment no other female athlete is forced to endure. I never imagined that after all my efforts to comply with World Athletics regulations for trans athletes, that they would bar transgender women from competing in international competition.

I never imagined that I would be banned from the Olympics.

But here's the thing. I'm not done fighting. The battle continues. I don't deserve this discrimination. I deserve a chance to compete on that world stage, just like any other female athlete. So, I will continue to run. I refuse to let them rob me of my joy. I refuse to let them take away my passion. I will fight this decision with everything I've got.

But it is not easy. Some days I want to give up. Some days it's hard to feel hope. Some days it feels like every time I take a step forward, there is always someone waiting to spew hate or threaten my rights. Some days it feels like I'm running on the edge of a knife, and the harder I push, the deeper the blade sinks into my skin, but I keep going, I have no choice, because at the end of my path lies what I've dreamed of for so long and so hard that I can feel it in every inch of my body. It's a dream I want not only for myself, but for the generations of trans and non-binary people who will come after me. I'm doing this to remind them that no matter what prejudice you may face, no one can stop you from living your truth. The road won't always be easy—in fact, it may be very difficult, incredibly painful—but it will be worth it. Because there *will* be people who love you for exactly who you are. And that love is more powerful than any hatred. Especially when that hatred comes from people who claim to be Christian but seem to forget the Bible verse that says "God is love. Whoever lives in love lives in God."

I'm fighting for love. It's love that fuels my survival. It's love that helps me push forward, even when I want to give up. It's love that got me to that NCAA Championship in 2019; it's love that led me to the most glorious moment of my career, when the crowd roared and a profound joy surged within me. And it's love that has gotten me through every moment since, no matter how many obstacles I face. I feel love for the world around me, for all my fellow humans, but especially for anyone who's ever felt alone or othered. Because I know what that feels like. I know what it feels like to be excluded, to be pushed to the side, to have people refuse to recognize your humanity. I've been in headlines across the United States and across the world, I've been named personally in anti-trans legislation, I've been honored by top LGBTQ organizations, I've been painted as a hero, as a villain, as a symbol, as a representative for an issue that has taken center stage in the culture wars. But when people are busy turning you into a symbol, they forget what you really are: a human being. A person with needs and desires, fears and hopes just like everyone else. At the end of the day, I'm just a girl with a dream. A girl with so much love in her heart.

And all I want, all I've ever wanted, is the freedom to run.

CHAPTER ONE

I'm six years old and I'm running, playing under the black mango tree in our lane. I dodge and weave, chasing my friends. Fruit hangs in heavy clusters above us. It's funny—black mangoes aren't black, they're purple. A deep violet, the color of a bruise. The fruit is ripe, dangerously ripe, it could fall at any minute, and hit us on the head. We're not supposed to play under the tree when it's mango season, but we do anyway. Sometimes I pick the fruit from the ground, bust the skin open with my fingers, and dig out the delicious meat inside.

I hear my auntie call my name. I know it's time to go. We're taking a trip today, but she won't tell me where. It's a secret. A surprise. But I trust her. Auntie Peaches loves me so much. But she's also one of those aunties you don't mess with. Her name is sweet, but she can be plenty sour if she needs to be. When she calls, you answer.

I break into a sprint. Run down the thin gravel road. Past the large houses that line the street, home to wealthy plantation families, with acres of farmland behind their properties. The lane is bursting with lush vegetation, and an endless variety of fruit trees; there's broad-leafed trees heavy with breadfruit, trees with bunches of glistening red cherries, trees boasting heavy bounties of guineps, or pineapples, or guavas. There's so much life, so much abundance, no matter where you turn.

I keep running. My feet pound the gravel.

And then I see it—one of my favorite places in all of Jamaica.

The house at the end of the lane.

The house is huge, one story, it seems like it stretches on forever. It's bright and beautiful, painted mint green. The pitched roof is framed on either side by mango trees, East Indian mangoes, and the fruit is big and hairy and so, so juicy. They're the most expensive mangoes if you buy them in the store, but we never do, because they grow right in our yard.

The house belongs to my grandfather. Or it did. Before he died. I feel an ache in my heart when I think of him. How much I miss him. It seems impossible that he's gone. Just yesterday I got to hold his hand.

I wish my mother was here. I wish she could hug me, comfort me. But she's gone. Gone to Canada. She's always flying there. For work. Usually she's gone for about six months. Sometimes longer. I'm not quite sure what her job is. I think she takes care of other people. People who are dying. I think she's like a nurse. She's working in Canada so she can send money back home, so we can have a better life here. But I miss her so much when she's gone. I wish she would just stay here with us, in St. Thomas, forever. Thankfully, I feel so loved by the rest of my family. It makes missing her hurt less.

The house at the end of the lane is a three-family home, but our one big extended family is the only family living here. Auntie Peaches lives there. Auntie Bella too. And all their kids— my cousins. When my mom is in Jamaica, she also lives with us here. Sometimes as many as fourteen people stay there at once. Family comes and goes, we all share rooms, and if we run out of space, we set up a cot in the living room. It's a bustling house, brimming with life. My sister and I love staying here, especially when our mother is here with us.

I run up to the driveway, where Auntie Peaches waits by the car. I hop in the front seat. She still won't tell me where we're going. *It's a secret*, she says, as the engine revs.

We pull out onto the lane. Gravel pops under the wheels of our tires and makes for a bumpy ride. I feel excited, but nervous too. I wish Auntie Peaches would tell me where we're going. We turn off the lane, and onto the main road. The ride is smoother now. The car speeds faster. So does my heart. We drive and drive. I peer out the window. See a giant parking lot. Beyond, a runway filled with planes. The airport. We're driving to the airport.

We make another turn. Approach a terminal. And there in the distance, I see her, the woman I've missed so much, the person I love more than anyone else on earth: my mother. She's home early. This is the best surprise. She's not supposed to be back yet. She waves at me. A big grin spreads across her face. I love her dimples because I have dimples too. I can see the gap between her front teeth. It's just like mine. We have matching smiles. She looks so beautiful standing there, with her strong, muscular body and long flowing dreads.

We pull into a parking space. I fling my door open. Rush toward her. She sweeps me into a warm embrace. Showers me with kisses. I feel so happy to have her home. So relieved. She's my safe place; nothing can hurt me when I'm in her arms. When we're together, there's no stronger force than our love.

Did you miss me, she asks.

Every day, I reply.

You happy to have me back?

So happy, I say. *But why are you back so early?* I look up at her. A sadness fills her eyes. I notice that they're red. Bloodshot. She's been crying. Suddenly, I know the answer to my question. I know why my mother rushed back to Jamaica, back to the bright green house at the end of the lane. It all makes sense now. She rushed back because her father is dead.

* * *

11

There's someone outside our bedroom.

Someone in our house. An intruder.

It's late at night. Pitch-black. I'm too afraid to speak. Too afraid to move.

But I have to pee. I try to hold it, but I can't. So I get up.

There are two beds in our room. My mother is asleep in the one next to mine. I walk softly, not wanting to wake her. I walk to the door. My heart is pounding. It feels like a bomb. Like it might explode.

I open the door.

He's standing right there. My grandpa.

Just earlier today, we went to the funeral, and I saw his casket, I saw him lying down in it. His eyes were closed. Peaceful. At rest.

But now he's standing in front of me. Looking at me. Not saying anything. I want to scream, but I can't. I can't speak. I can barely breathe. I'm so afraid. I'm stuck right there. Frozen. My legs won't move.

He doesn't say anything. He just stands there, in silhouette. I realize how much I miss him. I loved him so much. The whole lane loved him. He was my grandfather, but he acted like everyone else's grandfather too. He took care of everybody on the lane. Kids who didn't live in our house, their parents. Even the homeless people. He'd bring them small presents, or food, or whatever else someone might need. To my grandfather, everyone was family. And for this reason, the whole lane misses him. The whole community feels like they've lost a grandfather.

But despite my fond memories, his spirit still scares me. Standing right there in front of me. I wish I could make out his face, see his expression. But it's hidden in darkness.

I turn and run. I shake my mother, beg her to wake up.

Mom! Mom! Wake up. Grandpa's here.

What? She rubs her eyes.

Grandpa's right outside the door.

Go back to sleep, baby.

My mother doesn't believe me. Doesn't see Grandpa. But he's here. I can see him. I beg to sleep in my mom's bed. *You're too old for that*, she says, grumpy. But I keep begging. Finally she sighs and says yes, I can sleep next to her. I climb in bed, feel the warmth of her body. She squeezes me tight. She drifts to sleep. I love being in my mother's arms. I feel like I'm home. I feel safe. But even still, I can't sleep.

Because my grandfather is still here. Standing in the doorway. I hope he's watching over us. I hope he's here because he loves us. I wish he was still alive, still a part of our family.

Thank God I have my mom. I nestle deeper into her arms and pray she'll protect me.

Not just tonight, but for my whole life.

Everyone has chicken pox. Every kid in the house at the end of the lane spends their days scratching. My skin is on fire. It itches so bad. I can't stand it. I start whining, crying. My older sister is babysitting. She says we'll take a bath to make the itching go away. She sends my cousins out to pick leaves from the Neem trees on our lane. They return with big green bunches. She lets me hold a few leaves. They're coarse in my hands.

My sister brings out all the pots we have and fills them with water and puts them on the stove. When they start to boil, she puts in the leaves. Then she carries the big pots of water to the bathtub and pours them in. The bathroom fills with steam. It's warm and nice.

My sister lifts me into the tub. She tells me to stay in the water until the itching stops. But the water is too hot, almost scalding. It's searing my skin. I want to cry. But then, it starts to work. Before, I wanted to peel off my skin, to live in another body—that's how bad the itching was. But now, I feel comfortable in my own skin. I take a breath, relieved.

Then, the bath is over. My sister dries me off with a towel and wraps it around me.

Okay, get out of here, and get dressed. My sister shoos me away. *Now it's my turn.* She drains the tub and turns on the shower. I start to walk out of the bathroom but look over my shoulder and steal a glance at my sister as she steps under the spray.

Her body is beautiful. She looks just like my mother. I feel so happy. I know I'm going to grow up and bloom into my beauty and look like my sister, like my mother.

Because I'm a girl, just like them.

Mom is cooking today. No school, it's Sunday. She wakes me up and tells me to get dressed because I'm going to the market. We need coconut. *No time to waste,* my mom says to me. She's going to be cooking all day. And I'm going to help her. She wants to start at 9:00 a.m., so we can have a meal ready by lunch.

We need more rice too, Terrence calls out from the next room.

Okay, Terrence, I call back.

How many times do I have to tell you, my mother scolds me. *He's your father now. You're his son. Call him dad.*

Okay, Dad, I say, wanting to please my mother. I want to love Terrence as much as I love my mother. But I'm not sure I can. I'm not sure I trust him.

Me and my mother live with Terrence now. At his house. My sister has a different father than me, and she went to live with him, though she visits us frequently. Terrence lives on a quiet street, at the bottom of a hill. The house is one story, with beige siding and a flat concrete roof. There's a mango tree in the yard that I love to climb. I scurry all the way up the trunk, then hop onto the roof. I always have to be quick, because there are so many lizards hiding in the branches. And I *hate* lizards. It's so much fun to play on the roof—even though I'm not supposed to. Terrence doesn't want me up there, says it's not safe. I love the view; I eat mangoes that fall onto the roof and look out over the whole neighborhood. I have fun here, but I do miss St. Thomas and the house at the end of the lane.

But Mom wants to live here now, with Terrence, so I don't have a choice.

I call him Terrence because I don't want to call him Dad. I don't know who my dad is, but I don't really care. He's never been around. I don't miss him, because how can you miss someone who's never been there? All I need is my mom. I don't need a dad.

But my mom thinks I do. That's why we're living with Terrence now. She says I need a father figure. Someone to teach me to be a man. Which is confusing to me. I'm a girl, so how could I grow up to be a man? How could I grow up to be something I'm not? But I don't ask my mom these questions, because I'm worried they'll make her angry. She's more irritable these days, quick to criticize me if I do anything feminine. I don't think she likes that I'm a girl. She's always buying me big, baggy boy clothes. Sometimes, when people call the house and I answer the phone, they hear my voice but think it's her talking. She says I need to sound more like a boy, act more like a boy, dress more like a boy. But I'm *not* a boy. Still, I'm scared to go against what my mom says. So I wear the clothes she gets me. I try to act more like a boy, even though I'm a girl. I try so hard to please her, try to correct my behavior, even though it's so confusing, so upsetting—and sometimes it pisses me off so much. But even still, I do what she asks.

I say goodbye to Mom and Terrence and run out of the house. I bolt past the church in our neighborhood. It's Sunday, so cars are parked everywhere. The street is packed with people dressed in their finest church clothes. It's funny—even though Terrence lives so close to a church, he's definitely not a Christian. It's a big joke around here, *the Rastafarian that lives in the same neighborhood as the church.* But they coexist peacefully. Sometimes, when the church parking lot is empty on a Saturday, Terrence will set up two goals and play football with the neighborhood men and their sons. My mom is always pressuring me to join their game, but I don't like being with the men. I always feel out of place when I'm with them. Like I don't belong. The jokes they make, the macho culture, I just don't fit in.

I'm too pretty, too polite, too dainty. I can see other men talk to Terrence. I know they're talking about me. I know they don't approve of my feminine ways. I can feel that Terrence is embarrassed. He wants me to act differently, present myself differently. He has long dreadlocks, and he wants me to grow mine out too. Mom thinks it's a good idea. We can be a big happy Rastafarian family, with everybody in dreads.

Except I started going to church. Which Terrence didn't like. He called me a fake Rastafarian once. But I don't think I was ever a Rastafarian, so I don't know how I could be a fake one. I just like going to the church and hanging out with the kids in the youth group. I go every Friday night. After we're done, we go to the plaza and get chicken and chips at Rouney's. It's the one time I can eat meat, because all Mom cooks at home is vegetarian food, because Terrence is vegetarian, and she's cooking to make him happy. I like vegetarian food too because my mom makes it and she's a great cook. But *chicken*. And *fries*. Heaven. There's nothing better.

Except for my mom's rice and peas. That's what she's making today.

I run down the street. Some neighborhood boy yells at me as I pass. *That boy runs like a girl, that boy a battyman.* My heart beats faster. I'm terrified. If you're a *battyman*, you can get beat up. You can get killed. It happens all the time here. That's what my mother says. But she also says that those men are asking for it, because they're going against God's natural plan for our bodies. *Battyman*, the boy yells again. He runs after me, but I'm too fast for him. I leave him in a cloud of kicked-up dust.

People call me *battyman* all the time, make fun of the way I walk and talk and run. My mom worries about me; she doesn't like what people say. Even her friends and cousins and sisters worry about me, say that I'm too feminine. She always defends me, but sometimes it seems like she actually believes what people say. That I'm a sissy, a *battyman*. Sometimes she looks at me like she's not sure if she might hate her own child. She'll snap at me, and tell me to fix the way I stand, or walk, or talk, or move my hands. It feels awful when she's angry with me. I feel like I'll never be what she wants me to be. But even when she's being aggressive, I know it's just because she wants to protect me from other people. I try so hard to do what she tells me. Because at the end of the day, I just want her to love me like I love her.

But I don't have time to worry about all that. I run to the shops. I grab a bunch of coconuts, a bag of rice, and head straight to the cash register. I want to get back quickly, so we can get everything ready in time.

I hurry home. Find my mom in the kitchen. She pulls out the grater, a big bowl, and a cloth. *Hand me the coconuts*, she says. She takes each coconut and smashes it open with a small hammer. *Start peeling*. I take shards of coconut and peel off the skin, so I've just got the white meat in my hands. I sneak a small bite. I love coconut so much, even the raw bits. My mom smiles. I know what to do. I take the coconut meat and grind it against the metal grater. I grate and grate until my arm is sore. I always hate this part, but I know it's what we have to do to make the milk. I keep working until there's a big pile of white coconut on the counter. I put it in a big bowl. My mom boils some water and pours it over the meat. We let it sit. I'm excited. Coconut milk is incredible, one of the most wonderful foods. It can make any dish taste amazing, but I also love drinking it raw. Once the meat has soaked for long enough, we pour it into a strainer, so we can get rid of all the coconut bits and just have the milk.

You want a little spoonful? she asks.

I smile and nod. She feeds me a mouthful of the milk. It's still warm. Creamy and sweet. It's beautiful and delicate and I could drink the whole bowl. It tastes like love.

My mom hands me the bowl with the discarded coconut shreds. *You want a little coconut in a bowl?* I nod my head. *You want me to put brown sugar on top?* I nod again. This is one of my favorite treats. Coconut shavings with brown sugar. I snack on the coconut as she starts making rice and peas. *Pay attention now*, she says. *You need to learn how to make this.* My mom opens the bag of rice, pours it into a pot. *Can you grate some ginger for me?*

Back to the grater. But I don't mind. Because I'm helping Mom. Together, we're making a meal. A silence settles between us, but even though we're not talking, we're still communicating. The act of cooking is all we need to connect us. I take a deep breath and inhale the smell of fresh ginger and smile. I could stay in this kitchen forever, cooking with my mom.

I'm going back to Canada tomorrow, she says.

It's so sudden. No advanced notice. I don't want her to leave.

I feel a pain in my chest. I fight back tears as I peel ginger.

I pray that she changes her mind.

But she doesn't. She's gone again. It's just me and Terrence at the house. The next morning, he tells me that I need to pack a bag. *You're going to stay with Auntie Peaches*, he says. *She'll take care of you while your mom is away.*

We drive in silence. I'm not sure if I like Terrence or not. He's nice to me. Sometimes. He doesn't have any kids, and Mom says he wants to have kids, she says they're trying to give me a little baby brother or sister, but for now Terrence can have me as his child.

We arrive in St. Thomas and the house at the end of the lane. I miss it, so I'm happy to see it again. We park outside, and Auntie Peaches comes to the door. I run up to her and Terrence follows. *Thanks for watching him*, he says, handing her a fistful of cash.

Auntie Peaches doesn't say anything, just nods, and gives him this look. A tough Auntie Peaches look, the kind you never want aimed at you. *You just behave yourself*, she says as Terrence gets back in his car.

He slams the door shut. Starts the engine.

There are some things I don't tell Auntie Peaches. Things about Terrence that would make her angry. But by the way she's frowning at that car as it rolls down the lane, I can tell that she also suspects what I suspect: he sees other women when my mother is away.

Soon, the car is gone. We don't see Terrence again for two weeks.

Screaming. Crying. I jolt awake. It's my mother. She's yelling at Terrence. He roars back. Another fight. It's the same, every time my mom comes back from Canada. They've been locked in their bedroom since my mom came home. It's late, past my bedtime. It's always bad when my mother comes back from Canada, but it's never been as bad as it is tonight. I've never heard anyone scream like this before.

Crack. It sounds like a thunderbolt, but I know it's not. I think it's the sound of Terrence hitting my mother. I make a small cry, but I'm too afraid to make a louder sound. I want to do something; I want to defend my mother. But I'm afraid of what will happen if I try. I'm afraid Terrence will hurt me. I'm paralyzed with fear.

Crack. Another thunderbolt. Then, loud footsteps. Speeding down the hallway. They're fast and heavy. Terrence is screaming, my mother is screaming back.

I tiptoe to my door. Open it. I think I see him pushing my mother down the hall, out the door, and into the night. *If you don't like the way I run my house, then you can leave,* he yells and slams the door shut. Locks it. My mother pounds, but it seems to me like he won't open it for her. He turns around. I shut my door, praying he didn't see me watching. I listen to his footsteps. They slow down outside my door. I run to bed. Dive under the covers. Pretend to be asleep. He keeps walking, doesn't look inside.

I lie in bed. Terrified for my mother. She's locked outside. It's freezing cold at night. What's she going to do? She was wearing her pajamas. No shoes. I look at the clock. It's four in the morning. The sun will be up soon. But right now, it's dark, it's cold, and my mother is locked outside.

I don't know what to do. I'm afraid to leave my room. I'm afraid

Terrence will catch me. Yell at me. Hurt me. I stay under the covers, too scared to move.

And then there's a sound.

A soft knocking. I peer from under the covers. My mother is at the window. Knocking on the glass. Her face is wet with tears. I tiptoe to the window, open it for her. A cold gust of air rushes inside. I shiver. *Mom, are you okay?*

I just need a blanket. Or a towel. Something to keep me warm until morning.

I run back to the bed, rip off the blanket, and run back to the window. But right as I'm about to hand her the quilt, my door opens.

It's Terrence.

Stop, he yells. *Don't you dare. Don't you open* my *window, in* my *house, and hand her* my *blanket. Don't give that woman shit.*

I step away from the window. My mother does the same. I want to cry; I want to scream at him. But I just repress it. Swallow the anger like it's poison. I feel sick. I feel furious. My mom has been begging me to call Terrence "dad." But now I know I never will. That man isn't my father.

CHAPTER TWO

Today a teacher is coming into our classroom to teach us about sex. All the other kids in my fourth-grade class are giggling and laughing and making jokes. But I'm not. I'm excited, I have so many questions I want answered but I'm too afraid to ask my mom. I want to know about boys and girls. About the differences. Maybe I'll finally figure out why everyone calls me a boy, even though I know I'm a girl and I'm going to grow up to be a woman like my sister and my aunties and my mother. But if I learn all the differences between boys and girls, then I'll finally be able to explain why everyone else is wrong.

The teacher steps in front of our class. She starts talking about how girls have eggs. Boys have sperm. I'm riveted, I'm fixated. I'm determined to remember every single detail. Finally, I'll be able to understand the truth about myself, about my body, and all my confusion will come to an end.

She tells us that all girls get their period. That's when a girl becomes a woman.

And I know, from that moment, that I will get my period. Because I'm a girl. I'll get my period and that will be proof to my mother and sister and aunties and Terrence and everyone else that

21

I'm a girl. I'll get my period and all the wondering and waiting and strange stares and bullying will come to an end. I feel relieved. I feel such incredible joy. I want to run and tell everyone I know. *I'm going to get my period.* My mother won't have to defend me anymore, won't have to tell her friends and sisters that I'm not a *battyman.* She won't have to buy me baggy clothes, trying to hide my feminine curves. She'll let me wear dresses and makeup and I'll be free to be exactly who I am. She'll love me for who I am. A girl.

I'm going to get my period.

This is the answer. Praise God. I can barely sit through the rest of the school day. My classes are a blur. My heart is beating so hard it feels like it might break my rib cage.

The bell rings. I run out of class. Run down the halls. Push through the swarm of students. Burst out of the doors and into the courtyard.

My mother is waiting.

I rush into her arms. She gives me a hug. The courtyard is crowded with other kids and their parents, but for a moment it feels like it's just me and my mother. There's no one else in the world. Because we don't need anyone else. We have each other. We love each other. And she'll love me more than ever when I finally tell her the truth about me.

Momma? I break from our hug and look up at her.

She pats my head. *What is it, my baby boy?*

We had sex education today.

Oh yes, that's right. She seems distracted. Like something else is on her mind. Like something is worrying her.

I tug on her skirt to make sure she's paying attention. *I want to tell you what I learned.*

Okay, she says.

I learned that I'm going to get my period.

In my mind, what happens next happens so quickly I can hardly believe it: Did my own mother just slap me across the face?

I'm so shocked, I almost forget to cry. But then the pain comes rushing in. The tears follow. I'm crying and my mother is screaming at me. *What the fuck?* she yells. The courtyard quiets. Everyone is looking at us. My classmates and their parents too. I feel so ashamed. *Where the fuck did you get that? Only girls get their period. You're a boy. Don't you ever tell me that shit again.*

She grabs my hand and yanks me toward the car. I'm crying so hard I can barely see. I can barely catch my breath. She pushes me into the front seat. Slams the door. Gets into the driver's side. Starts the engine. I'm so confused. I know that I'm a girl, I know this is who I am. So why can't my mother see that? Why can't my mother love me? A feeling grows in the pit of my stomach. A realization. I know I can never talk to my mother about this again. I know I'll have to hide my feminine side forever. I know she will never accept me. And if my mother won't accept me, then how can I ever hope that the rest of the world will? I'll be alone. I'll have to live a double life. I'll have to keep the truest part of me hidden. I'm already trying to hide it in the car, right now. I cover my body with my arms. Crouch down in my seat. Try to make myself so small I disappear. But I can't disappear.

We ride in silence.

Then, my mother opens her mouth and speaks in a voice so calm and clear and harsh that I know she means every ugly word she says. *If you ever turn out to be a faggot…* She pauses and grips the steering wheel tight. *I'm going to kill you. Or hire somebody to kill you*, I think I hear her say. *Because I brought you into this world, and I can take you right back out.*

CHAPTER THREE

There's a problem. A math problem. And it's waiting for me across the field, sixty meters away. Our math teacher lines us up. The whole fourth-grade class stands alert, poised, ready to bolt.

The assignment: run across the field, grab the piece of paper in your lane, read the math problem, then solve it as you sprint back to your starting place. The first person to successfully complete the mission, wins.

We get into position. Wait for our teacher.

On your marks, she cries.

I tense my whole body.

Get set.

I focus my mind.

Go!

I tear across the field. Ripping up grass as I go. Passing all my classmates. I grab the slip of paper with my name on it. Read the math problem.

168 ÷ 8 = ?

I bolt back toward my teacher. My classmate is right behind. I push my body as hard as it can go. Past the finish line.

Quick, my teacher shouts. *What's the answer?*

24

Whoops. I forgot to solve the problem. I was too busy winning the race. But even though I don't have the answer, the victory still feels good. Like an affirmation. I can run like no one else. And this means a lot. In Jamaica, running is more than just a sport, it's a way of life. As soon as we can walk, we're running. From preschool on, running is a part of everyone's education. It's a part of everyone's life. It's our culture, our national pride. If you're good at track and field, if you can get to that elite level where you're competing internationally, then you will be adored by everyone in your country, everyone in the world, accepted by everyone, loved by everyone. And if everyone loves me, then maybe my mother will love me too. Right now, I worry that she doesn't. Things have been tense between us since she yelled at me in the school parking lot. I get the silent treatment at home. She barely talks to me.

I'm starting to realize that my mom is the other unsolved problem in my life.

But now I've found the solution: running.

The sign-up sheet has been posted. I rush toward the bulletin board. Other kids crowd around me. I see the paper. It's lined with blank spaces.

Tryouts for Sports Day.

Our school is divided up into five Houses, each assigned a different color. There's Red, Green, Yellow, Orange, and Blue. I'm in Orange House. Every week, we host House meetings before school, where the teachers make announcements, organize fundraisers, and prepare for Sports Day—the day when the Houses compete against one another to see who's the fastest in the school. Not everyone gets to run in every event, which is why there are tryouts. Our teachers want to see who the fastest kids are. Who can bring home a win for their House.

Next to the sign-up sheet, a pen dangles on a string. I grab it. Scrawl my name in the section devoted to the 400-meter dash. I know I have what it takes to represent my House at Sports Day. I know that I'm fast. I know that I'm good. Maybe I could even be great. Maybe I could make it past Sports Day. Maybe I could represent our school at Champs, the national track competition for kids my age. Maybe I could represent my country at the Olympics. Maybe I could join the ranks of the greatest female athletes in history. Maybe the thing I love could take me to unimaginable heights.

But first I have to make this team.

I made the team. Now, weeks of training have led me here—to the back of a school bus, packed into its seats with the rest of my classmates, on our way to Sports Day. My heart is pounding. It's almost competition time. The Orange House is amped up. One of the boys starts my favorite chant.

Soup! Soup! He yells out.

Pressure! Pressure! Everyone yells back.

Soup! Soup!

Pressure! Pressure!

We're driving to the athletic field. I'm wearing my bright orange jersey—our House color. Everyone else wears their jersey too. The bus is a bright sea of rowdy children, shouting and laughing as the breeze from the open windows hits our faces. The bus stops at a red light. A line of cars pulls up next to us. We yell at the drivers, make a ruckus. The drivers honk back at us, cheer for us, because they know it's Sports Day, they know that this event is where some of the greatest athletes get their start, they know it's possible that somewhere on this bus, there's a future Olympian. Maybe it's even me.

Soup! Soup!

Pressure! Pressure!

Yellow House under pressure!

The chant is about applying pressure to the competition. Applying heat. Like you would to a pot of soup. But even though we're calling out the Yellow House, telling them they don't have shit on

26

us, I feel like I'm the one under pressure. I feel the heat myself. I start to sweat in my orange jersey. I know my House is counting on me. I know I have to win for them. But also for myself.

The bus comes to a stop. We've arrived. The driver opens the door. Kids pour out, running toward the field. Clusters of tents line a dirt track. We sprint toward the area designated for the Orange House. The field becomes crowded with teachers and students and spectators. The Yellow House starts their own patois chant, aimed back at us.

A chicken back, a tun cornmeal,
A chicken back and tun cornmeal,
That's all Orange House feed pan,
A chicken back and tun cornmeal.

"Chicken back" describes the bony parts of the chicken no one wants and "tun cornmeal" is yellow cornmeal cooked in coconut milk. Both dishes are seen as poor people's food. They're saying this is all the Orange House eats, so the chant is designed to insult us. The Yellow House keeps shouting, and their words get under my skin.

I feel the pressure mounting. The day is a blur. I'm waiting for my event. Someone hands me a white crisp. All the runners eat them for extra energy before their event. It's funny—you can tell who's about to compete because their faces are dusted with chalky powder. All across the field, there are kids with white cheeks. Like it's been snowing in Jamaica. I place the crisp on my tongue. It's sweet—straight sugar. It dissolves immediately. I feel a jolt—my adrenaline spikes. My muscles tense.

Then—it's time for my event. The 400-meter dash.

On your marks! I take my place on the track. I feel the dirt against my bare feet. Small stones dig into my heels. *Get set!* I'm focused. I'm ready.

Boom! The gun goes off. I fly out of the blocks. I pass my competitors—muscles burning, lungs pumping. I give my whole body to the race. My whole mind. I push harder.

I cross the finish line.

I win the race.

The crowd cheers. The Orange House goes wild. My teammates swarm around me. I feel seen. I feel loved. I can't wait to run my next race.

I'm an *athlete*. The word is like a shield. It protects me from bullies. They've been a problem recently. Calling me names, making fun of me, threatening me after school. *Battymen* get beat up. But *athletes* are celebrated. Protected. Even bullies can't deny my talent on the track. People defend me. Coaches advocate for me. My teammates rely on me to help our team win. I'm making more friends. Gaining more respect. But I never dim my light. Never stop being who I truly am. I may have to hide who I am when I'm at home with my mother, but I never hide who I am at school. My status as an athlete protects me. I'm just as flamboyant and feminine and beautiful as I want to be. I never stop being all the things people hate about me, because no matter how much people may hate me, I never stop loving myself.

At track practice, I feel out of place with the boys. I can't relate to their roughhousing, their jokes, or their gross behavior. But because our practices are coed, I can train with the girls. I love running alongside them because I feel they understand me. They sense my feminine energy; we care about the same things, have the same sense of humor. I get to be myself when I'm around them. Like I'm just one of the girls.

My coach is amazed by my talent. I'm one of his favorites. He asked me to join the track team, to represent the school at different meets across the country. He puts me on the relay team, he says I could be an asset. Sports Day was just the start. Soon, I'm not just competing against my own classmates, I'm competing against other schools, I'm gaining a reputation for being a fierce competitor. Yes, I'm an *athlete*. Maybe I could even become a great one.

* * *

I run home from school after practice. I speed past the church. Terrence's house comes into view. But as I get closer, I realize something is off. It's the front step—the concrete has been painted with thick crimson splatters. A sick feeling overwhelms me.

I step closer, crouch down.

I realize it's blood.

My mother. I instantly think of my mother. I worry that Terrence has done something terrible. I run to the front door. Grab the handle. But it's locked. I pull and pull but it won't open. I pound on the door. *Let me in!* I scream. But no one is home. I whip out my cell phone. Call my mother. No answer. I call Terrence. No answer. I feel so alone. So terrified. So panicked. My heart pounds. My pulse races.

I turn back and look at the blood on the doorstep.

I burst into sobs.

I pray that my mother is still alive.

call my sister on my cell phone. She drives two hours, across Jamaica, to sit with me on that doorstep. We wait. And wait. What we're waiting for we're not sure. Will our mother return to us? Bruised and cut and broken? Or will it be Terrence who comes back, walking past the church with a deep sadness on his face, a grieving look that will confirm our worst fears? Is our mother gone forever? My sister lives in Spanish Town with her dad and his family. It's far from here, this front stoop stained in blood, and I worry about what will happen to me if my mother is gone. Could I live with my sister? Would her family have me? Or will I be forced to live with Terrence? There are no answers this afternoon. Only terrifying questions that swirl between us in the silence.

Dusk settles. The sun begins to fade.

My mother's car pulls up.

She tells us the story in a calm voice. Like nothing's wrong.

It started with a fight. She doesn't tell us what it was about, only that it was bad. Worse than their usual screaming matches. They were in the yard, right by the cluster of tall trees. Fat wooden vines snaked up their trunks. Thick as whips. A machete lay on the ground. It had been abandoned, after clearing brush from the landscape. The fight escalated. Terrence grabbed the knife. Chopped a vine from the tree. Dropped the machete. It all happened so fast from there, but my mother tells us that in her mind, this is how she feels it went down: Terrence picked up the vine and started whipping her. She screamed. She grabbed the vine, caught it in her fist and held it tight, trying to stop him. But Terrence ripped the vine right out of her grasp. It sliced her skin as it went, sliced her hand right open, right down to the muscle. She looked down at her palm. Blood poured from the gash. Fury possessed her. She scrambled toward the machete, snatched it from the ground. Terrence ran at her again, but this time she had the knife, she slashed at him, made contact with his hand. He screamed and dropped the vine.

The fight was over.

It was time to go to the hospital.

I'm fine now, she tells us in that strange calm voice. It's flat. Emotionless. She stares down at the bandage wrapped around her hand. *I fucked him up though. I taught him a lesson.*

But that doesn't make me feel better. I don't believe that Terrence learned any lessons. And she wants me to treat him like a father? I'll *never* see him as a father.

He's a man, she tells us. *A real man. And real men are aggressive. Sometimes they're violent. And when they go too far, you have to defend yourself. But I'd rather have a real man, than some sissy who doesn't know how to handle himself.*

We sit there and I listen to my mother. I can sense what my sister is feeling. I feel it too. The shock. The disbelief. There's only one ending to my mother's story that would make sense: the ending in which she leaves Terrence, and we're safe again, a family again, a *real* family, with no toxic man trying to pose as my father figure. But that's not the ending my mother has in mind. I've seen abuse like this before, in other families we know in Jamaica. Men are seen as heads of their household, they have the power, they can do what they please and not be questioned. Sometimes it seems like women are just supposed to accept violence from men, to remain by their husband's side, no matter how badly they're bruised. But I don't understand this. I think my mother should run. But it's clear from her tone, the way she's pretending nothing's wrong, as if getting beaten by your man is just what it means to be loved, it's clear that she has no intentions of leaving him.

She's going to stay forever.

CHAPTER FIVE

Our coach has good news. He's going to tell us after practice. First, we train.

I've been competing now for about two years. Getting stronger, getting faster. I'm in sixth grade, at Calabar Infant, Primary, and Junior High School in Kingston. I'm on the relay team. Our event is the 4 x 100 meters. We don't have a track at school, so we run drills in the parking lot of the East Queen St. Baptist Church, in the shade of the large redbrick building. Today, we're practicing our handoffs. I start the race, sprint my hundred meters, then hand the baton to the second person, who hands it off to the third, who hands it off to the fourth. He's the anchor. The fastest boy on the team. I'm the fastest of them all, but I'm not a boy.

I'm a girl who runs with the boys. I never say this out loud, but that's how I feel. I spend each practice grappling with the sensation of being out of place. Out of my body. I'm on the wrong team. But even still, I love running. This is something I'm good at. Something I love. It feels worth it—to hide who I am, in order to do something that brings me such joy. And there are some advantages to being a girl who trains with boys. The boys push me to be faster, stronger. They're good teammates. Supportive. When I'm training, I don't get the hate and harassment that I've become accustomed to in Jamaica while walking the streets. I don't get called *battyman*, I don't get threatened, I don't fear for my life. On the field, I'm respected. On the field, I'm an *athlete*. That magic word. My protection. It's a part of my identity now. My teammates admire me for my abilities, my friends stand up for me no matter what. I feel more confident in who I am.

We finish our practice. The coach tells us to gather around. He says our times today were good, but they can be better. And we're going to work to make them better.

Because our relay team has qualified for the National Championships.

My mom will miss the meet.

She's gone again, back to Canada to work. It's just me and Terrence at the house. He says he's happy for me, proud that I made it all the way to the national competition. But he can't come either. He has something to do that day. He doesn't tell me what it is. I don't ask. I think I know what he gets up to when my mom isn't around. I think he sees other women.

So, I'll go alone.

The day comes. The event is officially called Inter-Secondary Schools Boys and Girls Championships, but everyone just calls it Champs. The track team meets up at the school, where buses are waiting to take us to the meet. We load in, laughing and chatting and yelling. There's a nervous energy; the anticipation is like an electric current, buzzing through our bodies on the bus. We speed toward our destination.

Then, it appears: National Stadium. We crane our necks to take it in as we pull into the parking lot. It towers above us. A series of white concrete arches curve over the entrance, coming to points in the sky. Crowds of people file in, looking so small in the shadow of the stadium.

The bus comes to a stop. The doors open. Our coach leads the way to the entrance. We pass a bronze statue of Bob Marley, holding his guitar. We join the crush of bodies funneling their way into the stadium. I know that this is where some of the greatest Olympians in the world have competed. And now, I get to compete here too. I can feel the heat from the crowd, the excitement. But nothing matches the thrill I feel when I walk onto the field. It stretches on for what feels like forever. Our coach says the stadium can hold up to 35,000 people. The bright blue track encircles a vibrant green field. This is nothing like the dirt tracks we run on at school. I look up into the stands, imagine all the roaring crowds that have witnessed historic wins.

Spectators file into their seats, waving at my teammates. It seems like everyone else on my team has a group of loved ones there to support them; parents and aunts and uncles and cousins and friends fill the bleachers, shouting words of encouragement, holding up handmade signs.

But no one is here for me. Terrence is busy. Auntie Peaches is consumed, as she usually is these days, by the grind of being a single mother to young children, too busy with work to make a weekday meet.

I think of my mother. Wonder what she's doing in Canada. Is she thinking of me? I wish she was here. I want her to join all the other cheering family members in the stands. I want her to share this moment with me. I want to make her proud. I've made it here, to Champs. And I got here doing something I love, something I'm good at, something that other people find impressive. Why does it seem like she doesn't understand that? I feel so lonely. But I also feel more determined than ever to succeed. Maybe if I keep winning, maybe if I keep gaining a bigger and bigger reputation as an athlete, maybe if I work harder than I've ever worked before, maybe if I make it to the Olympics, maybe if I achieve something *so* remarkable, so huge, so undeniable, then my mother will *finally* support me in the way I wish she would.

Because sometimes I feel like there's a hole in my heart in the shape of my mother.

But I can't get distracted with these thoughts.

I have to focus on the competition. I am learning that to perform to the best of my ability, I have to clear my mind before hitting the track. I have to drown out the noise of the world. I have to focus on the task at hand and nothing else.

The time comes for our event. I'm the first sprinter in our relay. I go to my starting block, watch the rest of our team get into position. Our competitors go to their own lanes, preparing for the race. Silence falls over the field. Isolated cheers erupt from the stands. A stillness overwhelms me, a feeling of serenity, the feeling that I'm in the right place. This is what I was born to do. I'm at home here, on this track, the same track that's weathered the footsteps of so many world-class athletes before me.

I could be one of them. At some point in my life, somewhere down the line, I could be an Olympian. A dream begins to form in the back of my mind. A dream that one day this sport that I love will take me to glory. Not just for myself, but for my teammates, my family, and everyone I love.

But then, another thought enters my mind. A realization: They will want me to compete with the boys. Like I am now. If I ever make it to Team Jamaica, there's no way they will ever let me run with the females. And I know this because I know what it's like for me to live in Jamaica, I know how it feels to be bullied, to be called a *battyman*, to have people taunt you because they say you walk like a girl, talk like a girl. I know that Team Jamaica will never honor who I am and will never see my true self. I will have to lie about who I am to compete on the world stage. And that's just something I don't want to do. It's already painful enough to have to hide who I am today, on this field, with everyone watching, thinking that I'm just another one of the boys, even though I'm not. I'm a girl.

On your marks!

But I love this sport. Love it more than anything else in my life.

Get set.

Except for my sister. And my mother.

Boom! The gun goes off. I'm out of the blocks. Bolting down the lane. The baton is tight in my grip. It's just me and the track and my teammates. Adrenaline pumps through my system. All my thoughts dissipate, all my anxieties vanish. The only thing that matters at that moment: the finish line.

CHAPTER SIX

Something is about to happen. I can feel it. My mother is acting differently. We're doing things we don't normally do. Yesterday, we retwisted my dreadlocks. My mom wanted me looking my best for some reason, though she didn't say why. Today, we went shopping for new clothes. A suitcase. We got home and started packing it. I wanted to know where we were going, but I was afraid to ask. Afraid she'd be angry at me if I did. My mother doesn't tell me things until I need to know them. So I just wait, wondering how our lives are about to change.

Wake up, my mother says. I open my eyes and see her smiling face, close to mine. *It's time to go to the airport.*

Why? I ask.

Because we're moving to Toronto. To be with your brother and his wife.

I feel a jolt of excitement. I jump out of bed, start getting ready. I've been to Canada a few times. I have one other sibling, an older brother, and he lives in Toronto with his wife. She's pregnant with a baby boy, my new nephew. I can't wait to meet him. I love it in

Toronto. The city is amazing, there are so many different people from so many different backgrounds. Whenever I'm there, I don't have to worry about kids bullying me, or calling me a faggot or *battyman*. I can walk down the street without fear. Now that we're moving, I'll get to start over at a new school. Make new friends. And maybe I'll finally get to live as my true self—the girl I was born to be.

Still, a part of me is sad. I'm leaving behind the people who raised me—Auntie Peaches and Auntie Bella, all my cousins, friends, and neighbors in the community. These people are a part of my history. These people love me. But their love is a love I have to leave behind.

Because they will never accept me for who I truly am.

We load the suitcases into the car. Terrence drives us to the airport. But he's not moving to Canada. He's staying back here in Jamaica. My mom is going to send him money, to help him create a better life here. Their plan is to build a house on an empty plot of land in the countryside that my grandfather left her when he died. A place she can come back and visit, where she and Terrence can vacation. Because they're going to stay together, even though they'll be living in different countries. They're not breaking up. Sometimes I wish they would.

But I won't have to deal with Terrence anymore. Or, at least, I won't have to deal with him as much. Because we'll be far away in Toronto, creating our new life. My sister isn't coming with us either, not yet. She'll keep living in Jamaica with her father. Today, it's just me and my mother traveling to Toronto. An adventure we get to share. Just the two of us.

Terrence drops us off. I say goodbye and I do feel a little sad. For all the times he was so horrible to my mother, I can tell he also loves her. That he'll miss her. And I think he'll miss me too. He was good to me at times. But I'll never call him dad, because he never acted like a father to me. A real father wouldn't do what he did to my mother.

We're flying Air Jamaica. My heart beats faster as we board the plane. I've only ever been on a plane a couple of times, and I barely remember it. My mother and I settle into our seats. The plane takes off. My stomach flips. I look up at my mother. She smiles and holds my hand. I love traveling with her. I love having her all to myself. Because she's the one constant in my life. The other people—my sister, my aunties, Terrence—they come and go. But at the end of the day, I know that I'll always have my mother. For a moment, as we're flying, I make a wish. I wish it could be just the two of us like this forever, soaring through the air, our hearts filled with the excitement of the unknown. But I know eventually we have to come back down to earth.

We have to start our life in Toronto.

The apple tree is the first thing I notice. It's tall, lush, and heavy with apples. The front yard is overgrown, the grasses are wild and tangled. A cement walkway cuts through the green and leads to the front door of the house. It's two stories, with brick siding, and a pitched roof. We pull into the driveway. I step out of the car and take a breath. The air smells fresh, clean, with a hint of earth and grass wafting up from the unkempt lawn. My brother comes out of the house to help us with our bags. He's handsome, with clear dark skin, and a scruffy goatee. He smiles; he's got the same dimples as me and Mom.

We're all moving in today: me, my mother, my brother, his wife Samantha, and their three kids. Samantha steps out onto the front stoop. She's beautiful and light-skinned—half Black, half white—and she has a slight gap between her front teeth. She waves to us, caressing her pregnant belly. The baby is coming any day, and I'm excited to have a new nephew.

For the past three months we've all been crammed into a small apartment in Toronto, and even though I love my new life, I have to admit that the apartment just wasn't enough space for all those people. But now we live here, in Mississauga, a small city along the shore of Lake Ontario, in a house that my brother's wife has inherited from her mother. The death has been painful for her—and it hasn't been made any easier by her pregnancy. Her grief, the stress of caring for three children, and the knowledge that there's another on the way— it's too much. Sometimes, late at night, I think I hear my brother and his wife fighting. Sometimes, my mother joins in. They always argue about the same things: housework, childcare, money, who is carrying the weight of the family. My mother and I are often tasked with babysitting; I'm eleven years old, almost twelve. Old enough to watch my brother's kids, who are all younger than me. But I don't mind babysitting; I love my nieces and nephews, and they love me.

My brother helps us get our things inside, then gives us a tour of the house. There's a big living room, with a bright window that fills the room with light. Black leather couches line the edges of the room and face a large flat-screen TV. There's a dining room too—with a long table and six chairs tucked in around its edges. It leads straight into the kitchen, maybe the most beautiful kitchen I've seen in my whole life, with long granite countertops, tall white cabinets, and a massive silver fridge. The sink is massive, with two large basins. A window overlooks the backyard. I peer outside. The backyard is even bigger than the front; garden beds burst with a tangle of over-grown vegetables, tomato vines intertwine with cucumbers, spilling over into a small pumpkin patch. Rebellious onion stalks pop up at random intervals across the yard. There's a gorgeous cherry tree with low-hanging branches that stretch almost to the ground; it needs to be trimmed. The grass is overgrown here too—it looks like it hasn't been mowed in months. And it probably hasn't. Samantha's mother was too sick to care for her property before she passed away. There's work to be done. But I know we can do it. Together. The whole fam-ily. This is our new home.

And I love it.

My brother leads us past the stairwell. He motions upstairs and tells us that he and his wife and kids will take the upper level of the house. He then leads us to a large room on the bottom floor; this is where I'll stay with Mom. There's one big bed that we'll have to share. But I don't mind; I'm used to sharing space with my mother. There are two other rooms on the bottom floor as well. They plan to rent them out, to help pay the mortgage. Even though this house is huge, it will definitely feel tight. But I don't mind. I'm just excited to begin my new life, in a new country, in a new house, where it feels like anything is possible.

My mom and Samantha are in another fight. I feel like Samantha is in a fight with everyone these days. She's had the baby—it's a beautiful boy that she loves. But still, it's a lot of work, caring for a newborn and three other kids. Ever since she's given birth, it seems to me like she's always angry or depressed. She seems overwhelmed, even though my mother does most of the housework. It's a full-time job for my mother—watching the kids, cooking, and cleaning. But this was the plan: grandma gives up her career, moves to Canada, and helps raise the children. It made sense at the time; this is just the nature of so many Jamaican women I know—they step into a leadership role in the household. But they'll also remind you of all the hard work they're doing. They're not going to let you forget the sacrifices they're making. And Samantha doesn't like this. She feels my mother is always giving her a guilt trip. Judging her for the way she is (or isn't) caring for her own kids. Honestly, sometimes it feels like I pitch in more than Samantha does. I'm twelve, which means I'm old enough to help cook and clean and babysit when my mother can't. It's definitely a lot of work, but I never complain; I love playing with the children and watching over them. But for some reason, it seems like when Samantha sees the way I care for her children, it just makes Samantha even angrier. My mom says it's her hormones. I wonder if it's also the fact that Samantha is still devastated by her mother's death, too sad to step into the role of a parent herself, consumed by an anger that has no outlet.

So she lashes out at my mother. I don't know what their fight was about today. All I know is that we had to get out of the house. To give Samantha some time to cool off.

Which is why we're driving to Claudia's condo. It's where we always go, whenever my mom and Samantha get into an altercation. Claudia is Samantha's sister, and it seems like the two of them are always fighting as well. Even though Samantha can be cruel to me and my mother, a part of me feels bad for her. It seems like Samantha can't get along with anyone—she pushes away the people who are closest to her.

My mom and Claudia are close—nothing brings people together like a common enemy. But I think they also just genuinely love each other's company. I love Claudia too; she's warm and funny and she's always hosting parties at her condo. The building is tall and luxurious, with giant glass windows, bright apartments, and *two* pools— one indoor and one outdoor. I always look forward to an afternoon at Claudia's, because I know I'll get to swim in one of those beautiful pools.

But there's another reason I love going to her condo.

There's a boy who lives there.

And I have a crush on him.

I'm alone in the condo. My mom and Claudia are out at the grocery store, picking up some lunch. *Go ahead and use the pool if you want,* Claudia said before they left. *We'll be back in a little bit.* I brought my swim trunks along, but I don't want to wear them. I hate them— they're big and baggy, meant for boys.

Claudia has a daughter—she's sixteen, four years older than me. She's not here today, she's probably out with her friends. I tiptoe into her room. I see her dresser in the corner, walk over to it. Open the drawers. I dig through her clothes, heart pounding, until I find what I'm looking for: a bikini. I take it out, slip it on. I tie the top extra tight to make it fit. I look at myself in the mirror. I look beautiful. I look like myself.

I hurry to the elevator. Press the button. I have to be back upstairs before my mom and Claudia return. I can't get caught. I know my mother will be furious if she sees me like this.

Ding! The doors open. I jump in. My stomach drops along with the elevator. It opens onto the floor with the outdoor pool. I run out onto the patio, bare feet slapping against the concrete. The sun hits my face. I scan the pool and there he is: my crush. He's my age— around twelve years old. He's splashing in the deep end with his brother. His hair is wet, curls heavy with water. He looks so cute. I wade into the shallow end. He catches my eye and waves. Smiles shyly. I'm shy too. I wave back, too scared to swim over.

But the clock is ticking. My mother will be back at any minute.

I want to stay, but I know I can't. I climb out of the pool, grab a towel, and look over my shoulder. He's looking right back. I want him to run over to me, to beg me to spend the day with him. But he just stays there. I turn, saddened, and rush back to the elevator. Press the button.

Suddenly, I hear a voice behind me.

Hi, he says, almost in a whisper.

Hi, I say back, as he walks up next to me.

I've noticed you around recently.

My auntie lives in the building. We hang out here sometimes.

Cool, he says.

Yeah, it's pretty cool.

I... he hesitates. *I just wanted to tell you that I think you're pretty.*

Thank you, I say and blush. Our bodies move closer together; it's almost like we can't control them, almost like we're magnets and not people, like we're drawn together by some force greater than we can understand. He leans forward. He kisses me, soft and gentle. He caresses my body. I feel happier than I've ever felt. A boy thinks I'm pretty, and not only that, a boy sees me for who I am, he sees me as a girl. He sees my true self.

This moment feels like it could be the start of something new. I realize that I could be the narrator of my own story. I could take control of my own life. I could live authentically, and people would love me for it.

Ding! The elevator doors open.

I guess I'll see you around, I say.

Yeah, for sure, he replies.

I step inside the elevator. Wait for the doors to close. I fall back against the wall. A smile spreads across my face. I feel like I could fly, soar through the air, explode with happiness. I feel like I could light up the whole sky.

CHAPTER SEVEN

I love our life in Canada. I've lived here for one year, but sometimes it feels like just one minute. The rush of new experiences never seems to stop. I've started middle school and I love it; it seems like everyone in my class comes from a different background, it's so diverse, so multicultural, there are Black people and brown people and Asian people, and everyone is accepted no matter who they are or where they come from. I'm feeling closer to my mother, like she's almost a best friend; now that she's not leaving for months-long stretches, we spend so much more time together. We share the same room; we share household chores. I've helped my family make a home, I've watched Samantha's kids and cooked them breakfasts, and lunches, even dinners. I once burned a pan of eggs and the flames got so high that they licked the ceiling. Samantha was mad but my brother and I painted over the big black spot until you couldn't tell it had ever been burned. I've tended the garden in our backyard, I've pulled out weeds and made room for new growth. I celebrated my first Canadian Christmas, and the weather was colder than anything I'd ever experienced in Jamaica, but I felt so warm inside our big, beautiful house. We had a Christmas party, and I danced, and ate cookies, and felt so lucky to be here, in Canada, thousands of miles away from St. Thomas, thousands of miles away from all the pain I endured there. It's all in the past. I have a new home now. And when the house fills with love, when our family is whole, it feels like anything is possible.

My mother and I come home from the grocery store. My brother jumps when we walk into the living room.

I notice he has a new phone.

When did you get that? I ask.

Oh, this isn't mine, he says. *I…I'm just keeping it for a friend.*

Hm, is all my mother says. I can tell she doesn't believe him. I don't either.

And if Samantha asks, that's what you tell her too, he says.

My mother just nods. I don't say anything. It seems to me that my brother is asking us to lie for him. I know that we will. Because he's family, and you do anything for your family.

Samantha is yelling at my mother. They've fought plenty of times before, but never like this, never this intensely. I'm hiding in our bedroom on the lower level. My mother and Samantha are in the kitchen. I'm listening, terrified of what might happen. Samantha is furious about my brother's new phone. Apparently, he's been texting multiple women from it. Cheating on her. My mother repeats the lie we've been told—she tells Samantha that he's just holding the phone for a friend. *That's bullshit,* she yells. *I've read those texts and those texts are from him.* My mother defends her son, raises her voice. Soon, they're shouting over each other.

I step into the hallway. Hover closer to the kitchen. I watch from the doorframe. The women are only about one foot away from each other. Their faces are red. Their necks strained from yelling. I'm worried it could get physical. I'm worried Samantha could hurt my mother.

Their fight takes a turn. Samantha thinks it's disgusting that my mother can defend someone who's betrayed his whole family. *I don't want a man like that raising my children*, she shouts.

And what do you know about raising children, Samantha? my mother yells. *You don't raise your children. I raise your children.*

Don't talk to me like that in my house.

Samantha charges at my mother. From my vantage point, it seems like Samantha pushes her. My mother staggers backward. Her eyes widen in shock. Something is triggered inside me. Seeing someone seemingly attack my mother takes me back to Jamaica. Back to Terrence. Back to the time my mother's life was threatened, but I was too young to defend her.

But I'm not too young now.

I rush into the kitchen. Step in between Samantha and my mother. *Don't touch my mom!* Samantha comes at me. I swing hands. She swings back, but I'm too fast for her. My mom keeps screaming at Samantha. Samantha tells us to leave, get out, that we can never come back again. I'm shocked. Devastated. I'm so attached to the bonds we've formed since living here. So attached to the beautiful family life we've created. And relatives fight, of course, but not like this. How could Samantha kick us out? After all we've shared. It feels like me and my mother are all alone in this world. I hold back tears. And I realize, at this moment, that it's the last day we'll ever spend here, in the house I loved so much, the home I thought would be ours forever.

Now it's all gone.

CHAPTER EIGHT

It's just me and Mom again. On our own.

She has a good friend, Damian, who has a big house with an extra room. He lets us stay there while we search for another place to live. My mother gets a job at McDonald's, so she can try to save up. Plus, my sister has now moved to Canada. She doesn't want to live with her father anymore. So she's come to stay with us here, at Damian's house. But it's cramped. I try to stay out of Damian's way. Keep to myself. Our family doesn't want to outstay our welcome. We need a place of our own.

We're in a new neighborhood, so I have to transfer to a new school. I visit their website to see if they have a track team. My last school didn't, and I'm sad to discover that this school doesn't have one either. I miss track so much. I know that it's my calling, that God put me on this earth to run. I know that one day I'll get back to it. For now, I'll focus on being a good student. Maybe I'll search for another sport to play, biding my time until high school, when I'll jump at the chance to join the track team.

But despite my sadness, there's another part of me that's excited about this new school. I like starting over. I like meeting new people. New friends. I'm used to it by now.

Also, I have an idea.

At a new school, no one knows your past. You can be anyone you want to be. You can take control of your own narrative. You can show people your true self.

Which is exactly what I plan to do.

Do you want to come introduce yourself to the class? our teacher asks me.

It's my first day of school. Monday. I'm sitting at my desk. My pulse is racing, like I've just run the 400-meter dash. I nod, stand up, walk to the front of the room. I know what I have to do. This is the moment that will change everything.

Hi everyone. I give a little wave. I say my name. I'm sweating now. I stall for time, smoothing my white T-shirt and black slacks, thanking God that our school uniforms are unisex. Then, I say it: *I'm so excited to be the new girl.*

Yes, the new girl.

I look out at the class. A few people smile. Some kids looked bored. But no one questions me. They just accept me for who I am: a new girl, at a new school, excited for her first day.

Finally, I get to live my truth.

I sit back down in my seat, relieved and giddy. I'm filled with a sense of freedom. I get to be myself. Is there anything more beautiful than that? No, there isn't. Except maybe the cute boy who's sitting behind me.

His name is Andrew. I saw him in the hallway earlier today, surrounded by a crowd of people. He's tall. Athletic. Popular. It seemed like he clocked me then, gave me a little nod, but I wasn't sure. I look over my shoulder now.

He smiles at me.

And it's official: I have a crush.

* * *

The bell rings. It's time to switch classes.

I turn around. Face Andrew. My cheeks flush.

Do you know where the bathroom is? I ask him. Not because I really need to go. Just because I want to talk to him.

Sure, he says and shoots me another beautiful smile. *I'll take you there.*

Shit. I hadn't planned on this. We walk together through the halls. We're chatting, making small talk, but I can barely pay attention to what he's saying because I know what's coming: another moment where I'll need to summon the courage to be my true self.

We get to the bathrooms. He stands in between the two doors. On his left, it's the girls' room. On his right, it's the boys'. *Here you go,* he says, and I feel suddenly like he's testing me, like there is still some doubt in his mind about whether I'm a boy or a girl, and that my choice at this moment will confirm something for him.

I take a breath. *You've got this,* I think to myself. *Just live your truth.*

So I walk right into the girls' bathroom. Exactly where I belong.

I have something to tell you, one of my classmates whispers to me, as we walk to gym class in a gaggle of girls. *I think Andrew has a crush on you!*

I can't believe it. This week has felt like a dream. Everything is falling into place. One of the most popular boys in school has a crush on *me.* And it's not just Andrew who likes me. It's everyone. It seems like the whole school wants to get to know the new girl.

We all run into the gym. Our shoes squeak as we speed across the basketball court, toward the locker rooms. I slow down. Come to a stop. Watch as the boys roughhouse their way into one locker room, while the girls file into the other. I know where I belong. And at this point, I'm feeling more confident about living as myself. But each new test still fills me with fear.

What are you waiting for? a voice calls from behind me. It's our gym teacher. *It's time to get changed!*

I take a breath and enter the girls' locker room. Our gym uniforms are unisex too. Plain shorts and T-shirts. Even still, I feel shy about my body. I worry about getting "found out." I sneak off to a bathroom stall, to have some privacy. When I come back out, the girls are changing in front of their lockers. They're giggling, sharing stories about when their mothers bought them their first training bras.

When did your mom take you to get yours? one of the girls asks me.

She…she hasn't yet.

Oh, okay, the girl replies.

What size are you? I ask.

Why do you wanna know my bra size? she says, like I've offended her somehow. *That's private.*

It seems like we might be the same size.

We're definitely not. So stop being weird.

I'm not. I just thought if we were the same size, I would know which size to get.

The girl gives me a strange look, then walks out of the locker room.

Later that afternoon, I'm called to the principal's office.

I got a visit from one of your classmates today, the principal tells me. I'm sitting in her office, filled with fear. *She said she was made very uncomfortable by someone asking her about her bra size in the locker room. She said it was the new girl. I told your classmate that there isn't a new girl. There's a new boy.* I wish I could go back in time and tell everyone I was a boy, even though that's a lie. Anything to take away this terrible feeling in my gut. *But she confirmed it was you. She said you've told everyone that you're a girl. That you're going to the girls' bathroom, changing in the girls' locker room.* I want to disappear, vanish from this room, from this earth. *This is a problem. So, we're going to have to call your mother.*

Terror shoots through my body. I see a flash of my mother. A memory. From my fourth-grade year, when I walked out of sex education and told her that I was going to get my period. I remember how awful she was to me. I remember the terror that ran through my body. I remember thinking I could never talk to my mother about my gender again.

The principal picks up the phone.

She dials a number. Hands me the receiver.

I pray.

CHAPTER NINE

The phone rings. Adrenaline pounds at my temples. I wait for my mother to pick up.

I'll run away. That's the only solution. I can't stay at home; I know what my mother will do to me once she finds out what I've done. So yes, I'll run away. I don't know where I'll go. But I'll find somewhere. I'll sleep on the street, a park bench, under an awning. I'll have no choice. After this conversation with my mother, it won't be safe to stay with her. I won't have a home. My life as I know it will be over.

The phone stops ringing. Someone picks up. *Hello?*

My sister's voice.

Relief washes over me. I start crying, bawling right in front of the principal. *It's...it's me.*

What's wrong?

I did something bad.

My sister picks me up from school. She's furious, confused, appalled by what the principal told her. *Not a word of this to Mom, you understand?* She's scared for me. She's seen my mom's anger; she knows my mom's wrath. *I'm gonna deal with this. Because I know how Mom will react. And I don't want to see my little brother get hurt.* Those words: "little brother"; those words hurt too. I'm her little sister. But she doesn't know this. *Talk to me,* she says. *Why would you pretend to be a girl? Why would you go into the girls' locker room like that?*

I wish I could tell my sister the truth. But I know I can't. I know she'd never understand. So I stall for time. *I think I'm just…I'm just…*

I have an idea. Back in Jamaica, there were men we called *gyalis*. Players. Womanizers. *Man a gyalis,* we'd say when we saw a man walking down the street, surrounded by a posse of women, laughing and joking and flirting. These men were often pretty boys, sometimes even feminine. They took care of themselves, wore the finest clothes, and spent all their time seducing women. *I'm just so into girls.* My voice quavers, as I avoid my sister's skeptical stare. *A gyalis.*

Okay, she says. I can tell that there's a part of her that doesn't believe me, a part of her that understands the truth we're both too scared to articulate. *You were just being a little creep,* she continues. I can hear the relief in her voice. Her brother's just a player, like all the other boys his age. Trying to get girls however he can. *I'm gonna keep my eye on you.* She's no longer angry, she's almost teasing me now. Her little rascal brother. Boys will be boys, after all.

I won't ever do it again, I promise. I wish I felt relieved. But I don't. I still have to live this lie. I still have to live in fear of my mother discovering the truth.

You better not, she says. Her smile drops. *And we can never, ever, tell Mom about this.*

I'm standing in front of the class again. Just like I did on my first day of school. Only this time, I'm not filled with giddy excitement. I'm consumed by fear. I feel like I'm in a nightmare. I wish I could wake up. But I'm not dreaming; the disgusted stares from my classmates, the disappointment on my teacher's face—it's all real. Too real. This morning, on my way to class, it was all hateful looks in the hallway. The rumors about me have already spread across the school.

I just want to apologize to everyone, I say. My voice is small. About to crack. *I lied and told you that I was a girl, but I'm really a boy.* I fight back the sobs that are bubbling in my throat. *I should've told you all the truth…* But I can't hold it back any longer. I break down. Start bawling. No one comes up to comfort me. No one gives me a hug. I feel so alone.

Thank you, that'll be all, my teacher says.

I stumble back toward my seat, sobbing. My eyes are sore from crying. I can barely catch my breath. Andrew looks at me. He shakes his head. *What the fuck*, he mouths silently. I ignore him. There's nothing left to say. I sit down. Bury my head in my hands.

It's surreal. My first week at school was a dream. The best week of my life. I told everyone the truth: I'm a girl. And no one hated me for it. I was accepted, even celebrated. I was the intriguing new girl; everyone wanted to be my friend. The most popular boy had a crush on me. My life was like a show on the Disney Channel, and I was the star, the beautiful girl at the center of the frame.

But now, that dream is over. It's like I woke up to discover that everyone actually hates me. They think I'm a freak, the weirdo who wanted to sneak into the girls' locker room and ask everyone about their bra sizes. No one will talk to me. No one will look me in the eye.

The rest of the day passes in a blur. The teacher's voice is a drone. I'm lost in my thoughts, agonized, terrified of what will happen when the bell rings and I'm forced to leave the safety of the classroom and confront a school full of kids who hate me. I keep playing my apology over and over again in my head, getting caught on the same sentence: *I should've told you all the truth.* But here's the thing: I *did* tell everyone the truth. I told them the truth from the very beginning. I *am* a girl. I've always known it. It's who I am. And I love who I am. And despite the scorn from my teachers, and my classmates, and my sister—despite all of that, there is a part of me, a small hopeful corner of my heart, where I know that I did absolutely nothing wrong.

I never lied. I just told them a truth they weren't ready to hear.

CHAPTER TEN

School is hell. For the next three weeks, the threat of violence is constant. Slurs are shouted at me in the hallway. I see clusters of kids gathered around the school bully. I know what they're doing. Egging him on. Telling him to give me what I deserve—a beating. Every time he sees me, he gets up in my face. I try to suppress my fear, keep my head down, rush to class, avoid the fight that everyone in the school wants to see. I wonder how long I can take it, how long I can endure the awful onslaught of hate. I pray, every day, to God. I know that God sees me for who I truly am. I know that God loves me. I pray that God will protect me.

And then my mom breaks the news: We're moving. She's found a place for us to live. We don't have to stay with her friend anymore. We'll have a place of our own.

And I get to switch schools.

Not a minute too soon. I'll never have to face that bully again. I can say goodbye to the hateful stares from my classmates, the disapproval from my teachers. The relief is overwhelming. God has saved my life. My prayers have been answered. The Lord has delivered me, has proven that there is a force more powerful than hatred, and that force is called love.

* * *

Our new apartment is on Morningside Avenue. It's two bedrooms, one bath. Small, but I don't care. It's *ours*. We don't have to share it with anyone. And I love it. My mom and sister have their own rooms. I'm the youngest, so I have to sleep on the foldout couch. But I don't care—I'm just happy that our family has a home again.

One morning, before school, I sneak into my sister's room while she's in the shower. I know I have to be quick. I know the consequences if I'm caught. I know that my mother would do unspeakable things to me if she learned my plan. But I have to live as my true self. I can't keep repressing who I am. The pain is too great.

So there's only one solution: I have to live a double life.

I go into my sister's closet. Grab a pair of jeans. A top. I shove them in my backpack. Run out the door of our apartment. Yell good-bye to my mother, without stopping. Then I'm on the street, on my way to Joseph Brant Middle School, hoping that this school will be different from the last. Hoping that I can find people who embrace me. The true me.

I run to the bathroom before the first bell rings. I rush into a stall, lock the door, and open my bag. I pull out my sister's jeans and slip them on. They're a perfect fit. They hug my curves in all the right places. Next, I shimmy into her top. It's also tight, feminine; it shows off my body. I unlock the stall and look in the bathroom mirror. Yes, this feels right. I look cute, feminine; these jeans feel like they were *made* for my butt. I walk out into the hallway, a little nervous, but determined to live my truth. There are no school uniforms to hide behind here, so dressing up is a way to tell everyone who I am.

I'm gonna do it a little differently this time, though. I'm not going to make a big announcement. Because why should I have to? Why does my gender have to be this huge issue? Why can't I just live my life like everyone else?

So, I walk down the hall, head held high, just another girl on her way to class.

For the rest of the year, I live my double life.

At school, I'm free. Free to wear whatever I want, act however I want, say whatever I want. But when the school bell rings, I know it's time to live a lie again. I wait until most of the other students leave, slip back into the bathroom, and change into the male clothes my mother expects me to wear. Thankfully, I find a group of friends who I can confide in about everything I'm going through. Janell, Celina, and Aushia are my absolute besties. They love and support me—the *real* me. We live in the same neighborhood, so sometimes we'll walk home from school together, laughing, or gossiping about boys, or sharing makeup tips, or belting out our favorite hits by Christina Aguilera and Leona Lewis. We all *love* to sing, and Janell and I even competed in Joseph Brant Idol—a singing competition that was our school's answer to *American Idol*. Janell always says I have such an incredible voice, but I think *she's* the amazing singer; she's stunning, Filipino, with long black hair—if she ever entered Miss Universe, I *know* she'd win. Celina is also gorgeous, so funny and smart—she has a Latina flair that electrifies every room she enters. And finally, there's Aushia, maybe my best friend of all. We live in the same building—she and her mom are just one floor above me. I'm constantly hanging out at her apartment; her mother is always so warm, so nurturing, she treats me like I'm her own child. Sometimes she'll drive us all to the movies—me and Aushia and Janell and Celina—then pick us up when we're ready to come home, tired, happy, and full of candy and popcorn and soda.

I feel like I'm finally blossoming into the young woman I was always meant to be.

But the minute I get back to my apartment, I have to hide. I try to avoid my mother as much as possible. It seems like she does the same. Like if we steer clear of each other, we won't have to confront

60

the truth. Fortunately, she's gone from the apartment many nights, working late. But when she's home, I play the part of the good son. It's exhausting. I repress my femininity. That's a thing about living a double life. The truth always lives in a shadow, hidden from the people you love the most. I know that if my mother could just accept me for who I am, if she could just show me the care and attention that every daughter deserves, we would be unstoppable, we could accomplish anything.

But I'm afraid that day will never come. Yet I hold on to hope, no matter how much it hurts, no matter how many times my mother disappoints me. I want to believe that the space between us is a gap we can close. I want to believe that our love will be enough to bring us back together.

CHAPTER ELEVEN

High school is another fresh start. Some people might be exhausted by the constant change I've endured since moving to Canada, by the pressure of having to repeatedly carve out your identity in a new environment. But I view each fresh start as an opportunity to write the next chapter of my story, and a chance to grow further into my true self. For this reason, I feel it's important to seek out the right school, somewhere I can keep my inner light shining.

So I apply to Sir Wilfrid Laurier Collegiate Institute, one of the best high schools in Canada, and I'm accepted. It feels like a confirmation of something: I'm on the right path. I'm worthy of love, I'm worthy of support, and even if it sometimes feels like those things are in short supply at home, there are people out in the world who see what I see in myself: a bright young girl, with a passion for life, a talent for sport, and a potential for greatness.

It's my first day of school. The bell rings. Sir Wilfrid Laurier is a massive complex, a maze of interlocking buildings. The hallways flood with students, hurrying toward our first assembly. The faces in the crowd are so diverse, so beautiful, it feels like every culture on earth might be represented here. The school consciously promotes an inclusive environment; no bigotry is tolerated, every ethnic heritage is celebrated, and queer kids are made to feel welcome. I feel lucky to be among a community that clearly embraces difference. There are no bullies lurking by their lockers, no hostile stares from students. Just an atmosphere of acceptance.

I dive into the stream of students. Excited chatter fills the air. Footsteps echo across linoleum. In the distance, I spot Aushia, Janell, and Celina, huddled around a locker. I let out a little scream of excitement, then cut across the wave of kids. I hug my friends— we're all so thrilled to be here, at this incredible school. We don't have much time before orientation, so we lock arms and follow the crush of bodies toward the auditorium, sharing stories of first-day jitters, tough teachers, and cute boys. The campus stretches on forever; there's a football stadium, an Olympic-sized pool, and a massive outdoor track. It's bright red, not rubber but dirt.

It reminds me of those dirt tracks I'd run on when I was a child.

Back in Jamaica.

A longing fills my heart. None of the schools I've attended in Canada have had track teams. It's been so long since I've donned my spikes. So long since I've sprinted down a straightaway. So long since I've felt that runner's high, that overwhelming euphoria.

I miss it.

Soon, we're marching into a massive auditorium, with two balconies, large enough to fit the fourteen hundred students that attend Sir Wilfrid Laurier. We find seats and settle in with the rest of the crowd. School leaders welcome us, and after their opening remarks, we move on to announcements.

A teacher steps up to the mic. He says that if we're interested in joining a sports team, there will be sign-up sheets posted on a bulletin board outside the gym. He rattles off a list of teams we can try out for: swimming, basketball, rugby, volleyball. As he goes down the line, I feel ambition rising within me. I have this crazy impulse to join every team he mentions; I'm swept up in this sense of boundless opportunity. Here, at this new school, I could be anyone, do anything, accomplish dreams I never thought possible.

The teacher comes to the end of his list. *And finally, you can try out for track.*

I feel a surge of emotion in my heart. My focus narrows. Yes, I want to try it all, I want to discover what other sports might bring me joy. But I *know* that whatever else I may try, that track will always be my number one. It's in my blood, my heritage, my history. It's a love that's tied to my identity as a Jamaican; it's something that was bestowed upon me as a young child, this passion for running, and the idea that it could lead me to great things, that it could open doors across the world. But it's also complicated, because I was traumatized by so much of my life in Jamaica, there was so much abuse, so much hatred aimed at me, and the sense that no matter what I did, no matter how much I excelled at the nation's most treasured sport, no matter how much glory I brought to my country, the people within its borders would never accept me.

Now, here I am in a new country, a new school, with a fresh chance to do the thing I love more than anything else. But this time, I can do it as the person I truly am, free from the fear of expressing my femininity, free from the terror of not knowing if I'll survive the walk home from school, free to be authentic as I want to be.

I have to get on that track team.

The day of tryouts arrives. I stand amidst a nervous bunch of fresh-man boys. I wish I was with the girls, where I belong, but I'm used to this. I'm the girl that runs with the boys. It's been that way for as long as I can remember. We're all stretching, warming up on a patch of green, encircled by the red dirt track. I feel calm, confident. I'm Jamaican. This is in my blood. Whatever complexities I may feel regarding my heritage do not diminish the fact that this is what I was born to do.

The coach divides us into smaller groups. There will be multiple heats. The runners with the best times will be accepted onto the junior varsity team. *That's where all the boys start,* he says. *If you work hard, one day, when you're a junior or senior, you'll make the varsity team.*

The time comes for my heat. First up, is the 100-meter dash. The eight of us walk out onto the track. Focus. I can tell these boys are green. They don't have years of running under their belt. But I do.

Runners, on your marks.

These are words I know well.

Get set.

I'm focused, ready to execute.

Go!

I bolt out of the blocks. Pass every boy with ease. I hit the home stretch, and it *feels* like home, it feels like this is where I belong, on this track, and the rest of the world fades to the background. I'm in my element, so alive, so free, so connected to my body, to my true self, hurtling toward a bright and beautiful future.

I cross the finish line.

I win the race.

The nerves kick in the next day. Even though I dominated my heat, that doesn't necessarily mean I'll make the team. Coach is looking at times from *every* heat and choosing the runners with the best overall performances. The list will be posted after school, on the bulletin board outside the gym. My confidence fades as the day stretches on. It's difficult to focus in class. My thoughts wander. What if my time wasn't good enough? What if the coach doesn't see my potential? What if I've been dreaming the wrong dream this whole time?

My last class of the day is French. The hardest class. With the toughest teacher. I can barely focus. The foreign words just sound like nonsense. Our teacher tells me to pay attention. But all I can think about is the team, the list, and whether I'll see my name printed on it.

The bell rings. I jump up from my desk, bolt out the door. The hallways are packed with students. I push my way through the crowd. I turn the corner, see the bulletin board. The hall outside the gym is empty—I'm the first one to get here. I scan the list for my name.

And I'm shocked.

I didn't make the junior team.

I made varsity.

My double life continues. It starts every morning behind the bathroom door. I lock it behind me. Open the medicine cabinet. Pull out my sister's makeup bag. I've started wearing her makeup. Nothing too flashy, just a little eyeshadow. Some subtle mascara to lengthen my lashes. Maybe glitter for my cheeks.

Then I throw my hoodie over my head. Can't let Mom see my makeup. I dash out the front door. There is something energizing about the early morning light. The promise of the sun. I rush to track practice. We train every day before school, and I'm always among the first to arrive. I've been on the team for months now, so I've got my routine down.

I get to the track and start warming up. I take off my hoodie. I greet my teammates. They smile and welcome me to practice. No one gives me shit about my makeup. No one gives me shit about my femininity. Because they know how dedicated I am. They know how hard I work. I demolish every drill I'm given. I'll run the 200 meter ten times in a row, stopping for only sixty seconds between each repetition. They know what a fierce competitor I am. A prodigy, really.

The only freshman on the varsity team.

They respect me because they can see that I'm a true athlete. Not only am I on the track team, but I've also joined the volleyball team. Two sports are a lot to keep up with in addition to my academics, but I'm making it all work. It feels like there's nothing I can't accomplish. And because of my positivity, because of my joy, I can feel that other students are drawn to me, other students want to be around me. I'm just so happy to be in a place where I am no longer the outcast, where people finally accept me.

But things are different when we travel to track meets. Sometimes I hear boys from rival teams whispering about me. They mutter slurs under their breath as we make our way onto the field. They give me dirty stares when we settle into our starting blocks. And later, after the meet, in voices just loud enough so I can hear, they might ask: *Why is there a girl in the boys' locker room?* Even though I hate the prejudice in their tone, I often wonder the same question myself. Why *am* I in the boys' locker room? I feel out of place here, uncomfortable, disconnected from my body. I never take a shower with the boys. I wish I could be with the girls, train with the girls, run with the girls. But I've come to accept that this is just another part of my double life. Yes, I can wear my sister's jeans and makeup; yes, I can be as feminine as I want to be at my new school, and that does make me feel seen and loved and happy. Yes, so many people want to be my friend, they see the way I move through the world with an open heart and an open mind, and I inspire them to do the same. But despite all this, there's still the painful fact of my double life, the fact that when I'm doing the thing I love the most, I still have to repress a part of who I am.

Time for practice, my coach calls out. *Let's go!*

I follow the boys out onto the field.

CHAPTER TWELVE

Everyone is talking about sex: who's having it, who's not, which guys are good in bed, which girls are easy, when we're gonna lose our virginity, how we're gonna lose our virginity, and who is gonna take it. During all these discussions, one thing is crystal clear: having sex is cool, and virgins are not. So, sex. It's all my friends can think about. All I can think about.

School's out for summer, and there are no classes to distract us, no extracurriculars, no homework, just endless afternoons to sit in the park, or hang out at Aushia's place, or walk home from Bible study with Janell, or stand outside the movie theater waiting for Celina's mom to pick us up, sweltering in the hottest summer on record, sweating through our clothes, and giggling about cute guys who pass us on the street. No matter where we go, no matter what we do, it seems like all conversations lead back to sex. And that's when I get shy. Because I'm not quite sure how to express what I feel. I know I like guys. But I'm not gay. Because I feel like a girl. And I'm attracted to straight men. So, does that make me straight? I'm constantly having this internal dialogue with myself. Which is why I don't speak up when I'm with my friends. Because I'm still unsure. I'm still figuring it out. I'm not ready to voice any of this out loud.

I need to explore on my own.

The heat is worse than it's ever been. My mother's in a mood. *We have to get out of this apartment*, she says as she wipes the sweat from her brow. *We're going to burn up here. But Chantal's got air-conditioning.*

Chantal is one of my mother's best friends; they've known each other since they were kids back in Jamaica. We head to their house, which is just down the street. I've been there many times— Chantal's daughter Lisa is a little younger than me, but we often hang out together. My mother settles herself in the kitchen with Chantal and her husband, Mark. I wander into the living room to hang with Lisa. We watch TV for a bit, but I get bored after a while. *Mind if I go on the computer?* I ask.

Go for it, Lisa says.

I wander over to their desktop computer. I hit the power button. The screen lights up. I grab the mouse, drag the cursor over to their internet browser. But just as I'm about to click, I notice that they have MSN Messenger.

I have an idea. A dangerous one.

I look back at Lisa. She's engrossed in her TV show, not paying attention to me. I stare at the computer screen, mustering courage. I click the MSN icon. It opens. I know that MSN has public chat rooms. Chat rooms that anyone can join, from anywhere in the world. They're organized by conversation topics, and it seems like you could discuss just about anything on here. There are chat rooms devoted to gardening, cooking, writing, cars, pets, cameras.

And sex.

Which is what I'm here for. I use keywords to search for a chat room that will give me what I'm looking for. And I find it. A chat room filled with men talking about sex. Only this time, unlike all those nervous and giddy discussions my friends are having, I'm free to join the conversation. Because I'm anonymous. I can hide behind my computer screen. I can say anything, I can be anyone, and no one will question me or judge me.

I'm free to explore.

As long as no one finds out.

It seems we're always at Chantal's house that summer. Whenever Lisa's there we'll hang out, sometimes watching her younger brothers, Tim and Henry, or sometimes just chilling on our own. But when she's not around, I go onto the computer.

I've started messaging with a few guys. I found them in the chat rooms. But we're now talking one-on-one. We never do any video calls—that would be too risky. I don't want Chantal or Mark or one of their kids to overhear what I'm saying. Because we're really getting into it. And it's fun. It's hot. I'm free to experiment. Just like all my other friends are doing that summer.

One day, while I'm in a chat room, I feel a presence over my shoulder. Like someone's watching me. I turn. Through the window, I see Mark staring at me. Staring at the computer. There's a strange expression on his face. I jump in surprise, then turn around and shut MSN. A terrifying thought pops into my mind: He'll tell my mother. But when I turn back to look out the window—to explain, to beg him to keep this secret—he's gone.

I bolt out of their house. I don't say goodbye.

The phone rings. My mother picks up. *Hey Chantal, what's up?* My heart pounds. She listens to Chantal. I can't hear what's being said on the other line. But I can guess. My mother's face tells the whole story. First, it's filled with confusion, then shock, and finally, fury.

* * *

We're speeding in the car. Back to Chantal's house. We picked up my brother on the way. My mom says this is a crisis. A family emergency. She needs my brother there for protection. Because she's afraid things could get physical. Because they're saying horrible things about me. Her son. Things she doesn't believe. Things that I've denied, even though I secretly know they're true.

Chantal said that Mark saw me on their computer, using MSN. He saw a conversation I was having. Couldn't believe the sexual nature of it. So later, after I left the house, he went on the family computer. Went into chat history on MSN. And there they were: weeks and weeks of my conversations. All sexual in nature. All with men.

They're lying, I say between sobs, crammed in the backseat with my brother. *They're lying.*

Then why do they say they have proof? my brother asks. This is why we're speeding to Chantal's house right now. To see the proof. I keep denying that it exists. Keep lying, hoping that my lies will be enough to convince them, hoping that they'll finally just believe me, take my word for it and turn the car around. But that doesn't happen. Because I know, deep down, they both fear that this might be true. That I might be a *battyman*.

I...I don't know.

You better be telling the truth, bro. My brother narrows his eyes. It feels like he's looking right through me. *Because if you're lying, and if you're really talking to other dudes about sex, I'm gonna beat your ass.* I burst into tears. I look to the driver's seat. Hope that my mom will turn back, tell my brother to stop it. But she just stares straight ahead. She lets him say whatever he wants. I'm terrified—I start shaking, sweating. My whole body goes numb. And I realize: if it comes down to it, if they find out that Chantal is telling the truth, my brother *will* beat my ass. And my mother won't stop him.

I pray. Pray for God to protect me. Because no one else will.

We pull up to Chantal's house. *Let's go,* my mother says.

There's an awful silence as we crowd around the computer. Chantal, Mark, my mother, brother, and me. The air is heavy with tension. There's so much anger, unexpressed. Violence, waiting to be released. But the target of the anger and violence is yet to be determined. Because we're all waiting to see the proof.

Mark presses the power button. The computer boots up. The screen glows. I feel so humiliated. He clicks on the MSN icon. I know what's coming next. I know what will come up on that computer screen. I don't know what I'll do. How I'll escape. Where I'll go. Who will keep me safe from my own family.

The program opens. Mark clicks on "Chat History."

I close my eyes. Wait for the yelling to start.

But it doesn't come.

I open my eyes again. Stare at the screen. It's blank. The Chat History is completely empty. No conversations, no pictures, nothing. I'm in shock. It's impossible. I feel dizzy with relief.

What the fuck? my brother says.

I swear there were conversations here earlier today, Mark insists.

I saw them too, Chantal chimes in.

Well then where the fuck are they?

I...I don't know. Fear fills Chantal's voice.

This is bullshit. My brother is shouting. All that pent-up rage has an outlet now. *Fuck you. Fuck your husband. And if I ever hear you talking shit about my family again, there's gonna be a problem.*

Please. Chantal looks to my mother fearfully. *I swear we—*

Let's go, my mother snaps, interrupting Chantal, grabbing me by the arm.

You guys fucked up, my brother shouts as we storm out of the room. *Fucked up big-time.*

On the way out, we pass Lisa. She's sitting at the kitchen table.

She looks at me with a strange intensity; her eyes are filled with kindness and understanding. A little smile lights her face. She doesn't have to say a word. I understand exactly what she's done, exactly what just happened.

Lisa saved my life.

CHAPTER THIRTEEN

My mother is suspicious. It feels like she's always watching me. The episode at Chantal's house was a close call. Too close. And even though I narrowly escaped a beating, I can tell that there is a part of my mother that still fears her son is a *battyman*.

Aushia and I come up with a plan. Aushia doesn't like it at first. I'm desperate to convince her. She's nervous; she doesn't want to lie to my mom. But I tell her that I have to. That something terrible could happen if we don't. My mother could beat me. My brother could beat me. I could end up in the hospital. I could be kicked out of the house. Forced to live on the street. The plan: We'll say that Aushia is my girlfriend. That we're going to get married one day. It's not totally a lie, because we joke about it all the time. Aushia's always saying that she loves me more than she'll ever love any man, so we should get married and grow old together and be best friends forever. *We'll still get dick on the side, of course*, she'll say, and we'll laugh and laugh. *But you'll always be my number one.*

So I tell my mother that Aushia is my girlfriend. I can tell that she doesn't quite buy it. But she wants it to be true so badly. So she chooses to believe the lie. She tells her friends and my brother and anyone who will listen that her son has a girlfriend, that he's just like all the other boys his age. My mom has a script that works for her. But I have to be more careful than ever. My situation is precarious, and the double life I'm living is at risk of being torn open.

But I'm safe. For now. We're a family again.

Only, it doesn't really feel like it. I want us to share an authentic life together, I want to be embraced for who I am, I want my mother to be invested in the woman I'm becoming, I want my mother to see the same bright future that I see for myself. I want the intensity of affection and care that only a mother can provide.

I want love, but all we have is lies.

Aushia is my "girlfriend" now. It's not a difficult lie to sustain because we're already inseparable, going to the movies, or shopping, or hanging with Celina and Janell. We're also on the cheer team together, which takes up more and more of my time now. I still run track, it's still my passion, it's still something I believe could propel me to great heights one day. But there's still the same problem: I'm a girl who's forced to run with the boys. I don't feel comfortable when I'm with the males, I don't feel like my teammates truly get who I am. Volleyball is better; it feels like my teammates understand who I am and admire my athleticism, even if I have to compete on the male team.

But with cheer, I feel most at home. Boys and girls train together, perform together. Our cheer team isn't just pom-poms and chants. We're true athletes. Cheer, *true* cheer, combines tumbling and lifting and gymnastics and dance into one of the most rigorous competitive sports there is. I started because I thought it would be great cross-training for track, helping me gain strength and improve my overall performance. But I stayed because it feels like I found a sport where I can be my true self, where my teammates not only understand me, but *celebrate* me. A sport where I can forget—even if it's just for the length of afternoon practice—that I'm forced to live this double life.

Which is why I can never tell my mother about it.

*   *   *

Come here, right now, my mother calls from the laundry room. I recognize the anger in her voice. It fills me with fear. I'm terrified that she's discovered another one of my secrets. I wrack my brain—*what could it be?*

I slowly make my way through our new apartment. We've moved again. To be closer to my brother and his wife and their children. My mom and Samantha have finally buried the hatchet. They'll never be best friends, but as long as they're not living under the same roof, they've found a way to be cordial. My mother gets to see her grandkids, and Samantha gets the babysitter she so desperately needs. Our new apartment on the West End, in Mississauga, is about ten minutes from my brother's house. My high school is back on the East End, at least a forty-five-minute drive away from our new place, but I don't mind. I like the afternoons I get to spend watching the kids, taking them on walks through the neighborhood, buying them treats at the local Indian grocery store, or bringing them to Auntie Claudia's condo for a swim in the pool. My mother seems happier, lighter. It feels like maybe, after all the turmoil and hurt and misunderstanding, we might finally be a family again.

Which is why I'm filled with dread as I make my way to the laundry room, terrified to see what my mother has found. I arrive at the door. She's digging in the dryer. She pulls something out: my cheerleading uniform. Specifically, my shirt. It's long-sleeved, black, and studded with a whole constellation of sequins. It sparkles so brightly. Too brightly. I know what she's thinking: it's so feminine, so girly, no real man would ever wear something like this. I usually hide it from her, doing my own laundry to make sure she doesn't see it. But today I slipped up. Forgot that it was in with the rest of my clothes. My heart beats faster..

What's this? she asks, holding the glittering top far from her body, like it might bite her.

It's…my cheerleading uniform.

Wrong answer. She's shocked. *You're…a cheerleader?*

But it's not what you think. Lots of guys are on the team. This is different than the cheerleading you see at American football games—it's a competitive sport. I can tell she doesn't believe me. I can tell she's furious. She's quiet and tensed. But I have an idea. *Let me show you something*, I say.

I google Top Gun Allstars, my favorite pro team. I pull up a video on my phone. It shows them competing at the Cheerleading Worlds. I watch my mother watch the video. My pulse races. Her face is skeptical at first, but then it begins to shift. She sees that there are so many men on the team, and I can tell she's comforted by the fact that they all are so muscular, so masculine, so athletic. These men lift women up into the air, forming the foundation of human pyramids. These men leap, and flip, and perform wild tumbling passes where they seem to defy gravity. By the end of the video, I can tell my mother is impressed.

You can do all this? she asks me. *The flips and everything?*

I'm learning, I reply.

She nods, and smiles. Even this small morsel of approval feels overwhelming. I feel so relieved. Because for the first time, my mother has peered behind the curtain of my double life and not berated me for what she saw. Instead, she's accepted a truth I thought I had to hide. There are no threats today, only support. And if she accepts this one small part of who I am, maybe there's hope for more.

Today, our whole high school cheer team is headed to a special training gym. It's home to a local all-star team, the Ultimate Canadian Cheer Tigers. Our coaches have paid for and arranged private sessions with professional teachers here, to help us strengthen our skills.

The gym is huge, a large warehouse space with vaulted ceilings, tall white walls, and a massive blue mat that spreads across the floor. The room buzzes with activity; athletes catapult across the mat, leap into the air, yell words of encouragement to one another.

We have a two-hour training session with one of the UCC coaches. I've seen videos of their all-star team online, and I know how fierce they are. I want to impress these coaches. I want to show them I'm more than just your average high school cheerleader. I want to show them I have what it takes to be great. So I give them energy, enthusiasm; I'm willing to try anything they throw at me. I'm not scared of new tricks; I'm not intimidated by a difficult tumbling pass. I'm a copycat at its finest; I'll mimic any move. And even if it's not perfect the first time, I'll keep working until it is.

Our high school team returns to the gym two more times. At the end of our last session there, one of the UCC coaches pulls me aside as the rest of my team packs up their things.

You have real talent, she tells me.

Thank you, I say.

With enough work, you could potentially make our all-star team. You should seriously consider training here.

I would love that. I just don't think…I have the money to train here on my own.

Well, there are ways we could work around that. Sometimes the gym will sponsor athletes if we see the potential. And we definitely see potential in you.

That's all I need to hear.

The gym sponsors me, and I dive into cheer with a newfound passion. My schedule is packed—every day feels like a marathon, but I love it. I wake up every morning at 5:00 a.m., get ready for school, and take the bus an hour across town in rush hour to make it for the 7:00 a.m. bell. Then, it's a full day of classes, followed by track practice. After practice is over, I head to the bus station. I take a bus to a train to another bus to get to my cheer gym—at least another hour, but this is when I get my homework done. Then, I arrive at the gym; my sponsorship is a work-study program, so I'll do whatever tasks they need me to take on, whether it's cleaning the mats or teaching a class of toddlers how to somersault. Once I've done my chores, then I'm free to use the gym, take classes, and hone my skills. After

I've gotten my workout in, I head back home. It's an hour-long trip at least and involves another bus/train/bus connection. I get back home between eleven o'clock and midnight, then get up at 5:00 a.m. the next morning to do it all again.

I'm exhausted. But I've never felt happier. More fulfilled.

At first my mom is skeptical. She's suspicious of people willing to support me so much—she doesn't want me taking charity. But she doesn't get it; this isn't charity. I'm working hard. These people see my talent, my drive, my potential. All things my mother still refuses to acknowledge. She doesn't see how anyone could want to support me, because deep down, *she* doesn't think I'm worthy of that support.

But as time passes, she starts to appreciate how hard I'm working. She sees the way others praise me. She recognizes a work ethic that feels familiar, that feels Jamaican. I'm willing to push harder than anyone else around me. I'm willing to go to bed later, wake up earlier, do anything it takes to achieve my goals. Sometimes she'll even stay up for me on those late nights, waiting with a bowl of curry goat when I walk through the door.

But it still feels as if there's a wall between us. A distance I can never bridge, no matter how hard I try. There's a limit to her love. Because of our hectic schedules—me with school and sports and cheer, her with work—we rarely see each other. When we do, conversations at home are quick and to the point. Small talk about the day and not much else. Sometimes we don't speak at all, and she'll spend the night on the phone talking to Terrence. It feels like I'm in the background of her life. She never once drives me to practice. Never comes to pick me up. Never asks how I'm progressing. Never shows anything other than a casual interest in the things I'm passionate about. It feels like I could run for prime minister of Canada, and I would still be unable to get her to believe in my potential, to *invest* in me.

Finally, the day comes: UCC asks me to join their all-star team. All the hard work has been worth it and has led to this victory. I feel like I could cry. I'll now get to join some of the best cheerleaders in the nation, as they perform across the country. We'll train together, travel together, compete together. We'll be a family.

It's a sleepover trip. We're taking a two-hour bus ride to Niagara Falls, where I'll perform in my first competition. I'm nervous, excited, my mind is racing—I don't know how I'll ever sleep at the hotel tonight. I look across the bus at Shelly, who smiles at me. Shelly is a "team mom," one of those maternal figures who chaperones out-of-town trips, organizes fundraisers, makes travel plans, attends practices, and provides both emotional support and false eyelashes to every girl on the team. She's blond, middle aged, middle class, and has the spare time and money to mother not only her own daughter, Melissa, but also so many other athletes. I didn't have the money for the trip to Niagara Falls, so Shelly got together with a few of the other parents and pitched in to cover my travel expenses. I want to believe that if my own mother wasn't forced to work around the clock to keep our family afloat, that she would be on this bus, just like Shelly. I want to believe that if my mother had the chance, she'd show up for me. But I also know that even if she had all the money and time in the world, there would still be the part of her that refused to accept me for who I am: her daughter.

The bus comes to a stop. We've arrived at the hotel. *Let's go find our room*, Shelly says to me and Melissa. *Come on, girls.* It's just one simple word—*girls*—but when Shelly says it, I'm overwhelmed. The way she just casually uttered it. Treated me like I was just another one of the girls on the team, like my identity wasn't some big issue or crisis or problem to solve. I'm amazed. I don't have to say anything, I don't have to explain or apologize or beg her to see the true me. She already accepts who I am, unconditionally, the way I wish my own mother would.

We come to our room, and Shelly opens it with her key card. *Here we are, girls*, she says. Melissa and I rush in, throw our suitcases into a corner. Shelly gets one bed, and me and Melissa will share the other. It's late, so we start to unpack and settle in. We have an early morning tomorrow.

Is your mom coming to the competition? Shelly asks as she steams my uniform, carefully smoothing all the wrinkles.

She can't make it, I reply.

Well, I'm sure she'll be rooting for you from back home, Shelly says. I'm not so sure, but I stay silent. *And for the time being, I can be your Cheer Mom.*

I'd like that.

And if you're her Cheer Mom, Melissa chimes in, *then I get to be her Cheer Sister!*

From that moment on, we're a Cheer Family. The rest of the year feels like a dream. Shelly takes me under her wing, she treats me like her own daughter. *Our house is your house,* she always says, and she means it. *Anytime you want to sleep over, just let me know.* And I do. I spend so many nights at their house, so many evenings around their dinner table, eating, laughing, sharing stories. Shelly drives me to practice and team parties and local competitions. Sometimes, we spend hours in the car together, me and Shelly and Melissa, our little cheer family. If I need someone to talk to, I know I can go to Shelly. If I need a space to feel safe, I know that Shelly can provide it. I've often been low-key envious of friends who have families that embrace them for who they are; this is the first time I feel like I might have a family of my own to celebrate me. Even though Shelly is not my biological parent, she takes care of me, just like a real mother would. She makes up for that lack I feel. She fills the hole in my heart. She makes me feel seen, whole, and happy.

My real mother still holds me at an arm's length. She sees the way Shelly cares for me, and I think she respects it. She understands that other people are inspired by my passion, excited by my potential, and want to nurture me. I think she's happy for me. But it doesn't inspire her to step up to the plate and invest in me.

She doesn't come to a single competition, or a single practice.

She never sees me cheer. Just like she's never seen me run track. And I wish I could say this surprises me, but it doesn't.

We're moving back to Jamaica, my mom announces one day when I get home from school.

My heart shatters. This can't be happening. Not now. Not when I've finally found my community in Canada, not when I've created a life I love, not when I feel like I'm blossoming into the woman I'm meant to be, and yes, I still have to live this double life, I still have to hide my true self from my mother, but I've found a makeshift family that accepts me for who I am. I just can't believe that it comes to an end right here. And I have no say in the matter. My mom says we're moving, so we're moving. There's no discussion, no negotiating.

I put on a brave face. *It could be interesting to go back,* I say. *To see how Jamaica has changed since we moved.* But I don't really mean it. Inside, I feel nervous and anxious.

She says that she wants to reconnect with her family again. With Terrence. It's been so long since they've all lived in the same place. She's also saved up some money and wants to keep working on the house she's building in the country, on the land my grandfather left her. She says it'll just be for a short time. Just long enough for her to get some rest and reconnect with her people. Then, we'll figure out our next move.

But I don't want to live in Jamaica again. I want to stay right here, in Canada. I'm almost seventeen. Almost an adult. I wish I *was* an adult, so I could choose my own path, so I wouldn't be ripped from the life I've created here. Thrust back to Jamaica. The land where I endured so much trauma. A country that is not safe for someone like me.

I wish...I could...adopt you, Shelly says between sobs. We're both crying, huddled in the corner of the UCC gym. Moments ago, I said my goodbyes to all my teammates. That was hard enough; I stood in front of everyone, on the blue mat, and announced that I was moving away, that I was so sad to go, that I was so grateful for all their love and support and that's when I just burst into tears. Everyone leapt up, rushed to hug me, and I was enveloped in one big embrace, which made me sob even harder, because it just reminded me of what I was leaving behind: this beautiful warmth, this wonderful family, this love unlike any love I've ever known.

But saying goodbye to Shelly is so much harder. It feels like I'm losing my mother.

I really do want to, Shelly wipes away her tears. *I wish you could be my daughter.*

Then do it, I say. *Adopt me.*

Shelly looks slightly surprised, then saddened. *I...I don't think that would be realistic. You're leaving so soon.*

You're right, I say, rushed.

Besides, your mother loves you very much. She knows what's best for you.

I nod in agreement with what Shelly's said, but I don't know if I believe it. I'm not sure my mother knows what's best. I'm not sure my mother knows how to love me. I hoped that cheer might be the thing that would *finally* impress her, *finally* inspire her to invest in me. But no. It seems like no matter what I do, no matter how hard I work, no matter how incredibly I perform, whether it's on the track or competing with elite-level cheerleaders, my mother just does not care. And maybe it's because she's too overworked, maybe it's because she doesn't have the time. Or maybe there's a small, hard part of her heart that simply refuses to love me. Because of who I am, because I'm not masculine enough, because I don't fulfill her idea of how her son should act.

But I'm *not* her son. I'm her daughter. A daughter who deserves love from her mother.

But I've never gotten this love from her. How cruel to deny me that love. How awful to see all my potential, to see my talent, to see how I excel at so many things, and still deny me. I want my mom to embrace my skills and talent and athleticism. I want my mom to see me, believe in me. Invest in me. If she would just do that one thing, I know we could shine so bright together. And this knowledge burns in my heart, burns so much it hurts. If she would just nurture me, there's nothing we couldn't achieve together. There would be no such thing as an impossible dream. Because when you have a dream, especially as an athlete, when your dream is to be the greatest of all time, that's not only your dream, that's your parents' dream as well. That's your sibling's dream. That's your family's dream. And when they're all dreaming your dream with you, that force of energy is stronger than anything.

And I thought for a moment that maybe Shelly could be the woman to provide this love. Because she treated me how I want my mother to treat me. She saw me for who I truly am: a young girl, bursting with potential and passion, on the verge of something great.

I'm gonna miss you so much, Shelly says, as she wraps her arms around me, and holds me so tight it hurts. *Stay in touch, okay?*

I promise her I will. I promise I'll never forget her, that I'll always love her.

I fly back to Jamaica the next day.

CHAPTER FOURTEEN

I'm in survival mode. From the minute we touch down in Jamaica, I feel unsafe. In Canada I was coming into myself, my womanhood, my body, my curves, my femininity. Yes, I was forced to live two lives at once—the false one for my family, and the true one for myself—but there was freedom once I burst out of our apartment and onto the streets of Toronto. Not so in Jamaica. The woman I'm becoming is not welcome in Jamaica. This woman is at risk of being harassed, being beaten, being shot. I dim my light, I keep my head down, I try not to attract attention to myself. I act as masculine as possible, changing what I wear, and the way I walk, talk, and carry myself.

I begged my mom to attend Campion College, the most prestigious high school in Jamaica, with an immaculate campus, stunning facilities, an international student body, and a legendary track program. But she said "no." Instead, she puts me in a bad school in a bad neighborhood because my aunt is the bursar and can get us a discount on tuition. Once again, she refuses to invest in me. I've done everything I can to prove to her that I can excel at so many things—track, cheer, singing, academics—and she just denies me at every turn, as if these denials will somehow force her daughter to become the son she wishes she had.

This new school is in a dangerous part of Kingston. I don't feel safe there. I join the track team, hoping that people will be impressed by my athleticism, and that my identity as an "athlete" will once again provide me with protection. But not at this school. Track is no longer a safe haven. My teammates harass me. I'm afraid to use the locker room when certain boys are there, because these boys want to beat me up. And they're not the only ones. There are boys in my class who carry guns. Boys you don't want to cross. There's one bully who's targeted me, a boy who is not to be fucked with, a boy who is the son of the most notorious mafia *don* in Jamaica. He roughs me up, threatens me, demands money from me. I always give it to him, because I don't want trouble.

But it seems like trouble is everywhere.

I get hostile looks—on my way to the bus, outside the movie theater, leaving school. When I'm out in public, I try to act more masculine, hurry to my destination, avoid any alleyways or abandoned lots. *Go to school and go the fuck home.* That's my mantra, that's my strategy for avoiding violence. People call me names behind my back. I know my mother has to defend me against the gossip going around, I know she's still clinging to the lie I told her back in Canada: That I'm a boy who's attracted to girls. I wonder if she tells people about the "girlfriend" I had back in Canada. Or maybe she just stays silent, resigned, secretly agreeing with the whispers circulating around town.

Because people are talking.

Word on the street: I'm a *battyman*, which means the streets aren't safe for me. When you're a kid in Jamaica, you can get beat up for being a *battyman*. When you're older, you can get killed. My mom rarely lets me leave the house. We're living with Terrence again. His brother also lives with us. They keep a close eye on me. Sometimes, on the weekends, we head out to the house in the countryside, which is more of a construction site than a home. Other times, I'll stay with my aunt. But no matter where I stay, no one wants me to leave the house. There's this unspoken understanding that if I do, I might never return.

I need to be careful. I know I'm putting myself at risk. But I'm going to do things differently this time. I'm going to take precautions. My mom is out. So is Terrence. His brother is here, but on the opposite end of the house, and he rarely bothers me. The door to his room is shut. It's almost like I have the place to myself.

So, I pull a chair up to the computer.

I open MSN Messenger.

I can't be myself in Jamaica. I can't walk down the street without worrying about my life. But online, I'm safe. Free to be whoever I want.

Free to flirt with whoever I want.

I go back to the chat rooms I found when I was in Canada. Because let's face it: I'm a bored teenager, stuck at home. What horny sixteen-year-old *wouldn't* take this opportunity to message people online? I start chatting with a few people. Some are the same men I found in Toronto. Some are new. And it's fun to explore.

Suddenly, I hear a sound. Terrence's brother is in the kitchen. I close the chat window. But I don't leave, not yet. I don't want a repeat of the episode in Canada. Last time I was lucky. Last time fate and Lisa intervened. But this time, there will be no one to rescue me, no one to save me from my mother's wrath at the last minute. This time, I take every precaution.

I delete my history.

I've been waiting for this moment all day, all through school, all through choir practice. I've been anticipating the moment that me and my friends will walk to the bus terminal, approach the food truck that waits there every day, and order our fresh Jamaican patties.

I need two spicy patty, I say to the man, and he hands me two steaming patties, with golden brown crust that's so buttery and flaky that a little flurry of crumbs falls to the pavement. They're scalding hot, but I never wait for them to cool off. I eat the patty right away and it burns the roof of my mouth, but I don't care, because it's just so good, so flavorful. Steam rises from the beef, and I taste the fresh green onion, the scotch bonnet peppers. Joy spreads across my face. I turn and smile at the two friends I've brought with me today. They're friends I've made in choir, which is the one place I can let some of my inner light shine through. It's not all bad, this time around in Jamaica. There are pockets of joy, little moments like this one, where I can share the simple joy of a delicious meal, with two friends, on a beautiful afternoon in Kingston.

We board the bus. It rumbles to life. My stomach is full. I feel content and happy.

I arrive home, open the front door, and make my way down the hall. I pass the room with the computer, peer in. Terrence's brother is hunched over the screen. He jumps when he hears my footsteps. Turns around. Gives me a strange look. Almost like he's angry or confused.

I wave, then keep on moving. I try not to entertain paranoid thoughts. He was probably just surprised, annoyed that I'd scared him. Nothing more than that.

Later that afternoon, I see him in a hushed conversation with Terrence. I pass, and they both stare at me, silent, before returning to their discussion. I worry that they're talking about me. Have they found something on the computer? Something incriminating? An MSN Messenger conversation? But no, that would be impossible. I've been so careful. I've deleted my history every single time. There is not a trace of evidence on that computer, I'm sure of it.

* * *

Come here! my mother calls from the kitchen. I walk into the room. The look on her face fills me with terror. I can feel the anger radiate from her body. *What did you do?* she demands.

What...what are you talking about? I didn't do anything.

Don't lie to me, she says, her voice brimming with rage. *I'll give you another chance: What did you do?*

I recognize this tactic. My mother's done it before. She's giving me an opportunity to come clean. To tell her the truth on my own before she's forced to confront me with what she already knows. I wrack my brain. What could make her this furious? I can only think of one answer: somehow she's found my conversations on MSN Messenger. But how? There's no way. I've covered my tracks. I've been meticulous. *I swear, I didn't do anything*, I say.

Tony was on MSN Messenger the other day. A man started messaging him. All sorts of nasty disgusting things. Pornographic things, she shouts. Her fury echoes through the kitchen. *And this man was looking for you.*

I...I...that's not true. My heart is beating out of my chest. I'm so scared. There's no hiding this time. There's nothing I can do. I've been caught.

There is proof! You can't deny it, she yells. I burst into sobs. *It's right there on the computer. It's true, it's always been true, you were lying to me back in Canada, you've been lying to me this whole time.* She's screaming now. She moves to the kitchen counter. There's a machete lying there. Gleaming on the countertop. She grabs it.

Hatred fills her eyes. I'm shocked by what I see next: it seems to me like she's running at me, swinging the machete. *Mom, stop!* I yell through my tears.

Terrence appears. He grabs my mother. Holds her back. She flails in his arms, fights to get free. But Terrence doesn't loosen his grip. Doesn't let her go.

He saves my life.

But I feel no relief. Only terror. My secret has been revealed.

* * *

Terrence is taking my mother to the country house. He's not sure how long they'll be gone. He says she needs time to cool off. We can't be under the same roof. It's not safe. And they need to figure out what they're going to do with me. Terrence's brother is disgusted by me. Doesn't want to live with a *battyman*. He's leaving the house too. Just for now. Just temporarily. Until they figure out where I'm going to go. Because I can't stay here. Not in this house. And if word gets out, if his brother tells other people about what he discovered on the computer, then I can't stay in Jamaica, period. There will be an even bigger target on my back. My life will be in greater danger than before.

I'm now a problem to be solved.

I am grateful to Terrence. He saved my life that day. Despite all that we've been through—despite his horrible treatment of my mother when I was a child—he never once laid a hand on me. I don't forgive him for what he did to my mother, but I also don't think he's some sort of villain. I think a part of him really loves her. I think a part of him even loves me. I think a part of him wishes I was his blood, because he's always longed for a child. And I was so good growing up, I was the perfect obedient child. I always went to the store when he asked. I never got into trouble, never got mixed up in gangster shit, never got any girls pregnant. The only time he'd be mean or aggressive toward me was if I did something feminine, like overenunciate my words or gesture flamboyantly. He hated when I acted like a *battyman*.

And I can feel that hatred in his eyes now. I can hear the disappointment in his voice.

They leave me alone in the house. My mother doesn't say goodbye. They don't give me any money. There's not much in the cupboards. Only chicken and rice. I make it all, then ration it out. I'm not sure how long I'll need it to last. How long they'll be in the countryside. How long it will take for them to decide my fate.

CHAPTER FIFTEEN

If he stays in Jamaica, he's not going to survive until the end of the year, Terrence whispers to my mother, as I eavesdrop from the next room. They're back from the countryside. Things have cooled down.

We need a plan, my mother replies.

Soon, I learn their plan. Short term: I can no longer live with them in Terrence's place. His brother has a problem with me staying at the house. He says he doesn't want to live under the same roof as a faggot. Terrence is worried that he might hurt me. So they're sending me to live with my aunt. They're not telling her what happened. They're keeping it a secret. Because it won't be safe for me if word gets out. Which is why they've decided that soon, I have to move back to Canada or the United States.

Because I could get killed here.

I travel out to the country house. We're all going to be together for the weekend. My sister has flown in from Canada. My mother will cook. Terrence will be there too. I don't love the house itself—my mother and Terrence have built it from the ground up, and right now, it's still under construction, just a collection of nearly empty rooms, littered with power tools. But I love the land. It was a coffee farm at one point, though when my mother inherited it from her father, the land had been untended for years, growing into a tangle of weeds and vines and wildly overgrown coffee shrubs. At first, there was no house—my mother would have to build one—and our land stretched for acres, sloping up a steep hillside bursting with lush vegetation. We grew limes, oranges, plantains, mangoes, and tall stalks of sugarcane. I remember summers where my sister and I were recruited by my mother to cut out the weeds and overgrown grasses. We'd work the fields, gradually making our way up the mountainside, watching out for snakes and lizards that slithered underfoot. I loved walking along the river that flowed beside our property line, loved eating fresh sugarcane, snapping the thick stalk and sucking at the sweetness inside.

I like being out in the country. Things have calmed down. My sister's presence seems to put my mother at ease. I've told my mother that I'm bisexual. That I don't really like guys. That I was just curious, just exploring, that I really like women. My sister has been backing me up, advocating for me. My sister knows I'm in danger. Which is why she helps the situation. She doesn't want to see me get hurt. She's been getting into evangelicalism recently; she's committed to being a good Christian. She tells my mother that when she was younger, she also experienced desire for the same sex, but God eventually steered her in the right direction. It was just a phase that she grew out of, and she believes that I will also grow out of it. I know that I'm *not* going through a phase. Even still, I'm grateful to my sister for helping to calm my mother.

I walk along the river by myself, taking in the landscape. I stop under the shade of a mango tree; its branches are heavy with clusters of ripe fruit. I pick a mango from the tree, open it, and eat the sticky yellow meat inside. Here, in the quiet of the wilderness, I get a break from the stress of being with my family. I get a moment of peace.

I return to the country house. But as I'm walking up, I notice that there is a small group of people in the backyard. Our lush acreage stretches behind them. They're standing in a circle. My sister is there, along with my mother, my aunt, Terrence, and a few of my mother's friends. My sister waves me over. *Come on over, we want to talk to you for a minute*, she says.

I walk toward them, confused.

Suddenly, they begin to surround me.

This is a healing circle, my sister says. I'm trapped inside a circle of bodies. My heart begins to pound. *We're going to pray over you*, my sister continues. *Because you have the devil inside you, and we're going to drive him out*. I feel claustrophobic. Panicked. I can't breathe. My sister puts her hands on me. *God, take the devil out of my brother*. She begins to shake me. *God, I know these aren't my brother's thoughts, please take these impure thoughts from his mind*. She shakes me harder. It feels like she starts hitting me, slapping me. *God, please take the devil out of him*. I'm trapped inside this circle of people. And I'm so angry. Because what they're doing is wrong. This isn't what God wants. This isn't a prayer circle—this is an ambush. I know that my God would never do this to me. I know that my God loves me, loves *everyone* for exactly who they are.

I'm so furious. But there's nothing I can do. Nowhere to run. I just stand there and allow them to continue this awful ritual. They keep going, but I stay strong. Soon, my anger gives way to deep sadness. How can this be happening? How can my *family* do this to me? Instead of giving me care and affirmation, instead of loving who I am, they're trying to force it out of me. In the name of God.

But this isn't what God is about. God is love. And this "prayer circle" is nothing but hate. So I refuse to let it ruin my faith. I could walk away from this situation believing the lies they're all spewing, believing that God doesn't love me.

But no—God is speaking to me today. God is telling me that I am loved. God is telling me that I do not need to change who I am. God is telling me to be a warrior for my faith. Even if no one in my family affirms me, I know that God does. I will survive this. I will emerge stronger in my faith than ever. Because I love the woman I'm becoming, and I know that God does too.

The weeks pass. The prayer circle was a wake-up call. I need to watch my back. I stay locked into survival mode. I stay quiet. Neutral. Suppress my femininity. Suppress my sexuality. Suppress my authenticity. It seems like my family believes that the prayer circle worked. But of course it didn't. I'm so unhappy. I want to leave the country and never come back.

Then, my mother finds a job. In New Hampshire. Her friend Prudence helped her find it. Prudence lives in a small city called Lebanon. We'll stay with her family when we first arrive.

I'm ready. I feel hopeful. Because I have a plan. Once I've gotten my bearings, once I've adjusted to America, I know what I have to do.

I have to run away and start a life of my own.

CHAPTER SIXTEEN

I love it here in Lebanon. It's a city, but it feels like a town. It seems like everyone knows one another, and even if they don't, it's not uncommon for strangers to say hello as they pass on the street. There's an old New England charm to the buildings; houses have pitched roofs, big front porches, and healthy lawns. We live in a two-story home on Colburn Street, at the top of a steep hill, just around the corner from a small plaza with shops and restaurants and a beautiful brick church. Prudence has a big family; we share the house with her husband, her two sons, and her younger daughter. The older daughter is away at college, so me and my mom share her room. I love the tender chaos of the mornings, when the adults get ready for work, and the kids get ready for school, and the whole house hums with activity. Every weekend feels like a party; Prudence is Jamaican too, and she and my mom will cook food that feels like home, and everyone will gather around the dinner table to talk and laugh and share a delicious meal. Things have gotten better with my mother; now that we're out of Jamaica, the tension has faded. The move has brought us closer together, though I still hide my femininity from her.

We stay for the summer. I love it, but my mother is eager to find a place we can call our own. And I understand. We're living in someone else's home. She makes a friend at work, another Jamaican woman named Hermine, who is also looking for an apartment in Lebanon. The two women decide to hunt for a place together so they can save on rent. Hermine is sweet, Christian, and always kind to me. Eventually, Mom and Hermine find an apartment. The place is cozy, and my mother and I share the biggest room. I'm happy; things are so much better now that we're out of Jamaica. No longer do I feel like I'm risking my life by walking down the street. No longer do I feel like I have to hide who I am in order to survive. I feel free. I feel excited. I feel like there are endless possibilities here.

But my mother is already restless. She keeps talking about how much she misses her sister. She keeps saying that she'd love to live in New York City, so she could be closer to her sister, to her nephews. Closer to Toronto, so she could visit my brother, his wife, and their children. I can't imagine moving again. I've just started my new school. Lebanon High School, home to the Lebanon Raiders. I've started to make friends. At first, I was wary—I'm one of only three Black kids in the whole school. It's a very white community. But everyone is welcoming, everyone is curious about the new kid. I still live my double life, only revealing my true self at school; I play things low-key at first, gradually revealing my personality as I become more comfortable. I'm not bullied, I feel safe enough to run at night. Lebanon High also has an incredible track team; I can tell that this school is serious when it comes to sports—it could be a major step toward my goal of becoming a professional athlete. And so when my mother tells me she's thinking about another move, my heart sinks. *But what about us?* I want to say. *What about me? My life?*

But I never do. I just wait, hoping she changes her mind. Hoping we can settle somewhere for once, instead of packing our suitcases again, and uprooting our lives like we always do. I'm ready for stability, for permanence. I'm ready to find a place to call home.

* * *

Track tryouts. Everyone boards the bus. My classmates settle into their seats. There's a nervous hum in the air. But I'm not anxious. I'm ready to blow them all away.

We drive to Dartmouth College, a short fifteen-minute journey to Hanover, the next town over. The bus pulls into the parking lot of the Leverone Field House. This is Dartmouth's indoor track facility—and it's stunning. The building is one giant arch, gleaming white, held up by massive black metal scaffolding. I follow my fellow varsity hopefuls through the doors.

The facility is massive, immaculate. The roof is vaulted, arching, two acres long. Natural light streams in through the large, paneled windows. The red rubber track stretches around a field of green AstroTurf. I enter the stadium. I feel like I belong here, like my journey has led me to the right place, a place where I can truly shine, where I can pursue my calling.

In other words, I feel like a boss ass bitch.

And I'm ready to dominate.

Coach Andrew Gamble leads us through tryouts. He's aggressive, strict, no nonsense. But behind the tough coach demeanor, I can sense that there is real kindness and love. That he has a passion for what he does and a devotion to his athletes.

I want to impress him. And I do.

I make varsity.

At the end of tryouts, he announces everyone who's made the team. He calls us one by one and asks us to line up. Then, he goes down the line, assigning an event to each person. Giving us each an identity as an athlete, with one simple word. He points to each team member as he passes, announcing their position. *Sprinter, sprinter, jumper, hurdler, sprinter.* Then he gets to me and points. *Hurdler,* he says, and keeps moving.

I'm shocked. I've never hurdled before in my life. I can't do this. Hurdling takes such skill. I've only ever sprinted. There must be some mistake. I step out of line. Interrupt him.

Excuse me? I ask.

97

He stops. Gives me a stern stare. This is not a man who is used to being interrupted. *Yes?*

Did you say, hurdler?

Yes, he says, mildly annoyed. *Now did I tell you to get out of line?*

No, I say and hurry back to my position. He keeps going, like nothing happened. Like he didn't just upend my entire world. I was so confident walking into tryouts today, but now all I feel is anxiety. Insecurity. I don't have what it takes to hurdle. I *can't* do this.

I take a breath. I remember a cheer instructor I had back in Canada. If we ever said the word "can't" in her class, she would make us do push-ups. Punishment for not believing in ourselves, for not seeing our own potential. So I bite my tongue. Fight the urge to say "I can't."

Because Coach Gamble is choosing to invest in me. This is what I've always longed for. Someone to see my potential, to nurture my talent, to dream my dream with me. It won't ever be my mother; I know that much now. But it could be this coach. He's a man with so much experience. And if he sees a hurdler in me, then I'm going to become the *best* hurdler he's ever had on his team.

Oh, and you should know one thing, he says to us. *Our first meet is just one month away.*

We start with foam hurdles. They look like big blocks, the width of a track lane. At the top, there are strips of foam attached with Velcro. If I jump, and don't clear the hurdle, the foam strips will break away. That way, I don't injure myself. It gives me the freedom to experiment, to learn. And I'm grateful for that freedom, especially at the start.

Hurdling is difficult. The form isn't intuitive. It's not a jump. It's an elongation of your stride over a hurdle. You have to train your body to move in a way that feels unnatural. You have to train your mind to ignore the voices of doubt hovering in your thoughts.

But I'm determined to learn. Coach Gamble says that I have

what it takes to be a hurdler. I don't want to let him down. I don't want to let myself down. So I go hard. I hit those foam hurdles. I fail, fall down, make mistakes. But I always get back up. I don't have a choice. Our first meet is right around the corner.

I start to get better. My form improves. My body adapts. I've always been an expert copycat. It's one of my strengths as an athlete. It's how I became such a skilled cheerleader in such a short period of time. I listen to my coach. I watch the seniors, take note of their form, mimic their warm-ups. Soon, I'm barreling over hurdles like it's nothing.

Like I was born to do this.

Runners to your marks!

I walk to the starting block. My pulse is racing. I'm competing in the 60-meter hurdles for the first time in my life. I feel immense pressure. My team is watching. My coach is watching. Everyone is cheering me on. Screaming my name. I've seen my competitors during their warm-ups. I know they're good. I know this will be an intense race. But despite my nerves, I also feel an excitement start to build in my chest. I'm ready to perform, to prove myself. I'm ready to tear this track up.

Get set!

Boom! The gun goes off. And I'm gone. Out of the blocks. Soaring down my lane. Hurdle one is coming up fast. I spring forward, elongate my stride, and I'm up, up, up, and over. Adrenaline surges through me. Hurdle two is next. A sudden twinge of doubt surges through my body. I can't. I can't get over the next hurdle. It's too soon. I make a split-second decision. Run around the hurdle. Hope no one notices. Hurdle three is next. I have to make it over this one. I can't fuck up again. I focus. Push harder. And I'm over hurdle three. I pass a competitor. And another. Over hurdle four. One more to go. Every muscle in my body is burning. And then, I'm over hurdle five. The finish line is right there. I push, I lean, I pump my arms.

And then it's over.

I win third place. Score points for my team. Not only that, but my time has qualified me for nationals. Not bad for my very first time competing in the hurdles. I can hear my teammates cheering from the stands. Euphoria rushes over me.

But then I see Coach Gamble's face. Anger casts a shadow over his features. He calls me over. *What was that out there?*

What do you mean?

You ran around the second hurdle. You're disqualified.

But—

There's nothing more to discuss. You went around a hurdle. That's against the rules. So you're disqualified.

He walks away. The joy I felt just moments ago is replaced by rage. I feel betrayed. He's supposed to be on my side. No one else noticed that I went around hurdle two. If he just stayed quiet, I could've qualified for nationals.

But that would be cheating.

My anger fades. I feel disappointed in myself. I know Coach Gamble is right. I can't cheat my way to nationals. I have to play the game right. I make a vow right there: I can't let him down ever again. I need to show him that it wasn't a mistake to invest in me. That I have what it takes to be a star athlete. I'm going to train harder than ever and compete like my life depends on it. I want to make my supporters proud. This is a huge part of my drive as I start developing as a track athlete.

But for some reason, I can't regain my confidence. The indoor season is brutal. I compete in race after race, but I can't seem to win. Can't get a qualifying time. Everyone wants a spot in the state championships, which is why these qualifying meets are so important. If you make it through States, then you move onto New England Regionals, and then, finally, USA Track & Field National Championships. I watch as so many of my teammates win event after event, earning their spot at States. It feels like I've made one mistake, and now I'm paying for it for the rest of the season. It feels like I keep letting Coach Gamble down. I can't find my stride, can't gain momentum. I keep failing, until finally, I'm on the bus heading to the "Last Chance Meet."

The Last Chance bus is not a bus you want to be on. It's lonely there. Dispiriting. At the start of the season, our buses are packed with kids, rowdy, excited, all hoping to get qualifying times. But gradually, as people qualify, they stop coming to less important meets, so they can conserve their energy for States. Slowly, the number of runners on the bus dwindles, until there are only a few unlucky runners, pessimistic about their odds of becoming champions, heading to the Last Chance Meet, the final opportunity to qualify for States. And I'm here. On the Last Chance Bus, on my way to the Last Chance Meet, feeling like there's *no* chance for me.

We pull into the parking lot of the University of New Hampshire. Our small crew disembarks. We head to their indoor track. Find a spot to settle under the harsh glow of fluorescent lights. I check out the competition. I see them warming up. I can tell they're fierce. My confidence diminishes even further. I feel hopeless. Doubt swirls in my mind. Was it a mistake to believe in myself? Did I not push hard enough?

First there's prelims. Initial heats to narrow down the competition.

An announcer comes over the loudspeaker. It's time for the 60-meter hurdles. My event. I head to the starting blocks. Take my place. My adrenaline is pumping. Something shifts within me. My focus narrows. I still have this one shot left. Why waste it? This isn't the time to give up. This is the time to kill it, to put my whole mind and body into the race, to leave it all on the track. Yes, I could fall. Yes, I could fail. But fuck it. I have nothing to lose.

The gun goes off.

And I'm out of the blocks. Like a rocket. I cross the finish line.

I qualify for finals.

But I stay focused. It's not time to celebrate yet. The top athletes from this meet converge on the track for one last showdown. This race is all that stands between me and the State Championships. Once again, the gun goes off. Once again, I'm out of my blocks. Once again I dominate the race. Pushing until the very last second. Pushing toward the finish line. Pushing to overtake the boy in the lead.

I finish the race. I come in second. I qualify for State Championships. I'm so proud. More motivated than ever before.

From there, the momentum continues. I'm unstoppable. Coach Gamble was right to bet on me. Smart to invest. Because I'm proving that I have what it takes to be a great athlete. I sail through State Championships. Dominate the competition. I qualify for the New England Regional Championships. The underdog of the season is now leading the pack. I arrive at regionals with pride and gratitude filling my heart. I've made it so far. I've accomplished so much in my first school year in the US. I'm one step away from competing in the USA Track & Field National Championships. I'm close, so close I can envision myself racing, winning, standing on the podium to collect my medal.

But regionals doesn't go as planned.

I don't make it to nationals. But it's okay. Coach Gamble says that this is just the beginning, that he is so impressed with my performance this season. He starts training me as a decathlete—I picked up the hurdles so quickly, he's convinced I could excel at all ten events. He says I have a serious future in track and field, that the foundation we build together now could lead me to a future as a college athlete, as a pro, as an Olympian. After so many years of uncertainty, I finally feel like I'm in the right place, standing on solid ground.

Then, my mother tells me we're moving to New York City.

CHAPTER SEVENTEEN

I break down. Right in Coach Gamble's office. I sob, sitting across from him. I tell him that I can't believe I have to move again. I don't want to uproot my entire existence. I love Lebanon so much. I've found a place where I'm fully accepted, fully embraced, no bullying, no taunts, people love me, love my smile, love the bright energy I bring into every room. I have so many friends, I love all the relationships I've developed, I can't leave them behind. And this isn't the first time this has happened—I've been taken away from other supportive communities. It was gut-wrenching to leave them. I can't imagine abandoning another loving community. And finally, I say to Coach Gamble, I can't imagine leaving this track team. Not now. Not when it feels like I'm on the verge of something great.

Coach Gamble looks at me. His face softens. I can see the kindness in his eyes, the tenderness that emerges when he drops the tough coach act and allows a sweet father figure to emerge. *Well, it seems like you really don't want to move*, he says softly.

No, I don't.

Would you want to stay here? If you could figure out a way?

Yes.

Then let's come up with a plan.

* * *

Mom, I have something to ask you. I look my mother in the eye. She stares at me, expectant. I know this moment is crucial. I know the answer to the question I'm about to ask could affect the trajectory of my entire life. *Do you think I could finish out my junior year in New Hampshire? Stay here while you move to New York?*

She stares at me for a minute, considers what I'm saying.

Back in Jamaica I dreamed of running away from my mother once we hit American soil. But as it turns out, staying in one place is the key to gaining my independence. When it comes to our life together, my mother is the one doing the running—from one city to the next, from one home to another. I tell myself she's just trying to give me the best life she can. But sometimes I wonder if that's true, if she really does want the best for me. Because if she wanted the best for me, she wouldn't be forcing us to leave Lebanon, not now, not when I've found a community that truly embraces my talents and sees my potential and wants me to succeed.

Finally, she replies. *But where would you stay?*

I could keep living here with Hermine.

But what about rent?

I tell her that I've talked to Coach Gamble, that he also wants me to stay and finish out the year with the track team. He's teamed up with a few other teachers, and together they've pooled some money. Enough to cover half my rent for the rest of the year. But first, I'll need to figure out a way to pay the other half of the rent. *Do you think you could help me out?* I ask.

Not right now. Moving is expensive. She pauses for a moment, considering. *But I can help you later down the line, once I'm settled in New York.*

That's okay. I'll get a job in the meanwhile. Support myself.

Well, if this is really what you want, I'm okay with it.

Thank you, thank you. I feel a rush of joy. My mother has granted my wish. I get to stay here in New Hampshire for the rest of the school year, the rest of the summer, and—if I can figure out a way to become financially independent—the rest of high school. Without my mother present, I will no longer have to live my double life, and this brings a sense of relief.

But then, a wave of sadness comes crashing in. There is something bittersweet to this moment. Because this isn't what I *really* want. What I *really* want is for my mother to stay with me in New Hampshire. What I *really* want is for her to look me in the eye and say, *yes, you are my daughter, and yes, I'll do whatever it takes to help you embrace your true self. It's you and me against the world, and I'll never leave your side.* But instead, she's leaving me behind. Yes, I'm so grateful for everyone who has rallied around me, for the community of people who are stepping up to help me achieve my dreams. I'm so lucky for all their tender care and affection.

But it's not the same thing as a mother's love.

It's raining cash. With the amount of bills I'm racking up, you'd think I was a stripper. But I'm not—I'm an ice cream parlor girl. And all this money is from the fine paying customers at Dairy Twirl, the number one ice cream spot in Lebanon. It's a local favorite and happens to be directly across the street from my apartment. On hot summer days, the scene at Dairy Twirl is *lit*. The line stretches all the way through the parking lot, with people laughing and talking and hoping for a fresh breeze to cool them as they wait in the muggy Northeastern night. The building is classic New England Colonial, with bright yellow siding, white shutters, and a purple awning that hangs over the window where we take everyone's order. Next to the window is a whiteboard, with the day's flavors written in bright marker. We've got soft serve, hard serve, shakes, razzles, brownie sundaes, banana boats, and endless toppings. I'm there every shift from 11:00 a.m. to 11:00 p.m., working *all* the hours, eating *all* the ice cream, and getting *all* the tips.

Not to brag, but ice cream parlor girls are local celebrities. And let's be honest, sex sells. I love getting cute for work; beating my face, wearing my tight neon top, pushing my short shorts to the limit, giving customers something to look at when I'm scooping their sundae. Me and the other girls have an ongoing competition—who can rake in the most cash. We keep an eye on our tip buckets, see whose pile is bigger, watch as people throw in ones, fives, twenties, and sometimes, on a really busy shift, when I'm looking cute and turning out those cones, someone will throw in a fifty. There are nights when I walk away with as much as three hundred dollars, tired but energized by the fat stack in my pocket.

People start coming to see me specifically; they'll find out which line I'm working, and wait for a chance to say "hi," chat for a bit, see how my summer's going. Gradually, I get more and more regulars. I start sharing my story with them. There's a real sense that this community is getting to know me, getting to love me. And getting to tip me. It feels like the whole town is invested in me. Like they want me to win. Want me to succeed. A hardworking high schooler with a dream, in New Hampshire on her own, determined to become a track star. Sometimes I talk too much—my line gets long, and my bosses tell me to keep it moving. But I just love connecting with all these people—sharing a laugh as I dip their soft serve in sprinkles. The love in this community runs deep. Many families have lived here for generations; all my friends have known each other since they were kids. And it feels so wonderful to be folded into the fabric of this small town, to feel like I truly belong, like so many people are rooting for me.

My plan is already working. I've convinced my mother to let me stay in New Hampshire for the summer. She's happy I'm supporting myself, that I'm able to pay my half of the rent on my own. I tell Coach Gamble that I want to pay everyone back for the money they gave me, but he says not to worry about it, that I should pay it forward one day, when I come out on top as a successful athlete. I feel so grateful. I don't want to let him down. I know that I won't.

I'm also working a few shifts a week at Gusanoz, a Mexican

restaurant in town. I'm busy, but happy. It feels incredible to live on my own, to be free of my mother's judgment. I feel like God is looking out for me. With my mom in New York, I can express myself however I want, whenever I want, wherever I want. There's no more double life. I'm becoming the woman I've always wanted to become. Now that I've found my independence, no one can take it away from me. Everything I've ever dreamed of is just within reach.

CHAPTER EIGHTEEN

Senior year passes in a blur. I feel so much freedom and joy. But there is also an anxiety that lingers at the edges of my consciousness, an awareness that with this freedom comes an incredible responsibility. No longer do I have my mother by my side, however imperfect her parenting may be. My future is in my hands, and my hands alone.

For most of my classmates, this is their final year living in their childhood home, and it marks the transition out of adolescence and into adulthood. My experience is wildly different from theirs; my childhood home is a distant memory, we moved constantly during my youth, and I already live on my own, separated from my mother. I still live with Hermine; I don't have to hide my true self when I'm around her, she doesn't report my behavior back to my mother, even though the two of them stay in touch. Hermine shows me so much affection and support, but she's ultimately a roommate, not a parent. She's busy with her shifts at the hospital, so she doesn't have time to step into any maternal role. But I don't resent her for it. I know that's not her responsibility. It feels like I'm no one's responsibility, that no one is truly looking out for me, other than me. That's not to say I'm unhappy, only that my experience is something that I don't think my friends fully understand. I've never worked harder in my life; my days are filled with school, homework, track practice, and shifts at Dairy Twirl and Gusanoz. The pressure is immense; I feel like I'm hurtling toward the future blindly, with no time to stop and think about my destination.

Track is a refuge. One place where the finish line is something literal, painted on the rubber track. When I'm in my lane, there's no question about where I'm going, or how I'll get there. I just have to soar over those hurdles as fast as I can.

Coach Gamble keeps pushing me. He says I have what it takes to compete at an elite college level. With just one year of experience, I'm already one of the best high school hurdlers in New England. I go from meet to meet, shaving seconds off my time, qualifying for the most important races in the region. I'm regularly running a 14.1 in the 110-meter hurdles, a time that could attract interest from top colleges. Possibly even Stanford, a school that soon occupies a huge space in my imagination. Stanford has the resources I need to get where I want to go in life. Their track program is excellent, one of the best in the nation, and the school has produced so many Olympians.

My mother doesn't want me to go to college. Or, if I do, she wants me to attend a college in New York. She's agreed to let me stay in New Hampshire for senior year. She sees how hard I'm working to be independent, but she wants us to live under the same roof again. A part of me does miss her. But the answer is not sacrificing my dream to move to New York. Once again, my mother just fails to understand me. I'm left to figure out my future by myself. It's not like she's totally absent—she'll provide information I need for financial aid applications; she'll offer words of encouragement over the phone. But it's still not enough. It still comes back to the same issue: she is unwilling to dream my dreams with me.

All the other seniors in my class have parents to help them navigate the college application process. Parents who are invested in their futures, parents who've been to American college before, parents to help them compose admissions essays, parents who will pay for extra SAT prep, parents who are alumni of the elite colleges their children are applying to, parents who make significant donations to those same colleges to increase their child's chance of acceptance. I can't help but feel like the college game is rigged, that it favors applicants who are wealthy, white, and well-connected.

I make good friends with the guidance counselor, because frankly, I need guidance. We determine that I'll need to find a school that offers me significant financial aid. A full ride would be ideal. And I need a school that will invest in my dream of becoming an elite track athlete.

Coach Gamble offers advice when he can. But he has a stepson who's also going through the college applications. He doesn't have time to guide two children through this process. I work hard to not get overly attached to Coach Gamble, because he's already doing so much for me. And I understand that he's just my coach, not my parent, that there's a limit to the amount of care he's able to provide. So I look to my friends as well, see where they're applying, how they're navigating the process. But without a reliable parent, it feels like I'm all on my own, on the verge of one of the most important transitions in my life, fighting to keep my head above water.

It's not the first time I've been forced to grow up early.

But this time, it feels like there's more at stake than ever.

It's the same story it's always been throughout my athletic career: I run with the boys, but I hang with the girls. It's not that the guys on the track team don't respect me—they do. They're nice enough. Inclusive. But I know that I really belong with the female athletes. We can bond in ways that I can't with the boys, both on a superficial level—we do our makeup and nails, we can debate which guys in our class are the cutest—but also in a deeper, more profound way. We share the commonality that all female athletes share, the understanding of what it means to be a woman in the world of sports. Of course, I never articulate this explicitly. I never voice the fact that, despite having a male name and that I use male pronouns, I'm really a female. But I think they understand intuitively, I think they know without me having to tell them. We fit together so easily, and they accept me unquestioningly.

The girls just *get* me.

There's a sharp ache in my jaw. It hurts like hell. Something is wrong with my mouth. I go to the dentist. *Your wisdom teeth are coming in*, he says. *We'll need to remove them.* He promises it's nothing too intense, just a routine surgery. But they'll have to put me under anesthesia. *You'll want to take it easy afterward, and rest. So you should arrange to have your parents pick you up.*

I feel a surge of loneliness. The way he just assumes I have parents that will pick me up. I don't tell the doctor that this won't be possible, that I'm living on my own. That Hermine, my roommate, has to work, and won't be able to care for me after surgery.

Later, Georgia gives me a ride to track practice. She's one of my closest friends on the team. I tell her about the surgery. How I need someone to pick me up afterward. *Do you want my parents to pick you up? I'm sure they wouldn't mind.*

Which is how her mother, Dana Michalovic, ends up taking me home from surgery. She helps me into the car. I feel groggy and disoriented, but comforted by the fact that Dana is there to support me. Later, at their home, Dana helps me into bed. Her older daughter is away, working with the Peace Corps, so Dana says I can stay in her room. She tells me to call if I need anything, and that I should just plan to stay the night. Have dinner with the family. It's a small gesture, but I feel so grateful to be welcomed into another family's home.

From there, the Michalovics incorporate me into their lives in a way that deepens with every passing day. Every time Georgia and I have a track meet, they'll invite me to join them for dinner the night before. We'll eat delicious home-cooked food, talk about all our hopes for the competition, and sometimes I'll spend the night. In the mornings, Dana will pack lunches for Georgia and me, making sure we've got something that will sustain us for the meet. Dana teaches me to drive, taking me out in her sporty little Suzuki, and slowly I learn to navigate the roads of Lebanon. They even start to fold Hermine into their family, inviting her to cookouts and birthday parties and other gatherings. All these moments mean the world to me; the Michalovics are always so kind, so welcoming, and for this reason I know they will always have a place in my heart.

Perhaps, most importantly, the Michalovics help me navigate college applications. They invest in my journey. Dana works with me as I craft my essay. She helps me research the colleges that have the best track programs, that offer the best financial aid. They take me on campus visits, tour college facilities with me. They support me as I send off the applications. They know that Stanford is the dream. I have good grades, a fantastic athletic record, and I know that my application will be competitive. But still, the tension is high as I wait for an answer. The Michalovics do their best to ease my anxiety.

Finally, the envelope from Stanford arrives.

I'm waitlisted. So close. I hold out hope. But there's another girl in my school who is also waitlisted. Her parents both went to Stanford. She gets plucked off the waitlist. Accepted. And that's the end of my Stanford dream. I'm crushed, so disappointed, worried about what the future holds now that my ideal school is no longer an option.

But I begin to realize that I don't need Stanford. Because other acceptance letters also arrive in the mail. I will have alternatives. Which is good. Because college will be a significant financial strain on me and my mother. I'll need to go with whichever school gives me the best financial aid. That ends up being Franklin Pierce University, in Rindge, New Hampshire. Just an hour-and-a-half drive from Lebanon. This will make for an easier transition; I'll have a nearby support network, I'll be able to keep working in Lebanon. It's comforting to know that unlike so many other moves in my past,

I won't be completely uprooted. I'll be close enough to Lebanon to stay in touch with all the wonderful people I've met here. Franklin Pierce isn't Stanford, but that's okay. They have a track team, which is all I need. Because I have a dream, and I don't need Stanford to make it come true. All I need is two legs, a pair of spikes, and the passion that's burned in my heart since I was a child.

CHAPTER NINETEEN

Sunrise on a late-summer morning. The dawn air is crisp, slightly chilly. It's 6:00 a.m.—the streets are quiet. I'm standing outside my apartment building. All my possessions are packed up in duffel bags and boxes. In the distance, I see Dana's car approaching, that cute little Suzuki. Her headlights cut through the light morning fog. She parks in the driveway. I feel a surge of love and gratitude. Today she'll help me move into my college dorm.

She gets out of the car and gives me a big hug. We start packing her Suzuki, using every inch of available space—we jam bags into the trunk, stuff the backseat until we can barely see through the windshield. Once we've got it all in, we jump into our seats. Dana shoots me a warm smile. *You ready to go?*

Yes, I say.

We pull out of the driveway. Pass Dairy Twirl. The parking lot is empty at this hour. A stark contrast from the bustling scene that will develop in the afternoon, as inevitable as the sun and heat. A part of me will miss my shifts scooping ice cream. I like being one of the ice cream parlor girls. I'll be sad to leave their ranks. I've worked there this whole summer, eager to save up for school. I need money for supplies, for textbooks, for tuition that my scholarship doesn't cover. The Michalovics have been so wonderful to me—for every thousand dollars I earned this summer, they've matched it with a thousand-dollar gift to me. It is just one more example of the beautiful generosity of this family.

The drive to Franklin Pierce University is about an hour and a half. We fill our car ride with pleasant conversation, talking about my expectations for my first year of college. But underneath the chatter, there's a sort of bittersweet excitement. I'm thrilled at all the possibilities that college presents, but I'll also miss my community in Lebanon. I'll miss Hermine, who was always so kind. I'll miss all my friends—my fellow female athletes, and the ice cream parlor girls at Dairy Twirl. And perhaps, most of all, I'll miss the nights I spent at the Michalovic household, where I was made to feel like a member of their family. I'll miss Georgia, and Al, and Dana, the woman who feels like a mother to me, especially today, as she drives me to college, to support me as I make this crucial transition into adulthood.

We keep driving. Soon, Franklin Pierce appears on the horizon. It's stunning from afar—home to rolling green lawns, charming brick buildings, surrounded by lush green forest, and bordered by the rippling waters of Pearly Lake. Mount Monadnock looms over the campus, completing the pastoral scene. I feel nervous, anxious about moving away from this family that has given me so much love and attention. We pull up to my dorm. Granite Hall. It's a squat, three-story building, with a flat roof and concrete siding.

I'll be living with the boys. I wish I was with the girls. I feel uncomfortable, seeing the questioning stares from the guys in the hallway. But I ignore these feelings for now. Dana's by my side, supporting me, helping me make my dorm room as homey as possible. After we finish loading everything in, we walk around the campus together, eventually making our way to an orientation event. I imagine everyone who sees us is assuming the same thing, that I must be Dana's adopted child. In many ways, that's how I feel.

Dana is missing her own daughter's move-in day to help me. Georgia is attending a different college, and her move-in day happened to coincide with mine. I told Dana that she really didn't need to come, that I could move into my dorm by myself, that I'd figured out so much on my own already, that this would just be one more milestone I reached alone. Without my mother. But Dana insisted. She said Al would drop Georgia off, so she'd still have one parent there. She didn't want me to be alone on this day. I needed a parent too, she said.

We sit together at the orientation event, and I'm barely able to pay attention. Already, I'm beginning to think about our impending goodbye. Soon, the orientation leader says it's time for parents to leave campus. I know this moment has been coming, but now that it's here it feels so sudden. I'm not ready to say goodbye. I can tell that Dana isn't either. We stumble over our words, as the sun begins to set behind Mount Monadnock.

I guess this is it, she says.

Suddenly, I burst into tears. Soon, she's crying too. She pulls me into a fierce embrace. I feel the warmth of her body pressed against mine. I feel like I could stay here forever. Safe in her arms. But I know she has to go. We pull apart. She dries her eyes. *You're gonna be fine*, she says. *You're gonna be great here.*

I'm gonna miss you.

I'll miss you too, she says. *I love you.*

She gives me one final squeeze, then walks to her car. She smiles and waves. I know that this scene is one I'll never forget—Dana, outside my dorm, wiping her tears as she gets into her car. I know this moment will live on in my memory and in my heart forever, that it is representative of the love this family has shown me. I watch as Dana's Suzuki pulls out of the parking lot and weaves its way through the lush green campus. Once it vanishes, I take a breath, turn away from my past, and face the future.

* * *

I'm up the next morning at 5:00 a.m. It's still dark outside. My roommate is fast asleep. I've gotten to know him a little bit; he seems nice, we're cordial with each other, but I don't think he's exactly best friend material. I tiptoe through my room, so I don't wake him. Get ready in silence. Slide into my favorite pair of leggings. The ones that fit my ass just right. I put on a sports bra. Then, a tight green crop top. The look is complete. I feel like an elite athlete, a future Olympian. I feel like *that bitch*. I wait to leave the dorms until I see the sun, because even though I feel like that bitch, that bitch also realizes that she lives on a mountaintop campus, and that bitch does not want to be eaten by a bear.

But the minute daylight breaks over the tops of the trees, I burst out of my dorm, and into the brisk morning air. I accelerate, speeding past the lush lawns, until I arrive at a stop sign at the top of a hill. I pause for a moment. Take in the view. There, at the bottom of the sloping mountain road, I see the green expanse of the baseball field. Just beyond it—the lake. Early-morning sun ripples on the water's surface. No one else is up yet—it feels like I have the whole campus to myself, like it's a blank canvas waiting for my first brushstroke. My mind races. I realize that this is my moment. The moment to reinvent myself. No one here knows who I am. No one knows my history. I can be whoever I want. I can be my true self. I'm an adult now, in charge of my own life.

A ray of sunlight cuts through the branches of the maple tree above. The bright beam warms my skin. I resume my run. I feel energized; the whole campus seems to radiate with possibility. This is a place where I will excel. I'm going to be an incredible athlete, a star student, I'm going to live as my true self and in doing so, I'm going to help create a more welcoming campus for everyone like me, for every outsider. I'm going to be the change I want to see in the world. I'm going to be known on this campus.

And this is where it starts.

CHAPTER TWENTY

The first day of track practice. I walk toward the Fieldhouse, a large athletic facility on the edge of campus. It's home to the gym where the basketball and volleyball teams compete, and offices for all the coaches on campus. My shoes squeak against the polished gym floors as I walk toward the folding chairs set up on the court. Everyone finds a seat; the returning seniors, juniors, and sophomores all greet each other with hugs and backslaps. The freshmen are less confident, shyly lingering on the edges, still unsure of their place on a new team. I'm a little nervous too. But then I see Nikki Zeigler from across the room. She's unmistakable—with a shock of bright blue hair, a fresh set of nails, and a sprinter's body. She's got that track girl aesthetic—the same one I aspire to. We first met this summer—she was a lifeguard at the lake where I would swim on hot afternoons. She's a year ahead of me in school, and we struck up a friendship when we learned that we'd be running on the Franklin Pierce track team together in the fall.

Nikki! I yell across the gym. She sees me and her face lights up. She yells my name and runs toward me. We hug, then burst into giddy laughter.

All right everyone, take your seats! The head coach claps his hands to quiet us. Nikki and I find a couple of folding chairs. Coach Zach Emerson—or "Coach Zem," the nickname everyone calls him—is a commanding presence. He's tall with dark red hair, and a fiery beard. Right away, you can tell he means business—he's strict, aggressive, and driven to make a name for the track program he founded, a program that is just three years old. But despite the program's relative infancy, Coach Emerson has established Franklin Pierce as a school to watch. We've got a robust roster of coaches; Coach Zem is the distance coach for both the men's and women's team, then we have a sprinting coach, throwing coach, and a jumps coach. Already, all our rival schools in the Division II conference hate us because we're a brand-new team but we're good, no longer underdogs, and we're already dominating events.

Coach Emerson welcomes us all, introduces our coaches, and tells us that we're not actually training today, just meeting our fellow teammates. A feeling of anticipation radiates through my body. I'm ready to show everyone what I can do.

There's just one problem. Today's meeting is coed, the men's team and the women's team are all sitting together in the gym, but I know that soon we'll be divided by gender. And I'll be training with the men. Once again, a girl who runs with the boys. A part of me feels like I just can't take it anymore. I can't live a lie again, not now, not after that brisk summer-morning run where I looked out over the college campus and promised myself that I would, no matter what, live my truth. I deserve that much.

I'm just not sure how to get it.

I've got a lot on my plate right now. I'm sitting across from Coach Graham, another one of my track coaches, in his office. I'm trying to explain why I'm stressed. I tell him how I'm on my own, how I don't have support from my mother, how she didn't even want me to attend college, and because of this, I feel like I have to prove to her that this was the right decision. I've also started a job on campus, working as many hours as I can because I need the money. I have a good amount of financial aid, but I still have living expenses and tuition that's not covered by my scholarship. My mother helps out when she can, but it feels like the money is always late. I'm constantly worried that I'll be kicked out of school because it seems to me she's not paying on time. But I also can empathize with her, I know she's working so hard, I know she also sends money back to Jamaica, to Terrence, I know that college is just one more financial strain for her. So I feel this guilt. But mostly, I just feel like I'm on my own here at college, dealing with the biggest transition of my life without a mother to guide me. It's all too much; I'm keeping it together, but it also feels like everything could collapse at any minute. I'm walking around with constant anxiety, my nerves are shot, I don't know how much longer I can go on like this.

Coach Graham listens with quiet intensity. *It sounds like you do have a lot going on*, he says finally. *What if you redshirt your first year?*

I feel a small wave of relief. *I think that might be a good idea.*

You won't compete—so you won't have to deal with that pressure. It'll also free up your schedule so you can keep working. But we'll keep you in shape. You'll still attend all practices. You'll still train with the rest of the guys.

But what I don't tell Coach Graham is that I don't want to train with the guys. Because I'm not one of them. I don't tell Coach Graham that I hate running with the boys, that I've done it my whole life and I'm sick of it. I want to be with my fellow female athletes, my sisters. But I'm afraid he'll never understand. I'm afraid he'll kick me off the team if I even mention it. So I stay quiet. Keep my head down. Redshirt. I hope that, somehow, I'll gain the strength to endure.

Hold on, we're waiting for someone else, my friend Caitlin tells us. There's already four of us packed into Caitlin's car, so we're going to have to squeeze to fit one more. So far, it's me, Caitlin, and two other girls from the cheerleading team at Franklin Pierce. I don't cheer anymore, but I love hanging with the girls from the team. They remind me of all my cheerleader friends from Canada. They just get me, and I can truly be myself around them, which isn't always the case at track practice, where I feel like my male teammates simply don't understand me. Earlier today, Caitlin asked if I wanted to join them for open gym, just to hang out and maybe do a few tumbling passes. I said yes because it sounded fun. *Here she is*, Caitlin says.

The door opens. Another girl enters the car. I slide into the middle seat, as she presses up against me to find her seat belt. *I'm Sonja*, she says and smiles. During that first car ride, we don't say much to each other, don't necessarily hit it off. But gradually, as the weeks pass and we get to know each other, we start to form a real friendship. We share a similar background, so we bond over memories of island life, island food, island music. We connect over similar family experiences too—she has a difficult relationship with her father, I have a difficult relationship with my mother. But we share so much in common beyond our similar backgrounds. We're both athletes, we both have a passion for our sports. Soon, it feels like she's almost my long-lost sister, someone I wish I'd had by my side for my whole life, the supportive family member I've always longed for.

We become inseparable. She never questions me about my gender, never asks if I'm a boy or a girl. She just understands, from the very start of our friendship, that I'm a girl. Many of my new friends make this assumption, but Sonja becomes the first person to whom I confide the whole story of my journey with gender. The conversation is so simple, so easy, so straightforward. I don't have to explain or justify my existence. She just *gets* it from the start. She uses she/her pronouns without even thinking. It's like she knows exactly who I am, like she's always known. I feel an incredible freedom when I'm with her. Like I can be my true self, the woman I'm meant to be.

* * *

It's a cold winter evening. Me and Sonja are walking back from the dining hall after dinner, arm in arm, pressed against each other for warmth. I can see our breath—little clouds of vapor appear under the streetlights that illuminate the path to our dorms. We arrive in the redbrick courtyard, but we're not done talking yet. We stay in the cold, determined to finish our conversation. I'm venting my frustration to her, how I've been at school for almost two months, but I still sometimes feel like she's the only one on campus who truly gets me. I made this promise to live authentically as myself, but people still don't understand me, still think I'm just a boy, or that I'm gay. They still don't see my truth. *And they always get confused by my name*, I say. *Because it's a boy's name.*

Well, why don't you change it? Sonja asks me.

I'm shocked. How have I never thought of this before? Such a simple solution to a problem that's plagued me for my entire life.

But what should my name be?

Hmm. She thinks for a minute. Then her eyes light up. A smile spreads across her face. *How about CeCe?*

The minute she says it, I know that it's perfect. I know that this is my name. My *true* name. It fits. It's an affectionate pet name she's used for me since we first met. It's always felt right. And now I realize why: it's the name I've been waiting for my entire life. *CeCe*, I repeat. It rolls off my tongue effortlessly. *I love it. And maybe, for a little extra flair, we can add an accent over the final "e."*

CeCé! Sonja says. *Perfect!*

And as we say goodbye that night, under the gentle glow of the streetlamps, I feel closer to Sonja than ever. Yes, she's my best friend, but she's more than that. Our bond is deeper. She sees me in a way no one ever has. We've known each other for two months, but she understands me better than people who've known me for a lifetime. She understands me more than my own mother. I feel so grateful to have found her. My new sister.

* * *

I'm CeCé now, wherever I go. Well, I've *always* been CeCé. Now I just finally have my name. My true name. It feels so liberating, so powerful, to finally move through the world as myself. No more hiding. No more shame. No more double life. Just this one beautiful authentic existence.

I introduce myself to everyone as CeCé. I let my teachers know, I let my classmates know, I let the administrators know. If a professor uses my deadname or the wrong pronouns, I'll correct them. I'm not afraid. I have the support of the school therapist, who helps me navigate this new terrain. Franklin Pierce takes this very seriously, and I'm grateful for that.

I also tell my teammates. They're supportive as well. Respectful. They have to be. All our coaches make it very clear that if we don't support one another, then there's no team. Coach Zem has no problem kicking someone out if they're being disrespectful. But that's never really a problem. No one ever mocks or bullies me. From the very moment I introduce myself as CeCé, they treat me softly, sweetly, like they would any other girl.

But there's still one issue—I'm still training with the male track team. I'm still a girl who runs with the boys. And this creates a strange sort of schism in my mind. I'm living out loud, living as CeCé, no longer hiding. And yet, on the track team, in the sport that is my life's passion, I'm still forced into the male category. It's deeply painful, and yet, I don't know how to fix it. I'm not aware of anyone else like me competing in track and field at the college or elite level, I'm not used to seeing women like me in professional sports, I don't have a road map as to how to navigate this issue within the NCAA, the National Collegiate Athletic Association. Sometimes it feels like no one else could possibly understand what I'm going through—and that is a lonely place to be.

But I'm determined to carve my own path.

I'm determined to be myself *and* be a champion.

CHAPTER TWENTY-ONE

Bitch, I've arrived. Freshman year was just the test run. But sophomore year is *lit*. I bust out a jump split twerk at a party during the first month of school, and the crowd goes wild. People scream, cheer, raise their red SOLO cups in the air, and from that point on, everybody on campus knows my name. I'm invited to *all* the parties. Every time I walk into a room, people stare at me, so I *give* them a reason to stare. I'm serving you body, serving you face, serving you *all* of it. I have such a supportive crew of friends; I'm feeling more confident in who I am, more excited to express myself. I wear heels to every event, and clothes that show off my best feminine features. I *never* dim my light for anyone.

People stop me everywhere I go—friends, classmates, even students I don't know. People who just want to say "hi," to chat, to compliment me on my look. And I always make time for anyone who makes time for me. If you show me kindness, I'll show you kindness in return. Yes, I may be popular, but I never use that as an excuse to make anyone feel excluded. I'm *that* bitch, but I'm not *a* bitch. I want to use my visibility on campus to make sure everyone feels comfortable, especially the LGBTQ kids, or anyone else who might feel like an outcast. Because I know what it feels like to need that positivity, to need a safe space to exist.

Don't get it twisted. I'm partying, but never in a way that distracts from my academics or track. This year, I'm no longer redshirting, which means that once our fall preseason is over, I'll be competing with the team in January. During the week I'm all business—going to school, doing my homework, killing it at track practice. I also work part-time to support myself, taking shifts at the Raven's Nest—which is the pub on campus. I'm so busy that the first semester feels like it goes by in an instant. I blink and it's Halloween. A huge party weekend at Franklin Pierce. The campus buzzes with activity, excitement, anticipation; people have brought friends from other schools, cousins from out of town, brothers, and sisters, and anyone who wants to come take part in the wild festivities.

Saturday night is the big bash. I get ready in my friend Lillian's dorm. She's a freshman this year, new to the track team. She's a serious competitor on the field, but she's so funny and sweet when she's off it. We bonded almost instantly, and I welcomed her into our female athlete crew. We're all in the girls' bathroom, beating our faces, getting into our costumes.

I look in the mirror. Tonight, my costume is a naughty schoolgirl, and I'm serving up the whole fantasy. I'm in heels, thigh-high stockings, and a short plaid skirt. I'm looking fierce, feeling fine. Once everyone is ready, we hit the streets, strutting off campus, on our way to the party.

We arrive at the house, and the music is already blasting. We push our way through the crowd spilling onto the street and make our way inside. We head straight to the bar, to fix ourselves some drinks. As I'm mixing a cocktail, I make eye contact with a guy who is standing across the room. He smiles at me. I blush. He's so cute. He's wearing a bright yellow Baby Shark costume from the viral video, but let me tell you, there is nothing babyish about him. This is a full-blown *man*. I can see the muscles underneath the costume,

I can tell that he's probably an athlete. We keep making eyes at each other throughout the party. I try to get up the courage to talk to him, but I'm too shy. Still, I keep looking his way. Keep hoping.

Finally, he comes up to me.

What's up? he asks. *I'm Manny.*

I'm CeCé, I tell him. *I like your costume.*

Baby shark, doo, doo, doo, doo, doo, doo, he sings, and we both burst into laughter.

How did you find out about the party?

I'm friends with Greg, he says. Greg is one of my teammates. A senior. Manny tells me that he used to go to Franklin Pierce, he used to be on the track team. He stayed friends with Greg, and a lot of the other guys on the team. *I'm just visiting for the weekend.*

That's nice.

I'm gonna go say "hi" to some people, but I should get your number, he says. *Don't wanna miss my chance with the cutest girl at the party.*

Okay, I say, trying to keep it cool, even though I'm freaking out inside, because this fine-ass man wants *my* number. *Here you go.*

He's all I can think about for the rest of the party. He keeps glancing my way, keeps smiling that beautiful smile. But then, at one point, I notice that he's talking to Greg. They're both looking at me. Talking about me. The party keeps raging. It's getting late, people are getting drunker and drunker. Suddenly, Manny is back at my side.

Hey, he says and puts his arm around me flirtatiously. *I missed you.*

I missed you too. I smile.

You wanna know something? he whispers into my ear. *I would totally go bisexual for you.*

I pull back. *What do you mean you'd go bi for me? I'm a girl.*

I just thought...

I realize what Greg and Manny were talking about, back when I caught them looking at me. When you've been treated a certain way your whole life, you can see a microaggression from a mile away. I know that Greg must have told him that I'm not "really" a girl, that I

126

just look like one, that I'm "actually" a guy. And I'm so pissed. Greg is my teammate, and he says he's supportive of me, he says he sees me as a woman, but if he really sees me as a woman, why would he tell his friend that I'm not one? Why would he disrespect me that way?

Manny can see that I'm hurt. *I'm sorry*, he says. *I didn't mean to upset you.*

It seems like he's truly sorry. So I give him the benefit of the doubt. *It's okay*, I say.

Can I walk you back to your dorm?

Sure.

We leave together. The sounds of the party get fainter as we walk down the street. The trees are bright orange—the fall foliage glows under the streetlights. Dead leaves crunch underfoot. It's a brisk fall evening. We make our way back to Greg's place, where Manny is staying for the weekend. We're a bit tipsy, but not drunk. There's just a slight buzz that makes everything feel more vibrant, more romantic. Manny is kind, and very inquisitive. He asks me all about my life on campus, my school year, how track is going, how I'm adjusting to my new life. He tells me a bit more about his life too, how much he loves his family, his sister. The hurt I felt earlier begins to dissipate. It seems like he's a good guy, sweet and caring.

We arrive at Greg's house. But we're not done talking yet. Greg's already back home, asleep inside, so we find a spot on the front porch, sit on the stairs together, bodies lightly pressed against each other. Our arms slowly intertwine. And then, in one small tender movement, he takes my hand. Holds it tight. I feel so happy, so giddy.

Can I walk you back to your dorm? he asks.

And all I'm thinking is: *Of course you can walk me back to my motherfucking dorm! That is literally all I want!* But I play it cool. *Sure*, I reply.

Before I know it, we're standing right outside my room.

Can I come in?

Yes, I whisper. *But there's just one thing—I have a roommate. So we have to be quiet.*

Okay, he whispers back. *That's cool.*

I open the door slowly, trying not to make a sound. The room is pitch-black. We enter. I close the door behind us. My eyes adjust to the dark, and I can see my roommate sleeping on the other side of the room. Or, at least, I pray that he's sleeping.

I turn back toward Manny. Our faces are almost touching. *Can I kiss you*, he whispers.

Yes, I reply. And then his lips are on mine, and they're the softest lips, and he kisses me so gently, so tenderly, just like a woman should be kissed. A thrill rushes through my body.

And then my roommate coughs. And coughs again. And again.

He's awake. And he's giving us a not-so-subtle warning that we can't hook up here.

We sneak back out of the room, giggling under our breath.

I don't want to say goodbye, he whispers once we're out in the hallway.

Me neither, I say.

He kisses me again. Grabs my waist. Pulls me close. His arms are so warm, so strong, so comforting. We kiss for what feels like forever. Unwilling to let this moment go.

But then he pulls back. *Sleep tight*, he says, then walks down the hallway.

I'm so happy, I feel like I could faint. I tiptoe back into my room. I can still taste him on my lips. Desire overwhelms me. I close the door, then close my eyes, reveling in the magic for just a minute longer.

Did last night actually happen? This is the first thing I think when I wake up the following morning. Sunlight warms my face, as memories of Manny come rushing back. I text Lillian, tell her I'm coming over, because I have something to tell her.

I rush to her room and knock on the door. She lets me in, we sit on her bed. I immediately launch into the story of Manny, and my dreamy evening with the finest man at the Halloween party. She listens, rapt, giddy, so thrilled that I found someone.

Well, what are you going to do now? she asks when I'm finished telling my story.

Should I text him?

Yes! Lillian squeals.

It's Sunday, so I know he's probably leaving today, heading back to wherever he lives. Still, I'm hoping that maybe there's a chance I could see him for one brief second before he goes, just to say good-bye, maybe even steal one final kiss. I start composing my text. I tell him how much last night meant to me, how it was so wonderful to get to know him, how amazing he is, how incredible I felt after we kissed, and how I hope I get to see him again sometime soon. Once I've finished writing, I stare at my screen, pulse pounding.

Then I press send.

Lillian and I wait. We pass the time with more stories and gossip about the party. But the whole time, I'm just waiting for that response. Waiting for my phone to vibrate.

And then it does.

Girl, he texted back! Lillian screams.

I grab my phone. Open my messages. And my heart sinks. He's written an epic text, the length of a book. It's not good. He says that I'm so sweet, but last night he wasn't himself, he was drunk and wasn't thinking. He says we can't hang out; we can't talk, we can't be friends. He says that this has nothing to do with me, that I'm wonderful, he just has certain things going on in his life, things he can't tell me about, but things that will prevent us from being together. He says he's sorry for leading me on. He wishes me the best in life. He tells me to take care of myself.

He says goodbye.

Girl, I'm so sorry, Lillian says when I show her the text.

I have a feeling that Greg has something to do with this. That Greg has warned Manny against me. The heartbreak I feel in this moment dovetails with hurt, anger that my teammate would betray me in this way, would discourage his friend from dating me. Last night was almost magical; there was such an incredible spark between us. I hoped that his text back would confirm this, that he'd want to continue exploring our connection. But now I know this will never happen.

Later, I find Manny on social media. I see that he has a girl-friend. I realize that this must be part of the reason he couldn't see me. That perhaps Greg was concerned for this reason, he didn't want his friend to cheat on his girlfriend. This makes me feel slightly better, though I think a part of me will always feel let down by Greg. If I'd been any other girl, would Greg still have discouraged Manny? Or would he let his bro have a pass for just one night, a little anonymous fun at a college party? It feels terrible to be treated this way because of who I am, to be forced to deal with prejudice that none of my female friends face.

I keep scrolling through his profile. I see photos of him at a conservative evangelical church. My heart breaks for him. Because I know that there is a deeper truth about who he is, a more expansive idea of who he might be able to love, that he will never experience because of his religion. I hope he finds a path out of conservative Christianity, a way to freedom. And I'm just so thankful I've discovered my truth, that I've embraced who I am, and that I know that God loves me just as I am.

No amount of heartbreak or hurt will take that away from me.

CHAPTER TWENTY-TWO

illian is nervous. She doesn't want to be alone. So I agree to accompany her to Planned Parenthood. Lillian plans to get a routine sexual health checkup. We walk into the clinic, she signs some forms, and we take our seats in the waiting room. We chat, passing the time, but I can tell that in the back of her mind, Lillian is thinking about the impending doctor's visit. Then the nurse calls her name. I squeeze Lillian's hand. Then she's gone.

A little while later, Lillian emerges. She smiles and waves me over to the checkout desk. The check-up went well, nothing to be concerned about. I give her a little hug. She and the receptionist have a brief exchange about birth control. The receptionist hands Lillian a bottle of pills. A thought occurs to me and sets my heart beating just a bit faster. I ask the question before I have a chance to second-guess myself. *Do you think I could also get some birth control?*

Sure, she says, then roots around on her desk for some forms. *Give me just one second.*

I've been regularly taking birth control for a while now. When we moved to New Hampshire, I had a friend who wouldn't take her pills on certain days and give them to me. I asked her for them because I did a little research, and I learned that they contained estrogen. I thought the hormones might help me feel more like myself, and I was right. When I started taking them, I felt more at home in my body, more in touch with my womanhood. Now I'm always on the lookout for girls who have a couple extra pills they can part with. But I'm tired of always having to ask other people for favors. I want my own supply of birth control. I can't believe it could really be this easy.

We'll just need you to fill this out. The receptionist hands me a form.

Suddenly, her colleague clocks me. *Wait a second—are you doing this for, like, hormone replacement therapy?*

Yes, I reply, a little nervous.

Oh sweetie, she says. *We can get you on the real stuff if you want. Put you on an actual HRT regimen. With estrogen injections and testosterone blockers. Only if you want, though.* I always had a feeling, in the back of my mind, that there was a more official way to go about this. I just never had the language for what someone like me needed. But now, hearing this nurse talk about hormone replacement therapy, it all makes perfect sense. She smiles at me, and she's so kind, she so clearly wants to help me embrace who I am, that I'm suddenly overwhelmed by emotion. I burst into tears. Lillian does too. I'm so happy to have someone by my side right now, supporting me during this milestone. We both instinctively understand that this is the next step in my journey, that this will be a moment we will both remember forever, another milestone on the journey to embracing my truth.

The receptionist says that today will be free of cost, but moving forward, I'll either need insurance or have to pay out of pocket. I know that it will be difficult for me to afford this, I'm already living on a budget, working so hard at the school pub just to get by, but I'm determined to figure out a way.

We leave Planned Parenthood, and I feel a rush of happiness. I start my HRT regimen and gradually feel myself coming into my own. I feel ready, I feel excited. My body is transforming, my skin is softer, I begin to develop breast tissue. My mind is more at ease, confident that I am taking the right steps to fully embrace who I am. With every passing day, I feel more like me. Like CeCé.

Someone my mother doesn't understand.

Which is why, when she calls me up and says that she wants me to visit her in New York over winter break, my anxiety spikes. In the days leading up to the trip, I begin having panic attacks. I worry that she will see how I've changed and be furious with me. Disown me. I borrow a male teammate's clothes, making sure they're baggy, so I can hide my new feminine curves. I take out the beautiful, long extensions I've started wearing in my hair, because my mother will hate them. I start practicing more masculine mannerisms, altering the way I speak, and walk, and gesture. I feel such dread in my heart. A sadness. Because I know that the woman whose love I desperately seek will refuse to see the woman I'm becoming.

Meet Nigel, my mother says to me, with forced emotion. *He's my boyfriend. And I want us to all be a family.*

Something about this situation feels weird and forced. I don't know why she thinks I'm immediately going to accept this new boyfriend as a family member. We're not related. This man isn't my father. My father is a man named Tonto. I've never met him in person, but my mother made it a point to tell me about him back in high school. We've spoken on the phone a few times. He's sent money occasionally. He was out of the picture by the time I was born, so I've never been close with him. Nor have I felt the need to develop a relationship with him. But I know that he's my father, and that the man standing across from me right now is definitely not family.

Nice to meet you. I give him a hug. But my heart's not in it.

It's nice to meet you too, Nigel says and smiles. He seems sweet enough. I almost feel bad for him. He's an old flame of my mother's from Jamaica, someone she saw when she was younger. I think maybe she wants financial support from him, wants a place to stay, and wants to use this idea of a "family" as a bargaining chip to get these things. To push Nigel into playing a fatherly role. I hate having to go along with whatever scheme this is. I hate being here in this man's house, reinforcing my mother's facade of some "big happy family," when I could be back in New Hampshire, living the authentic existence I've worked so hard to create. Instead, I stay as quiet as possible, and try to make myself invisible. I worry that anything I say or do could betray the truth that my mother refuses to accept. It is so mentally exhausting to live in constant fear of her wrath. And on top of all this, I'm forced to pretend a stranger is my family.

Later, when we're alone, I confront my mother. *Why are you forcing this weird idea about us all being a family?*

I'm doing this to keep a roof over our head, she snaps. *Don't you say a word.*

We're at H&M. Going shopping with Nigel. My mom wants him to buy me some school clothes. It seems like there's tension between them, like maybe they've been fighting. Does he suspect that he isn't the only man in her life? Or maybe he also finds this whole "family" act strange? Regardless, I don't want to get involved. The whole thing feels sad and weird and wrong. I want to go back to New Hampshire, back to where it feels like my life is finally taking off.

Just before coming here, I was spending winter break with Hermine in Lebanon, keeping up with my training to maintain the strength and stamina I've gained during our preseason. Coach Zem expects all the athletes to find track meets near their hometowns during winter break, so we can get one practice meet in before we officially start competing as a team in January. So I competed at Dartmouth Relays, one of the most prestigious track meets in the region. It was my first official meet now that I'm no longer redshirting, and I came in fourth in the 400-meter open. A great start to my season. I've put in the work, I've trained so hard, I've improved so much. Now it feels like finally I am on the verge of accomplishing something great. I'm ready to dive into my first indoor season this January, I'm ready to kill it, to make a name for myself. Which is why I want to get out of this H&M, out of New York, out of my mother's world.

But as long as I'm here, I might as well get some free clothes.

I wander the store by myself, while my mother and Nigel talk outside. I sneak into the women's section, looking over my shoulder to make sure my mother doesn't see. I find some leggings and a pair of booty shorts that I know will make my ass look fine. I head to the dressing room to try them on, and sure enough, my ass is popping in these leggings, with these little shorts on over them. I'm looking cute, feeling feminine. I walk out of my changing room to get a better look in the mirrors on the floor, and find my mother and Nigel waiting for me.

What are you wearing? my mother snaps. *Take that off. Those clothes are for women.*

They're not, I insist. I feel a sharp pain in my heart. This feels like just another instance of the same battle we've been fighting for years. The same battle we'll always be fighting. I wish it would somehow get easier, but it doesn't. Each time my mother refuses to acknowledge who I am, it hurts just as bad as the first time. *They're for running*, I lie.

He's right, Nigel says. I detect a kindness in his eyes. Regardless of whether we're really family, I can sense that this man is a caring person. He wants to embrace me. Defend me. *It's weird, but I see male runners wear this type of thing all the time.*

I look at my mother. I can tell she wants to resist what he's saying, but she can't because he holds the power. She doesn't want to upset him. She doesn't want to risk it. This whole situation could crumble at any minute. *Okay*, she says. *As long as they aren't for girls.*

Nigel pays for my clothing. My mother and I stand behind him. She turns to me. Doesn't say a word. But from the look in her eyes, I can tell that she's angry, that somehow she'll find a way to punish me for this moment.

* * *

I feel claustrophobic. My mother keeps a watch on me at all times. She never wants me to leave her side. I know she doesn't trust me and doesn't want to think about what I could get up to on my own. And she's obsessed with creating this fake family, trying to force this situation to work. It's so toxic, grungy, weird. I hate being trapped in this house with them, forced to sit through awkward "family dinners" where my mother keeps pushing me to talk to Nigel, to form a bond I want to escape. I want the freedom to be myself, to not feel like I have to pretend to be someone else for my mother. I want this loneliness I feel to be relieved somehow. I want comfort.

Which is how I end up on a dating app.

I've been on the apps before, back in New Hampshire. But in small towns like Lebanon, that are so white, so cis, and so straight, there aren't a lot of options for a Black girl like me. Someone exploring her sexuality and gender. The only people I found back in New Hampshire were people who wanted to fetishize me, who saw me only as a sexual object. So I never met up with them. Because I know I deserve better than that. But it still left me longing for comfort. And maybe in New York, maybe in a bigger city, there will be more options out here.

I scroll through photos. Pass over men who don't interest me. Finally, I see him. He's Dominican—tall, muscular, with smooth skin and the cutest goatee I've ever seen. He's just my type—it's almost like I dreamed him up. I message him. He messages back. My heart beats faster. We start chatting, then flirting. He invites me over to his place. I agree. A nervous thrill courses through my whole body.

Then, my heart sinks. How am I going to get out of this house? What am I going to tell my mom? But I am *not* passing up this opportunity, this man is *way* too fine. So I slip on my new leggings, my new booty shorts, and I walk into the kitchen to confront my mother. She sits at the table with Nigel. *I'm gonna go for a run*, I tell her, not mentioning that what I'm really going to do is run my ass to this man's house.

No, you're not, my mom says. *I don't want you out in the city on your own. It's not safe.*

I look at Nigel. I pray that he's still my ally. That he'll have my back on this one too. *Oh, let him go*, he says to my mom. *He's a runner. He's in training. He needs to run.*

My mother sighs. Overruled by Nigel again. *Fine*, she says. *But take your phone. And text me when you're on your way back.*

I burst out of the house and onto the street. Make my way to his house. Get to his door. Knock. My pulse is pounding. I wait. I hear footsteps. Then, he opens the door. It seems impossible, but this man is even sexier in person. He's also sweet and charming. He invites me inside. We flirt for a little while. Then, he kisses me. His goatee scratches my face. His lips are delicious. Goose bumps ripple down my arms. The afternoon passes, we do things grown-ups do, and when we're done, I feel so blissful. I say goodbye, knowing that I'll probably never see him again, but happy that he could bring a little pleasure into an otherwise stressful and depressing trip. I'm grateful for this one beautiful afternoon.

I'm spending the day with Auntie Bella. She moved to New York from Jamaica a few years ago. She now lives in Brooklyn with her two daughters, and their children. It's a full house, but a happy one, most of the time. My mother moved to New York to be closer to Auntie Bella and her family, though their relationship is rocky at times—sometimes she and my mother fight.

I love Auntie Bella. Out of everyone in my family, she's always been the kindest to me. Though she never says it outright, it seems like she embraces me for who I am. She doesn't ask me to change. She defends me when my mother attacks me. She feels like my one connection left to a family that doesn't understand me, the one person out of all my kinfolk who might be willing to love me for who I am.

Today I'm headed to a big Jamaican party in the Bronx. It's dancehall themed, and Auntie Bella is one of the hosts for the event. I meet her at the venue—a nightclub she's rented—and it's already lively with activity. Dancehall music blasts from the speakers as vendors set up their stations along the edges of the dance floor. She's brought my cousin along as well, and the two of us help her set up her table, lining it with bottles of liquor, cigarettes, snacks, and other little things for sale. The crowd gets bigger, and my cousin and I help Auntie Bella keep up with all the customers. We joke and laugh and dance in our little booth, having a great time. I love having this moment of genuine family connection, especially because things are so tense with my mother. It feels like a light in the darkness. I'm so grateful for Auntie Bella. And she knows how to throw a great party!

More and more people file into the nightclub. Suddenly, angry male voices erupt from a group in the center of the dance floor. The crowd parts. The two men keep shouting, louder now. I can't quite understand what they're fighting about. But I can tell they're drunk. That they're not listening to reason.

One of them pulls out a gun. Fires a shot into the air.

People scream, run for cover. Run for the exits. I duck under the table with Auntie Bella and my cousin. We crouch and wait, fearful.

Slowly, we stand. Someone is breaking up the fight. No one is hurt. But the vibe is ruined. People are leaving in droves, scared for their safety. Auntie Bella shakes her head. *Let's just go home*, she says. *Everything's ruined.*

The party is over.

It's almost time to go back to New Hampshire. I can't wait to leave. I hate it here. I hate the fake family situation my mother has forced me into. I won't miss New York; I won't miss a single person here.

Except Auntie Bella.

On the final night of the trip, we all go over to Auntie Bella's house—me, my mother, and Nigel. We all hang out for a while, sharing a meal and conversation. Soon, it's time for bed. I'm spending my final night here because it's closer to the airport. Auntie Bella offers to help me get settled in my room.

But once we're alone, her expression gets serious. It sets me on edge. She seems concerned, upset. She sits on the bed, next to me. She smiles, but it's a sad smile. *Listen*, she says, *I love you. But I'm worried about you.*

Why? I ask, afraid.

Your feminine ways, she shakes her head. *You have to stop that. Your mother told me about the shopping trip. The women's clothes you bought. But it's not just that. There are so many things that have happened over the years. Your mother tells me everything. About the way you act like a girl. The incidents with men online. I try to defend you to your mom, but I just can't anymore. You have to stop this feminine behavior.*

I just stare at the ground, filled with grief. *Okay*, I say.

I just want you to have a family. The real way. The right way. With a wife.

My heart shatters when she says this. I love her so much. But I know this is the end. She was the last thin thread tying me to my family. She was the only person who seemed like she might actually be able to accept me for who I am. But now the truth is clear. I know she'll never understand. And I gave up on my mother years ago.

As I sit there, staring into her eyes, I realize a painful truth: I can't be in this family anymore. This is the last time I'll ever see them.

CHAPTER TWENTY-THREE

I throw myself into training. When I'm out there on the track, pushing my body to the limit, every frustration, every disappointment, every bit of anger and sadness—it all disappears. It's just me, the rubber beneath my feet, and the finish line.

The track team is back at school two weeks early. There's nothing to distract us. No classes. No extracurriculars. *You have nothing to do but train,* Coach Zem reminds us every day. *Take advantage of this time.* We have early-morning practice, then breakfast, then another practice, then lunch, then a third practice, a snack, a fourth practice, dinner, and then we're done. Our bodies are depleted at the end of every day. I love it. I love having this deep sense of purpose. I love feeling exhausted at the end of the day, knowing that I'll be stronger because of it. I love putting every ounce of energy and passion I have into this sport.

I live in the Bubble now, basically. That's the nickname for our training facility, a seven-story airframe structure that looks, as its name suggests, like a giant white bubble. The domed ceiling is made of heavy-duty industrial fabric and is held up by structural beams and air pressure. It provides athletes on campus with somewhere to work out during the winter season, a massive 72,000-square-foot facility that is our cardio/strength training facility, free weight area, complete with two tennis courts, two basketball/volleyball courts, and areas for track and field.

Our first track meet is a week after we return. The Spartan Regional Preview at the Ocean Breeze Athletic Complex in Staten Island, New York. I feel strong, ready, driven. I sail through the prelims in the 60-meter hurdles and qualify for the finals. Not bad for my first meet of the season. During the finals, I run my race just like I've been trained, and come in sixth place. There's still definitely room for improvement, but it's a great start to the indoor season.

I keep pushing. I train hard. Keep competing. I bond with my teammates, both male and female. We go to meets together, socialize together, become a tight-knit unit. Mama Holmes—a nickname we give to the mother of a boy on my team—becomes a sort of "team mom." She'll host giant barbecues in her backyard after meets, for all the students and coaches, sometimes up to ninety people. She's taken a special interest in me, and is always so warm, so accepting, so supportive.

I cut out other extracurricular activities. Track and academics—that is all I have time to focus on. I show improvement in every track meet. I'm making a name for myself within the conference. People know me as stiff competition. I'm always striving for a better time, a better ranking. I want to be the best runner at my school, in the conference, in the nation. Coach Zem is impressed by my dedication, my ambition, and my talent. *You have what it takes to become a national qualifying athlete,* he always says to me. *Keep it up, kid.*

But there is something holding me back. Something bottled inside me. The pressure mounts with every meet. I can see the way people look at me. I can see the double takes, the moments where people are confused—*why is there a girl on the boys' track team?* Because still, after all these years, after all the work I've done to live authentically as myself, I'm still the girl who is forced to run with the boys. It feels unbearable to be in this impossible position—track is both the cause and the cure for this excruciating pressure. When I'm running, it feels like the ultimate release: my mind is clear, my body is performing like it's been trained, and it's just me and the track and nothing else. But the minute I cross the finish line, reality comes crashing back in. I look around at all the male athletes surrounding me, and I feel trapped on the wrong team, with the wrong gender. I love track. But I hate being stuck in a position where it feels like the deepest part of who I am is denied every time I do the thing I love. The pain is too great. I want to be recognized as CeCé within the NCAA. I no longer want to hear my deadname—that name I was assigned at birth but no longer use, a name that has so much pain associated with it—blasted over the speakers at every meet I attend. I no longer want to line up with the men.

I need a way out.

But as the year stretches on, I don't feel any closer to finding one.

CHAPTER TWENTY-FOUR

I'm prepared for a battle.

At the end of every school year, students are asked to put in a request as to where they'd like to live the following year. This request is then processed by the housing department, and if you're approved, you get to live with whoever you wish, wherever you wish. Usually, this is a rote administrative procedure, a simple process where the housing department tries to accommodate as many students as possible. But I know that my case is unique, that they've never dealt with someone like me before. Because of this, there is a chance it's just an oversight, a bureaucratic error. But there's also a chance it's intentional, that they will refuse to let me live with the girls. In campus housing records, I'm listed under my deadname, assigned to live with the wrong gender. I hate living in the boys' dorm. I feel so out of place, so unwelcome. It's bad enough having to compete at track meets with the men, but then coming home, and having to live with them too? It's taking a toll on my mental health.

Which is why I'm ready to fight.

I need to live with the girls, I tell Sonja.

I know you do, she agrees. *And I'll support you no matter what.*

*I'm just afraid that the housing department won't see me. Won't
understand me.*

Which is why we're gonna write them a letter, explaining everything.

I compose a letter to the housing department, saying that I've
been living as a woman ever since I arrived at Franklin Pierce, and
not only that, but I've been a female since birth, so it only makes
sense that I should also live with other women on campus. Sonja
cosigns it, saying that she wants to be my roommate. We read and
reread the letter, making sure it expresses just how important this is
to my well-being.

It's good, Sonja says, once we're finished checking the letter one
last time. *It's really good.*

What if they say no?

Then we fight the decision. Together.

I'm sitting in the waiting room of the Residential Life offices. I
clutch my letter in my fist. The paper is damp with sweat. My heart
is pounding. I'm so nervous for this confrontation. But I'm ready to
defend myself, to assert my right to live freely. Even still, I'm terrified. This feels like the first step in an important journey. I've been
living as my true self on campus, living as CeCé, living as a female,
and all my peers have accepted me. But I've yet to receive this acceptance on an administrative level. The housing department has yet to
acknowledge that I'm a woman. And though that may sound like
boring bureaucracy to some people, these administrative decisions
deeply impact my life.

I look around the waiting room. Try to calm my breathing. A
woman steps out of her office. *CeCé?* she says.

Hi, I say, trying to suppress my nerves.

Are you ready to chat?

Yes, I say. *Let's go.*

* * *

Her name is Sally Pierson. She has kind eyes, a gentle yet firm demeanor. I plead my case. I show her my letter. I pray that she understands. After I finish speaking, she looks at my letter for a moment, then looks up at me and smiles.

You know, I don't think we've ever officially met, but I've seen you around campus, she says. *You're doing such great things on the track team. And I can tell from your records that you've also got a great academic standing.*

Thanks, I say, still nervous, eager for her response.

And yes, I also think it's a good idea for you to live with the girls, she says. *You'll just need letters from anyone else who wants to be your room-mate. But other than that, we're good to go!*

I'm shocked. I don't know what to say. I came in prepared for a fight. But instead, I'm getting a warm welcome. I feel the emotion rise in my throat. I wipe away a tear. I never imagined it would be this easy, that all I would have to do is ask, and that someone would simply say, *Yes, I affirm you. I see you for exactly who you are, and I will make sure we create a space where you feel comfortable and accepted.*

I feel so lucky to be at Franklin Pierce. Never has an academic institution acknowledged me in this way. This is such a far cry from that middle school in Canada, from that traumatizing experience where I attempted to live my truth, but was shut down by the school administration. Now, I'm fully supported, seen, and safe. This is a moment that will forever change my life.

CHAPTER TWENTY-FIVE

Another New England summer. The best yet. The humid days fly by, relieved by cool summer nights. I'm back in Lebanon. I can't go and visit my mother in New York. I've promised myself I'll never go back there, and that is a promise I don't intend to break. And I can't stay with Hermine—she's moved into a one-bedroom apartment and there isn't room for me. So I'm living with a girl named Riley—one of my coworkers at Dairy Twirl—and her parents, Ralph and Connie. She's my age, also in college, and we've spent a lot of hours scooping ice cream together. There's a spare room in her family's house, now that her older sister has officially moved out. Her family is so welcoming, and in many ways, it feels like I'm their daughter for the summer. Their house is so warm, so welcoming. Some nights we'll all gather for a meal that Connie's made, or sometimes I'll cook something, treat them to a Jamaican feast with rice and peas, or boiled dumplings. We'll have wine nights and movie nights, where we cozy up on the couches together, just me, Riley's family, and their three adorable cats.

They're about two miles from Dairy Twirl, so I run to work whenever I have a shift, burning off all those excess calories that you consume when you work in a place that gives you free ice cream every day. I also join a training gym, right across the street from Dairy Twirl, so I can stay in shape and go into the school year stronger than ever. The gym is hilariously named Wayne's World, because the owner is named—you guessed it—Wayne. Sometimes, when I have a work shift after training, I'll convince everyone to walk over to Dairy Twirl with me for some post-workout ice cream.

Dairy Twirl is lit as ever that summer, and me and my fellow ice cream parlor girls are back in the game, looking cute, and raking in the cash. I still keep in touch with the Michalovic family, and they'll often stop by to say hello, order some sundaes, check in to see how I'm doing. If Riley and I work the same shift, she'll give me a ride home, and we'll laugh and gossip as we count our tips. Some days we'll head to the beach to bask in the sun and when we get too hot, take a dip in the icy Atlantic waters. Some nights we'll head to local parties—Riley always seems to know where the best ones are at, and we'll stay until we're buzzed and tired and ready to go home, where we'll tiptoe up to our rooms, suppressing our giggles, careful not to wake her parents.

Such a beautiful summer.

But soon it's August. The days get shorter. It's almost time to head back to Franklin Pierce. I feel an end-of-summer sadness tug at my heart. But I'm excited for the new school year, excited to finally live in the girls' dorm, to share a room with my best friend.

There's still the issue of the track team, the fact that I will be returning to compete alongside the males. But I try not to think about that. I try to push it down, ignore the anxiety I feel, just power through.

After all, I don't have a choice. Not if I want a shot at my dream.

I get back to campus two weeks early. I'm living in the Mountain View dorm in one of the towers, which are private four-person apartments reserved for juniors with good academic standing. I live there with Sonja and our friends Nikita and Chanel. I absolutely love living with my girls, we all support and care for each other. We're also all student leaders, which is one of the reasons I'm back on campus early. We've volunteered to help with freshman orientation, guiding students on campus tours, and helping at events.

I love being a student leader. It's an opportunity to create a space where everyone feels welcome, especially LGBTQ students who might be nervous about whether they'll be accepted at college. Also, many kids come from environments where they've never met a trans person before, so this is a chance for me to share my experience, and maybe change hearts and minds. For this reason, I think that Franklin Pierce is smart for choosing me as ambassador. I can provide comfort to kids who are still finding themselves, who are still exploring their gender or sexuality. My presence signals that this school is a community where you are protected, where you can experiment freely. Because ultimately, I feel like this is the gift that Franklin Pierce has given to me—the space to blossom into myself. So I want to let every student know that the same thing can be true for them, that it's safe for them to embrace their identity here.

I meet with so many students during orientation. Hear stories about where they come from and share my own. I tell them about how Franklin Pierce is a place where I am fully embraced, fully loved for the woman that I am.

Except, of course, on the track team. But that feels too painful, too personal to share with these wide-eyed freshmen. So I leave that detail out. Push it down. Pray that I can withstand the pain and confusion of another year competing with the men.

The Silfen Invitational. The first track meet of the outdoor season. Connecticut College is hosting the event. It's April 15, a balmy spring day in New England. The track has a stunning view as it overlooks the Thames River. A small cluster of sailboats float idly in the water. I'm on the field, warming up, getting ready for the 110-meter hurdles. I tie my spikes, making sure they're firmly on my feet. I've had these shoes forever, since my high school coach first taught me hurdling, and they're well-worn. Maybe *too* well-worn.

I look around the track. American International College (AIC) is one of our competitors, and a group of men from their team huddle on the field, laughing and pointing at me. They're out of earshot. I can't hear what they're saying. But I can imagine. Some of the boys are Jamaican, and I can sense that they're the ones driving the taunting.

The announcers call us to the line for the men's 110-meter hurdles. I walk over to get my bib number for the race. I can see confusion on the officials' faces. *What is she doing up there?* I hear someone say. *Why is she in line with the guys?*

I walk to my lane. I see confusion spread through the crowd. People point. Stare. I know they're all wondering the same thing: *Who is this person? Is that a girl or a boy?* And I know what they're thinking, because it's been the same story at every meet this year. I get the same invasive stares. I hear the same cruel whispers, from competitors, from parents, from race officials. They comment on my gender, or make fun of me, or tell me I don't belong in the sport that I love. I hate standing up in front of a crowd and feeling like everyone is questioning who I am. I can't do this anymore. I can't run with the men. Each track meet is tainted with anxiety and dread and dysphoria. And it's not just on the track that I feel this unbearable stress, I feel it during warm-ups and during every practice, when I pay extra attention to my form, holding myself back, because I worry that if I push too aggressively, go too hard, I will be perceived as male. I feel it when I'm changing into my clothes for every meet, wanting to select the perfect outfit to make sure that I pass as an athletic girl, hoping that if I look feminine enough, it will prevent at least a few people from misgendering me. I feel it when I debate whether or not to go to the girls' bathroom to change, fearing that a parent will see me and make an official complaint, or worse, directly confront me. And I'm doing my best to push all of this anxiety from my mind as I walk onto the track, trying to click into that tunnel vision focus that gets me through every meet. But when I take my place at the starting blocks, I'm struck with a thought. An epiphany, really.

I have to run with the women. On the women's team.

And I don't know if it's the hormones, or just the fact that I'm sick of all the stress that's been building up, tired of dealing with all this bullshit, but I am struck by a moment of absolute clarity: if people are going to point and laugh at me while I line up, then I'd at least prefer that they point and laugh while I line up with my fellow female athletes. Not the men.

I have to run with the women. It's such a simple solution to a problem that's plagued me for so long. I don't know why I haven't thought of this before. Probably because there are no other women like me competing in track. Or, at least, none that I'm aware of. No other models of elite trans female runners competing as their true selves, out of the closet. But I could be that person. Instead of waiting for the world to change, I could *be* the change I want to see.

But how?

On your marks!

My focus narrows. I crouch down, back myself into the blocks. A boy from AIC is in the lane next to me. He mutters under his breath. Calls me a slur. Tries to intimidate me at the starting line. Anger courses through my body. But I don't react. I don't respond. I'm not worried. Because this boy can call me whatever the hell he wants, but at the end of the day, when it comes to this race, I'm gonna beat him. And that's when he'll truly be sorry he ever put my name in his mouth.

Get set!

I narrow my focus. Nothing matters now except the track, those hurdles, and the finish line.

Boom! The gun goes off. I bolt out of the blocks. I'm flying, fueled by adrenaline and anger. I clear hurdle after hurdle. Gaining on the boy who tried to intimidate me. Determined to pass him, to pass them all, and win the race.

I approach hurdle six. My feet leave the ground.

Which is when my right shoe falls off. One of my old spikes, that I haven't replaced since high school. Another jolt of adrenaline surges through me. But I don't give into panic.

I keep running. I pass the boy who harassed me. Leave him far behind.

And I win the race. With only one shoe.

I'm in hell. Technically I'm at UMass Lowell, standing under a tent, on a field, waiting for the 400-meter hurdles, waiting for them to call my deadname over the sound system, waiting for that name I no longer use to echo across the field, to remind me of all the pain I've endured to get to this point. But really, I'm in hell. This is hell. Competing with the men—hell. The past year—hell. It's been a year of people cheering my deadname from the stands, it's been a year of suspicious stares, a year of slurs, a year where I improved so much, a year where I gained a reputation as an athlete to watch in our conference, but a *male* athlete. There's a spotlight on me, but I hate the glare of attention. I'm climbing in the rankings listed on the NCAA website, but they list my deadname, list me as a male athlete, and I hate being assigned the wrong gender on this public platform. It is such a mind fuck. At school, I'm CeCé—I'm living fully as my female self. But the minute I hit the track for a competition, it's like I'm back to the double life I worked so hard to eliminate. I'm forced to live a lie again. People use the wrong pronouns, the wrong name, treat me like I am a male. I feel so out of balance, out of place, so anxious, so uneasy, so sad and depressed. Gender dysphoria is something I've struggled with my whole life, though I didn't have those words to describe it when I was a child. But never has this feeling been so intense, so amplified, as it is right now.

Dysphoria overwhelms my mind. I'm not here on this field. I'm not present in my body.

Suddenly, I feel the urge to pee. But just then, the announcer comes over the loudspeaker. It's time for my event. It's too late to go to the bathroom now. The announcer calls my deadname over the loudspeaker. Anxiety, dread, and fear brew in my gut. The dysphoria intensifies.

On your marks!

I get into the blocks. I feel numb. I feel like I'm floating above the track, looking down at my own body, only it doesn't feel like my body, it feels like it belongs to a stranger, like I'm just a spectator, watching myself from afar. There is no sensation in my limbs, no feeling that I am controlling them, it is all muscle memory at this point, like my body is a machine that will run on its own.

Get set!

I can't run this race. I can't do it.

Boom! The gun goes off. I'm out of the blocks. Adrenaline takes over. Maybe I can do this. I'm sprinting already. This isn't how I've been trained to run the race. This isn't the strategy. I'm supposed to be holding it at first, maintaining a solid pace, then pick it up. But I'm sprinting from the start. HRT has affected my performance recently, and I'm feeling it today. I'm slower, quicker to lose my breath, and my heart races faster than before, beating irregularly, which is the result of the arrythmia I've developed. But even still, I'm flying over hurdles. I pass every boy on that track. Soon, I'm in the lead.

I come up on the third corner. My speed starts to lag. Dysphoria hits again. I go over a hurdle, but I'm not in my body, not present, not in the race. I'm somewhere else, my mind is gone.

My leg clips the fourth hurdle.

I stumble. Momentum hurls me toward the ground. There's nothing I can do.

My entire body slams against the track, hits it so hard, at such a high velocity, that I actually bounce, my body is airborne for a brief second before it crashes back onto the track. The pain is wild. I'm in shock, facedown on the rubber. I don't know if I can get back up. I've always been taught to finish the race no matter what. But I'm not sure I can.

I see my coach running toward me. *Fuck, fuck,* fuck is all I can think. *I have to finish this fucking race.* I haul my body off the ground. And I push through. I push through the pain, the agony, the confusion, the dysphoria, until finally I cross the finish line, dead last.

People cheer for me. They're proud that I got up. That I finished my race. But I feel nothing but anger. I limp over to the medic. I tell him that it feels like my organs have shifted inside me. He laughs, says that that isn't possible. But he looks me over and asks a few more questions. I answer them, but I'm not really present, the pain is too great.

And I still have to pee. So, I excuse myself.

But when I get to the bathroom, when I start peeing, the pain is unlike anything I've ever felt. And that's when I realize, it's not piss in the toilet bowl.

It's blood.

The doctor says my kidney is bruised. He gives me pills, and says I need bed rest and plenty of fluids. If I do everything right, the blood in my urine should disappear within a few days. I'm shaken, but relieved to know that I'll be okay.

It's the end of April, and we're in the middle of the outdoor season. I'm supposed to be training harder than ever. But I sit out. I don't go to practice. I miss our next meet. But instead of feeling sadness, I feel a strange sort of relief. Because of this injury, I get a break from the hell that I've been living in.

This injury is a wake-up call. A realization starts to dominate my thoughts. I bruised my kidney because my head was out of the game, my body was on that track, but my mind was far away, far above, so disconnected from the race. The dysphoria—that's why I fell. I can't keep competing like this. I can't risk another injury, the next one could be worse, maybe even debilitating. I need to get my mind right. I need to focus on my mental health.

I need to quit the track team.

CHAPTER TWENTY-SIX

But I don't. After I heal from my injury, I finish out the school year, competing on the men's team. Just two more competitions. Then, I'm done.

Next year, I tell myself. *Next year is the year I'll quit.* I'm realizing that I don't know who I am without athletics. Without track. And a part of me is afraid to say goodbye to that facet of my identity. So I hold on for the rest of the season. Ride it out.

The summer comes. I stay on campus, working two jobs—one at the recreation center and one in the admissions office. I save up money. I keep training at the facilities on campus. Even though I want to quit track, it's difficult to just stop running. This sport is in my blood, it's been my purpose for so long, it just feels strange to abandon it. Maybe I'm not as ready to let go as I think. My coaches have no idea that I plan to quit. They think I'm coming back in the fall.

Time passes. I sign up to be a student leader again, to help with orientation. Sonja does too. We love being ambassadors for the school. We love making students feel welcome.

We're living together this year. We lucked out in terms of housing—the two of us have an entire apartment tower suite to ourselves, in the Sawmill dorms. We both have strained relationships with our families, so we seek comfort and support from each other, loving each other with an intensity we wish our biological relatives could match. We do everything side by side. We've tried to sync up our schedules, take the same classes. We go to all the parties together. Meet up for breakfast and lunch and dinner every day. We share everything we're going through. It feels like it's us against the world. We always say: *We got each other, so ya'll ain't got nothing on us.*

I need her support now more than ever. The year has just begun, and already I feel uncertain about the future. I know that I want to quit the track team, that I want to take time for my mental health. But when it comes to pulling the trigger, I just can't do it. I know that I'm going to have to have a conversation with my coaches, but I worry they won't understand. That they'll be angry. That they'll see me as a quitter. And I think a small part of me is afraid of what will happen to me once I've given up my life's purpose.

But before I can do anything, I get an email from my coaches.

They want to meet with me. I'm not sure why.

I walk into Coach Zem's office. All four track coaches are sitting there, waiting for me. They have smiles on their faces. On the desk, there's a pile of papers and a pen. I take a seat.

Hi CeCé, Coach Zem says. *Thanks for coming by. We have something we want to discuss with you.*

Okay, I say, nerves jangling, unsure of why everyone seems so eager. *What's up?*

Coach Graham, another one of my coaches, speaks up. *We see so much potential in you, CeCé. The way you've grown as an athlete over the past few years has been remarkable. You're so hardworking, such a good teammate. You're regularly scoring points for the team at our meets. And we think you have what it takes to go all the way to nationals. Which is why we want to make you a sponsored athlete.*

A sponsored athlete? I say. The news is so strange. Here I've been dreaming of ways to quit the team, to release myself from the awful pressure and pain of competing with the men, while my coaches have been dreaming of ways to formally sign me with a contract.

Congratulations, Coach Graham says, with a big smile, and pushes the stack of papers toward me. *We'll just need your signature on these.*

But there's something suspicious about his demeanor, how overly enthusiastic he is. I stare down at the papers and start leafing through them. *Can I take a minute to read through these?*

Sure, Coach Graham says. *Though it's all pretty straightforward stuff.*

And how much financial aid would I be getting as a part of this?

You'd be getting five hundred dollars a semester, he says.

Five hundred dollars? I ask, shocked. *That's it?* All four coaches look around the room, to the ground, to the ceiling, to the door. It seems like they're looking just about anywhere but straight in my eyes. Because they know this is such a low sum. I think, though I'm not really sure about the specifics, that all the other sponsored athletes on the team get significantly more money per semester (even though we are technically discouraged from discussing scholarship money with our fellow athletes, people can't help themselves from gossiping a little, and word eventually gets out about who gets what money). My coaches know that many of these athletes aren't even scoring the team points, when I am. They know I'm a greater asset to this team than people who will be getting much more scholarship money than me. Of course, I would love a scholarship, and it would be a relief to have a certain amount of financial stress taken off my plate. But five hundred dollars is barely enough to make a difference—and there are significant strings attached to those five hundred dollars. If I'm a sponsored athlete, my coaches will have greater control over me, the expectations will be higher, they'll want to micromanage my training schedule, they'll want me to cut out all my activities outside of track, they'll try to overwork me, they'll want me to make this team my entire life. All for just five hundred dollars. At a time when all I want, all I *need*, is a break from this team, from track. From competing with the men.

I'm not signing this, I say.

What? CeCé—this is a great opportunity for you, Coach Graham insists.

No, it's not. I get up from my chair.

Wait—where are you going? Coach Graham is raising his voice now. *Let's talk about this.*

I don't want to talk. I don't want to sign my life away for five hundred dollars when everyone else gets so much more. In fact, I don't want to be on this team anymore.

CeCé—stop!

But it's too late—I'm already gone.

I need my sister. I need to talk to Sonja. I search our apartment—but she's nowhere to be found. Out with another guy, probably. Something has shifted in our relationship recently. She has become distant; it seems like there's been a breakdown in our communication. I'm not really sure why she's putting up this wall. I'll call or text and she won't respond. We'll make plans and she'll flake right before we're supposed to meet. It seems like she'd rather hang out with guys she's dating than make time for me. I know how tough things are with her dad. I know they've been fighting, that things have been toxic. And when she's going through a rough patch with her dad, she always seeks comfort from men. I wouldn't mind that, if it didn't feel like suddenly, my sister doesn't have time for me. Now, when I need her support more than ever, when it feels like my world is turning upside down, she's not there for me.

The next day, I'm called into Coach Graham's office. It's just the two of us, this time. The tension is unbearable. But I have to remain strong. I've been pushing my feelings aside for so long. I've been prioritizing the team, my track career, and my coaches, over myself. Over my mental health. But no more.

I'm not signing the contract, I tell Coach Graham. *I don't want to be a sponsored athlete.*

That's concerning to me, he says. *I'm concerned about your commitment to the team.*

Well, I need to take a break from the team.

A break? he asks.

Yes. For my mental health. I want to say more. I want to tell him about the torture I've endured for the last year. I want to tell him how dysphoric I've felt. I want to tell him about the war going on inside me, the battle between my mind and body. I want to tell him about the excruciating pain that comes with being forced to live a lie, in order to do the thing you love. I want to tell him about my darkest thoughts, how deeply my depression has impacted me. But I don't have the strength to say any of this. *There's just…a lot I'm dealing with right now*, I continue. *I need a break.*

Well, we expect full commitment from everyone on the team. There's no such thing as "taking a break." You're either on the team, or you're not.

Then, I guess I'm not on the team.

He reconsiders for a moment. Hesitates. *How long would you need?* he asks.

I'm not sure. I just need space.

I can give you three days.

Three days? I say, shocked. Insulted. After all I've given to this team, after all the sacrifices I've made, Coach Graham is really going to look me in the eyes and tell me that I have *three days* to take care of my mental health? *That's not going to work for me. I can't put a timer on my mental health.*

Then I guess you're off the team, he says.

I guess so. And with that, I get up and walk out of the room and off the track team. I feel no ambivalence, no regret, no fear. The only thing I feel at this moment: total freedom.

* * *

I get back to the apartment. Throw my shit on my bed. Once again, Sonja is nowhere to be found. I'm beginning to wonder if this is a one-sided friendship, if I've overestimated our familial bond. She rarely wants to hang out anymore, steers clear of our daily rituals, and even avoids going to parties with me. I can sense she's going through a hard time personally, so I tell her she can open up to me, confide in me about what she's going through, but she says she's fine, she says she doesn't want to talk. But I miss our heart-to-hearts. I'm going through so much right now, all I want is to vent to my sister about my problems, to get her advice, but it seems like she just doesn't have time. At the beginning of the year, I truly believed that nothing could come between us. But now I'm not so sure.

I strip to my underwear. Go back out to the living room, where I always do my sit-ups and push-ups. Exercise feels good. A way to purge the anxiety that is starting to creep into my consciousness. *Did I really just quit the track team? What does this mean for my future? Who am I now that I'm no longer a runner?* All these thoughts race through my mind as I push through my workout. The pain feels good; I'm grateful for the rush of endorphins that flood my system.

Hey, CeCé.

I jump in surprise. I turn around, to see Sonja come out of her bedroom, also in her underwear. *Oh, I didn't realize you were home,* I say.

Yeah, we've just been in my room, she says, and suddenly there's a man, wearing nothing but a towel, standing in the doorway next to her.

Oh, I say. I feel exposed. I'm here in my underwear, and suddenly, there's a random man in our apartment staring at me, nearly naked. *I can give you guys some privacy.*

I go into my room. Wait until he's gone. My temper flares. I hear a whispered goodbye, hear the front door click shut. I come back out, into the living room.

I was in my underwear, Sonja, I say. *Do you think you could've given me a heads-up that you had a guy over?*

Sorry. She shrugs. *I guess I didn't think it was that big a deal.*

I just felt exposed. I need my privacy. And, if I'm being honest, it's been a revolving door of men around here recently.

Excuse me? Sonja says, her tone sharpening.

You don't have any boundaries, I snap. *You just bring dudes through whenever you feel like it.*

Well, maybe you're just jealous, she fires back. *Because you can't get any men.*

Jealous? I'm not jealous. I could get a man if I wanted. I just have standards, unlike you.

Well, maybe you should lower your standards, she shouts.

How can you tell me to lower *my standards?* I shout back. *You're supposed to be my best friend. You can't say shit like that to me.*

I can say whatever the hell I want, she's yelling now.

Well, that's pretty shitty. And I guess I expect more from someone who says she's my family. I'm so tired of feeling like you don't support me. I'm vulnerable with you. I'm here for you when you need me. I'm ride or die. I'm your sister, but you don't treat me like it.

Well, maybe that's because I'm not *your sister.*

That is such an awful thing to say. I storm into my room. Slam the door behind me. Because I'm afraid of what will happen if we keep fighting like this. I'm afraid it'll get physical. I throw myself onto my bed. Burst into tears. I feel overwhelmed. I need my sister now more than ever; I need her support, her guidance, her love. She still has her real mother, her real sisters, she still has family in her life that she can talk to. But I don't. She *was* my family, my *only* family. And maybe it's unfair to put that expectation on her, maybe that's too much pressure to put on someone you aren't related to. Maybe friends can't be family members. But regardless, I feel so alone. I worry that I've lost her forever.

CHAPTER TWENTY-SEVEN

The campus is empty. Covered in a blanket of snow and slush. Everyone is gone for winter break. But I've chosen to stay behind. I can't visit my mom. I don't have anywhere else to go. Sonja is visiting her family. I'm grateful to have our apartment to myself. Things have been tense between us. We've tried to avoid each other. We've gotten to the point where we can be cordial, but we've decided that it's best if we don't live together anymore. We're waiting for housing to approve our request for a room reassignment. But even though I'm relieved to have her gone, a part of me is also sad. I feel so alone.

A few friends asked me if I had a place to stay over winter break. Asked me if I wanted to come home with them. But I lied. I said I was going to visit my cousin. The truth: I didn't want to spend winter break with someone else. Didn't want to bear witness to another family's happy holiday, knowing that it wasn't my own. I thought I needed time to myself.

But now I realize it was a mistake to stay here.

An awful depression weighs on me. Deepens with every day. There are days I miss track, or miss Sonja, or miss them both. But then I remind myself of why I abandoned those parts of my life. I tell myself that I'm better off now. That I'm free to figure out who I want to be. So why does my heart hurt so much?

I'm running out of money. Campus is closed, so they don't need anyone to work at the recreation center or in the admissions office. I don't have a job, which means I don't have cash. I'm trying to stretch out the little I have in my bank account, so I can afford food for the entire three-week break. I'm worried I'll run out. I'm worried I'll go hungry. Because I also have to pay for hormones. I don't have insurance to cover them, and they recently increased the price.

It feels surreal to be here by myself, with nothing to do, in the dead of winter. Most days I just stay in bed, staring at my phone, too depressed to move. The weeks pass. Christmas comes—I don't have anyone; I don't go anywhere. New Year comes—I don't have anyone; I don't go anywhere. I just stay in my room, and retreat deeper into the most intense darkness I've ever felt.

I'm afraid of what I might do to myself.

One day, it's particularly bad. I know I shouldn't be alone.

Which is when I get a call from Larry Leach. Not a moment too soon.

Larry is the right-hand man to the president of Franklin Pierce, works as vice president of alumni affairs, and also heads up a lot of the diversity programs on campus, making sure that every student feels welcome. Ever since my sophomore year, he's been a sort of mentor figure to me, going out of his way to make sure I feel seen, safe, and supported. And I've never needed more support than I do at this moment.

Hi, CeCé, he says when I pick up the phone. *How would you feel about coming out to our house and spending the weekend? We're celebrating Chelsea's birthday.* Chelsea is his daughter, a fellow Franklin Pierce student and one of my friends. Spending the weekend at their house sounds exactly like what I need right now.

I'd love that, I reply.

Perfect, he says. *I'll come pick you up.*

Soon, Larry pulls up to my dorm, and I jump in his car. But from the moment I get in, he can tell something is wrong. *Are you okay?* he asks once we've gotten on the road.

I tell him everything—it all just pours out of me. My fight with Sonja. Quitting the track team. I tell him about my depression, the darkness, the loneliness, the fear, the anxiety, the dread. I tell him how it's all too overwhelming. That I feel like I can't live with these feelings anymore. That I don't know what to do. That I'm scared, and alone, and lost.

Why didn't you call me? Text me? he says, sweetly. *I would've come and gotten you a lot sooner.*

I didn't want to bother you. Or your family.

You never bother us CeCé. We love you.

Eventually, we arrive at his home. His wife, Judith, meets us at the door. She sweeps me into a warm embrace. *I'm so happy to see you*, she says. Their dog bounds up to me, slathering me with kisses. I laugh and pet him. Already, I'm feeling better. *Dinner is almost on the table*, she says.

She guides me to the dining room. Chelsea's there, along with her sister, Lindsay, and the two of them greet me with hugs. We pull up seats at the dining table. Larry pours some wine. Judith comes out with a big, steaming bowl of pasta. She scoops some onto everyone's plate. I dive into the food—it's so creamy, so rich, so delicious. At some point, a birthday cake appears on the table, and we all sing to Chelsea. The family folds me effortlessly into their dynamic— it feels like I'm at home, like I belong here. We chat, and laugh, and eat, and drink, and the night passes in a beautiful blur. I'm so grateful for this distraction. It feels so good to be around other people, people who love and support me, instead of by myself, with my darkest thoughts. We linger over dinner, and eventually everyone gets sleepy. Larry takes me up to the guest room. He asks me if I need anything else before I go to bed. I tell him that I'm good. He turns to leave. I tell him to wait. I tell him how thankful I am that he welcomed me into his home tonight. I tell him that it was exactly what I needed. A distraction. A beautiful escape. A reminder that I am loved, I am blessed, and that life is worth living.

The first students to come back to campus are the athletes, the basketball team, the lacrosse team, and, of course, the track team. They're all here to train before school officially starts. I try to avoid my ex-teammates as best I can. And I know that they're avoiding me too. They travel in a pack, eat together, train together, compete together. They have their group, their bubble, and I'm no longer a part of it. My choice, I know. But it still hurts to see them all together. Still hurts to remember what I've left behind. I wish there was a way to get it back. I wish there was a way for me to be my authentic self and compete in the sport I love.

Eventually, the rest of the students come back. Sonja comes with them. The break has done us some good. We're not anywhere close to being sisters again, but things are a little less tense around the apartment. Now, instead of anger, I just feel sadness. This is our senior year, and we were so excited to spend it together, side by side, attending all the parties, and games, and bonfires, and cookouts, and commencements. But that's no longer possible. The best I can hope for is a tight cordial smile as she passes me in the hallway.

A few weeks later, I move into a Lakeview townhouse. These six-person housing units are for seniors only and, as their name implies, they all have beautiful views of Pearly Lake. I share a room with my friend Caitlin. All the girls in the house have been welcoming to me, and even though I miss the closeness of my friendship with Sonja, I'm grateful that everyone in my new dorm has been so welcoming.

The rest of the year is uneventful. I attend my classes. Go to senior events. Party with friends, though Sonja always remains just out of reach, cordial and cold. This is not the triumphant senior year I imagined, this is not the victory lap where I fully blossom into an elite athlete, this does not feel like the culmination of all the painful but necessary growth that has marked my college experience.

Something about this year feels incomplete.

But there's nothing I can do. And before I know it, it's almost time for graduation.

I have to lie to my mother. I have no choice. I'm afraid of what will happen if I don't.

I'm on the phone with her now. It's one of our regular check-ins, conversations that give me anxiety because there's always so much left unsaid. She's asking about my graduation. About the date of my commencement. I don't think she'll actually come. My mother has rarely come to important events in my life, and I have no reason to believe she'll start now. But still, the idea that she might show up to my graduation terrifies me. I begin to panic when I imagine what might happen if she sees me collect my diploma in heels and a dress. Will she yell awful slurs, pull me off that stage, attack me, embarrass me in front of the entire school?

I can't have that.

I want the freedom to be myself at my own graduation.

So, I have to lie to my mother. I give my mother a date. A false date—a week after graduation. I feel relief, knowing that this lie will ensure my safety. But I also feel a deep sadness. Once again, I'm forced to live this double life. Because I'm scared of my mother. But that's not all. There's another fear that burns in my heart. I worry that if my mother learns the truth about me, it will destroy her. And despite all the shit she's put me through over the years, I don't want to hurt her. I love her. I want her to love me. So I lie to her. I continue to carry the burden of this secret. A secret that's killing me.

Graduation comes. I feel happy to walk down the aisle in my cap and gown, happy to find my seat amidst all my fellow seniors, happy to hear my name called, my *true* name, happy that Franklin Pierce is a place that, for the most part, supported my journey as I blossomed into womanhood. I'm happy to collect my diploma, happy to celebrate with all my friends. Yes, this year didn't turn out quite the way I expected, but I'm still so proud of how far I've come.

My mother isn't here. I try not to think about her absence. I try to focus on the positive. I have so many supporters in the crowd. Fellow students who've supported me throughout my time at Franklin Pierce. Friends from back in Lebanon, from Dairy Twirl, from high school. I'm touched to see that Lynn Hill, and her daughter Anna, have made it here today. Lynn was a Dairy Twirl regular who became a close friend, and almost like a surrogate mother to me. She opened her home to me many times over the years. During that idyllic summer before junior year, I would go to her house to hang out with Anna. They had a big, beautiful cabin in the woods that bordered a lake; Anna and I would spend entire afternoons jumping off a giant rock and into the water. When finally we were done, we'd head back inside, wrapped in towels, shivering from the water. Lynn would always have something prepared for us, snacks and drinks, and we'd watch the sun set over the lake. I'm so grateful to have Lynn in my life—she always saw the good in me and wanted me to succeed. Her presence here today, at graduation, just confirms this. She knows my story; she loves me just as I am. I can tell, thanks to all these small gestures, all these moments of quiet support and the way she's welcomed me into her home and into her family, that she's invested in my future.

What's the plan for the rest of the day? she asks, as the graduation crowd begins to thin.

I just have to move out of my room, I say.

Want some help?

I'd love some, I say.

Which is how we wind up back at my dorm room, in a sea of cardboard boxes, laughing and chatting as we pack up my clothes and books and toiletries and sheets and comforters. Larry Leach and his daughter Chelsea have joined us too; with all this love in one room, I almost forget that I miss my mother.

I can't believe that it's all over; that college will soon be nothing more than a memory. I try to enjoy the moment, to savor the company of Lynn and Anna and Larry and Chelsea. I try not to think about the uncertainty of the future. Finally, we finish taping up the last box. My room is empty. The bed is stripped bare. There's a short lull in the conversation. A silence falls over us. Then, Chelsea looks at me. *Your mom couldn't make it?* she asks.

I didn't want her here, I say. A pang of hurt constricts my chest. *I don't want her to know the truth about me...*

I understand, she replies. *But don't you ever wonder about what would happen if you did tell her the truth? There can be a lot of freedom in coming out—*

I don't want to come out to my mom, I say. *I know she'll never accept me.*

But can you really keep going through life hiding from your mother like this? Don't you want to at least try to tell her the truth? she asks.

Of course I do. All I want, all I've *ever* wanted, is to tell my mother the truth. To have her accept me, support me, fight for me, to see me as her daughter, her baby girl, the girl who loves her so much it hurts, and only wants to feel that same love in return.

Maybe, I reply.

Think about it. Lynn's eyes fill with kindness. *If you call her now, we'll all be here with you. Supporting you, staying by your side, no matter what happens.*

We've got you, CeCé, Larry chimes in.

Okay, I say, *I'm gonna do it.* And suddenly, I'm filled with adrenaline, with a newfound strength. With everyone's support, I can do this. I *have* to do this. I can't spend my whole life lying to my mother. I can't live with this fear in my heart forever. And how wonderful would it be if she *did* accept me? I can't even imagine the profound joy and relief that would fill my bursting heart.

I pick up my phone. My heart races. I dial my mother. The phone rings.

Hello? Her voice comes on the line. I start crying—I can't help it. *My baby boy—what's wrong?* I can hear the concern in her voice. The love. It gives me hope to continue.

*Mom...*I say, before bursting into a fresh wave of sobs.

Talk to me, she says tenderly. *I hate to hear you crying like this. Whatever it is, it's going to be okay.*

I pull myself together. Prepare myself to tell my mother the one thing I swore I never would. *Mom, I love you so much. I know you think you have a son, but I've actually been your daughter this whole time. My whole life, I've been your daughter.*

Silence on the line. I wait. My pulse beats faster. Finally, she speaks. *I don't understand,* she says. *I don't understand what you mean.*

I'm...I'm a woman.

No, no I can't accept this.

Mom, please just listen—

No, you can't turn your back on God like this. You can't give into the devil. This is the devil's work! You can't give into this lifestyle! She's yelling now. I'm grateful we're hundreds of miles apart. Grateful that she can't physically hurt me. Her words are enough. *You're gonna die,* she shouts. *You're gonna die of HIV. Go straight to hell—*

I hang up the phone. Throw it on my bed. Burst into tears. Bury my head in Lynn's arms. She holds me as I sob. Everyone gathers around me in support. My phone vibrates. It's my mother. Calling back. I let it go to voice mail. She calls again. And again. And again. My screen floods with a string of furious texts, filled with slurs and curses. I break from Lynn's embrace. Turn off my phone.

Suddenly, there's a knock at my door. I look at everyone in surprise. I catch my breath. Wipe my tears. Open the door.

A campus security guard stands outside. *We got a call from your mother,* he says. *Saying that you were in danger? Is everything okay?*

I can't believe it. I can't *believe* that she called the campus police. On her own daughter. I'm disgusted. *I'm fine,* I tell him. *Totally fine.*

168

I explain the situation. Lynn backs me up. And soon, he's on his way, leaving us alone.

Everyone comforts me. They tell me they're so sorry. They pull me close. I'm so grateful to have their support at this moment. I feel so devastated, so heartbroken, so angry.

But I don't feel regret.

Because my double life is over. Forever. No more lies. No more evasive conversations with my mother. No more sneaking around. No more fear that someone might tell her the truth before I do. Now I can live and act however I want, without fear of how it will affect my mother. Yes, there is so much unbearable pain in this moment. But there is also a small amount of relief. Because, I realize, I've been living my life for my mother. Up until today, I denied who I was whenever I was in her presence, because I was afraid that I'd hurt her or anger her or embarrass her or make her feel like she's failed as a parent. I took on that burden for her. I took on that excruciating weight. That awful stress of pretending to be someone else. All to protect my mother's feelings. But I can't take on the weight of my mother's feelings. That weight is for her to bear. Her prejudice is not my problem. Not anymore. Because I'm no longer living my life for my mother.

Now, I get to live my life for me.

CHAPTER TWENTY-EIGHT

Lillian can tell something is wrong. *Is everything okay?* she asks. We're stretching on the grassy field of a local high school track, which is just a few miles from Franklin Pierce. I can smell the freshly mowed lawn. Our teams train here during the outdoor season and summer because Franklin Pierce only has indoor track facilities. Of course, I'm no longer on the track team, and I've graduated from college. But I've decided to live on campus for the summer. To save up money while I figure out my next move, where I'm going to live, what I'm going to do with my life. Lillian has stayed for the summer too. We're living together in student housing, working together at the admissions office, and training together. She's got one more year of school ahead of her, one more year on the track team, so it's important that she stay in shape during the summer, so she can come back strong for her preseason. But me, I'm not coming back to school in the fall. I'm not sure why I keep training. Other than the fact that running is all I know, such a huge part of my identity. I'm not sure who I am without it.

You seem distracted, she continues.

It's just...I miss track, I say.

I'm sorry, she says. *I know how hard it's been for you to give it up.*

Yeah, it's been really tough.

Well, I know you're thinking of coming back to school to get those biology credits, she says. And it's true—I've been considering a return to Franklin Pierce for an extra year. I want to become a nurse—taking care of others is something I love to do, something I think could give me a new purpose. But to qualify for nursing school, I need a few more credits in biology. *What if you do another year of track?*

First of all, I don't even know how I'll afford another year, I say. *But even if I found a way to make it work, I could never go back to competing with the guys. It's just too painful.*

But what if you didn't compete with the guys?

What do you mean?

What if you competed with the girls? On the girls' team?

Is…is that even possible? I wonder. Of course, this thought has crossed my mind before, but I never saw it as an actual possibility. In my whole running career, I'd never seen an out trans woman compete with any female track team. Not at the high school level, not at the college level, and certainly not at the elite level. It just seemed impossible, like I'd sooner defy gravity than compete on a team that confirmed my true gender. The world of sports is one that is steeped in queerphobia and transphobia. I've seen it up close, experienced it throughout my life, and though things seem to be changing slowly, I never imagined that I could be a part of that change.

Until now. Suddenly, I feel hopeful. A surge of energy flows through my body, infusing me with a sense of purpose, and the drive to act immediately.

Just because something has *never* happened, doesn't mean it *can't* happen.

It's worth talking to Coach Zem about, Lillian says. *And I'll back you up one hundred percent. I'll fight alongside you, if I have to.*

It's just scary. I don't know if anyone has done this before.

But that's why you should try, she says. *You could make history.*

* * *

I wait outside Coach Zem's office. Lillian's there too. Sitting next to me. She squeezes my hand. I feel vulnerable, afraid I'll be rejected, that coach will tell me I can't compete with the female team. I've never asked for something like this before. No matter how much I've lived into my truth in every other area of my life, I've never dared to demand that the track world see me for the woman I am.

CeCé? Coach Zem comes out of his office. *I'm ready for you.*

I get up. Give Lillian one final look before I go in.

You've got this, she whispers.

I tell Coach Zem everything. My whole truth. I tell him that I quit the team last year because my mind and body were at war, because it was so painful to be deadnamed at every track meet, to have everyone in the NCAA think I was male. I tell him it was like someone else was competing out there, someone that wasn't CeCé. I tell him about how I felt outside my body all the time, during practice, at meets, in the locker room. I tell him how my dysphoria led to depression, how I worried that I would need to be checked into a mental health facility. I tell him about how I crashed after I quit the team, how I felt so lost. I tell him about that winter break, where I drifted into such darkness, that I worried I would take my own life. I tell him that, at the center of all this pain, there's one key problem that's never been resolved, a problem that's lasted my whole life: I've always been a girl that's been forced to run with the boys. And now, I've realized there's a potential solution: I could be a girl that runs with the girls.

I tell Coach Zem that I want to come back for one final year at Franklin Pierce. We'll call it my victory lap. A year where I finally join the women's track team, as CeCé, she/her, competing in the female category, where I belong.

He pauses, considers all I've just told him. A brief silence settles over the room. My heart is in my throat. Because deep down, I know what he's about to say. I know he's gonna tell me that it's just not possible, that it's never been done.

Finally, he says. *I've been waiting for this day. Ever since you first stepped into our office freshman year, and you introduced yourself to the coaches with your deadname, we were all surprised. But we all thought, okay, if that's how she wants to identify, we're not going to ask any questions. We followed your lead. But the truth is, we've always seen you as a female, CeCé. From day one. So I've been waiting for this day. And I would love to have you on the female track team.*

I'm absolutely stunned. Speechless. Overwhelmed by emotion. I can't believe it was just that easy. It makes me wonder why I waited four years to have this talk. The lifelong pain that's been lodged in my heart has been relieved with one simple conversation.

Finally, I will get to compete as my true self, in the sport I love.

CHAPTER TWENTY-NINE

It's the first team meeting of the season. We're all packed into the Bubble, waiting for Coach Zem. I'm sitting next to Lillian. *Girl, it's so good to finally have you here, where you belong,* she says. And it feels so good, so right, almost surreal. An impossible dream, realized. There's definitely been more work that's gone into getting me here. I worked with administrators and the financial aid department to score a last-minute scholarship, a full ride for my final year at Franklin Pierce. I'm so profoundly grateful for this support; it has given me a life-changing opportunity. Any misunderstandings last year regarding my coaches' previous sponsorship offer, all feel far in the rearview mirror. I feel so much excitement, so much momentum moving forward. I've also had to complete a lot of documentation, to officially join the female team. As it turns out, the NCAA has requirements for transgender athletes across all college sports. As a part of this, I will need to test my hormone levels every month, making sure I meet their protocols. My testosterone levels must stay below 5 nanomoles per liter. Thankfully, I've already been following these NCAA rules without realizing it. My trips to Planned Parenthood and my HRT regimen have kept me on track. So, finally, everything is in order.

Even still, I'm a little nervous.

Most of the returning girls know me and support me. But I'm not sure that everyone is one hundred percent on board with me training and competing alongside the female athletes. I'm especially worried about new students, who definitely don't know my story. I'm worried that they won't be accepting, that they won't want me on their team.

Coach Zem walks into the room. The chatter dies down. *Hello everyone!* he says. *I just wanted to have a meeting to welcome you all and kick off the season.* He launches into a fairly standard speech, introducing all the coaches and the athletic director, setting the expectations for the year ahead. *And there's just one more thing I'd like to mention,* he says before wrapping up. I feel my heart flutter. I know what's coming. *I want to introduce you all to CeCé Telfer. Most of you know her, but for those who don't, she's a very talented female athlete on our team, who happens to be transgender. Now, if anyone has any questions about that, they can come talk to me in my office. But I wanted to let you all know that she has the full support of every coach here, and I expect everyone on this team to have her back. Just like she has your back. Because we're a family here. That's what it means to be a team. Got it?*

I look around the room. A couple of the new girls have doubtful expressions on their faces, but other than that I can tell that almost everyone is excited for me, happy that I'm going to be their teammate. I feel a little conflicted; I don't love being singled out like this, but I also know that Coach Zem is smart for nipping any potential issues in the bud. He wants to create a safe space for me and ensure that I'll have the smoothest transition onto the female team.

All right, now let's have an amazing season!

Everyone claps and cheers. Lillian looks into my eyes and smiles.

Later, as we're all leaving the Bubble, Coach Zem pulls me aside. *This is gonna be your year,* he says, with a determined look on his face. *Let's go straight to the top.*

* * *

The Reggie Lewis Track & Athletic Center in Roxbury, Massachusetts. It's Day One of the NEICAAA Indoor Track & Field Championships. Today we've got prelims, tomorrow will be the finals. This will be my first competition running with my fellow female athletes. I'm surrounded by my teammates as we file into the stadium. We walk through the massive glass entryway, and into an atrium that's flooded with light. My heart is in my throat. I look to my teammate Paola, who flashes me a look that says: *You've got this, girl.* We've become so close during preseason training—I call her my Mexican sister. She has long brown hair, beautiful dark eyes, and a bright smile. She's from Querétaro but came to the US to follow her dream of becoming an Olympian high jumper. She is such a talented athlete, with an incredible work ethic. On the field, she's one hundred percent focused. But off the field, she loves to joke and laugh with me and Lillian. We're a small little track family, and I love these girls so much. I don't know if I could do this without their support. I've had no contact with my mother since that awful phone call after graduation, so it means the world to be embraced by this tight-knit group.

We walk into the field house—a massive indoor facility with a blue rubber track bordered on either side by rows of bleachers. Already, people are packed into the stands. I make my way to the field for warm-ups, nervously sizing up the competition, wondering what they're saying about me. I recognize many of the athletes from other schools. These athletes are used to calling me by my dead-name, used to seeing me compete with the men, and I know they're going to be caught off guard when they see me running with the women. I worry there's going to be hate aimed in my direction.

How are you doing? Lillian asks, as we start stretching.

I'm okay, I reply, grateful that I have Lillian and Paola by my side. Even still, I feel a twinge of loneliness. Yes, I'm finally on the female track team. But I'm the only trans girl, and not just the only trans girl on our track team, but the only trans girl on a college track team in the whole conference, in the entire United States, possibly the world. There's no one I can reach out to and ask for guidance, no one who can tell me: *I've been there before, girl, and I understand what you're going through.*

I see Paola over by where the guys are warming up, talking to her boyfriend Trevor. He's the captain for the men's track team, and we've been running together for years. He's an incredible athlete—hardcore, fast, and aggressive. He desperately wants to qualify for nationals. We all do, of course, but Trevor seems to be gunning for it the hardest. Sometimes I worry he's pushing too hard, that if he doesn't relax, he'll never reach that goal he longs for so badly. But even though I have so much respect for him as an athlete, I worry that he doesn't have that same respect for me, now that I'm competing with the women. This year feels different; it seems like he might be avoiding me, like he might not support Coach Zem's decision to let me run as my true self. And I worry that the other men might also feel the same, that they'll follow the lead of their team captain on this one.

On the track, time for the women's 200 meters, the announcer says over the loudspeaker.

Fuck it. I don't have time to worry about everyone else. I have to focus on my event. And you know what? If people want to talk shit, that's fine with me. They can worry about whatever they want to worry about. All I have to do today is focus on myself, run my race, dominate my heat, qualify for finals, then get the hell out.

On your marks.

I crouch down, into my starting block. I shift my thoughts to the people who *do* have my back. All my supporters that helped me arrive here today.

Get set.

I'm going to win this race for them.

Boom! The gun goes off. I'm out of the blocks. Pure speed. Eating up that track. Pushing like I've never pushed. Pushing to prove the haters wrong, to prove to myself that yes, this is where I belong, this is who I am. I was born to run with women.

I cross the finish line.

I come in first place. First in my heat, but also first out of all the women in 200-meter prelims. I've made it to finals. Now, I feel like I'm on a roll.

Then, it's time for the 60-meter hurdles. I know I've got this. I'm ready to crush it. And I do. I leave it all on the track. Come in first in my heat. Fourth in the overall prelims, but still a great time. I've made it to the finals in this event too. And I'm ready to kill it. I feel unstoppable.

After the meet, the whole team files out of the stadium, tired and ready to get something to eat, then rest up for finals the next day. As we pass athletes from another school, I hear one of them mutter something under his breath. I'm too far away to get exactly what he said, but I can tell by the way he's looking at me that it wasn't nice. But I rise above. Ignore him. Still, it hurts. I look back over my shoulder. Which is when I see something unexpected: Trevor, confronting this guy, standing up for me. They exchange a few tense words, then he jogs to catch up with our group again.

Fucking asshole, he mutters under his breath.

What were they saying? I ask.

Doesn't matter what they were saying, he says. *What matters is that I told them to shut the fuck up.*

Thanks, I say.

He smiles at me. *You killed it out there today.*

Finally, I feel seen by Trevor. This warms my heart a bit. I never thought he would be the one to stand up for me. Maybe I was wrong, maybe he does really support me. And even if he still feels conflicted, I'm grateful that at least he is making strides toward accepting me, that a part of him sees who I am, and is willing to fight alongside me for my right to compete.

We're at finals. I'm on fire. Ready to dominate.

First up, the 200 meters.

On your marks.

I line up with the eight other women who've made it to the finals. Suddenly, I'm struck by emotion. Tears well in my eyes. I say a prayer of gratitude, thank God for this opportunity, thank the other girls for seeing me, for letting me line up with them. And even if some don't truly accept me right now, I pray that they'll accept me in the future. Regardless, I'm grateful to be here. This is a meet I'll never forget. The meet where I competed as myself for the first time.

Get set.

I wipe my tears. Focus. I'm not here to cry. I'm here to win this event.

Boom! The gun goes off.

I win the race.

But the day's not over yet. I stay in competition mode. It's time for the 60-meter hurdles. I dominate again. Win another race. I feel euphoric.

I did what needed to be done. I won first place in both my events.

After the 60 meters, Trevor comes bounding up to me. *CeCé!* he yells.

What?

Your times qualified you for nationals.

I've qualified for nationals? I yell.

You've qualified for nationals!

Lillian, Paola, and Trevor, all surround me, loudly celebrating and laughing. I feel so much joy at this moment. And once again, I'm surprised by Trevor. He didn't qualify for nationals today. It's okay—there are still many other meets in the season where he'll have a chance. But I know how badly he wants to go to nationals, and I know it probably wasn't easy to see someone else achieve his goal before he did. But he put all that aside to acknowledge my achievement. This makes me feel seen, supported, and loved. It's incredible—it's the first major meet of the season, my first meet competing as my true self, and already I've qualified for the NCAA Indoor National Championship. It feels like a confirmation that I'm on the right path, that everything I've ever dreamed is finally within reach, that maybe, one day, CeCé Telfer will compete at the Olympic Games.

The backlash has started. My coaches, my athletic director, even the president of Franklin Pierce warned me that this might happen. Before my first competition, they met with me and asked me if I was prepared to deal with the negative fallout that could occur. I told them yes, that it was worth it to me, that I could handle whatever hate came my way.

But now I'm not so sure.

There have been articles in local papers, school papers, national papers, articles that express outrage that I was allowed to compete with the women, articles that deadname me, call me a man, and question the NCAA's decision to let me run as myself. Some parents are outraged, and a group of them have started a petition to kick both me and Franklin Pierce University out of the NCAA. My coach is getting death threats, his wife too. They just had a baby and people online have threatened their entire family. And, of course, I'm also getting death threats.

I try to keep my head down. To shut out the noise from the haters. To just focus on training. Since I've already qualified for nationals, my coaches are being selective about which meets they send me to. Technically, I don't need to compete again until the National Championships, but my coaches still want me to attend some high-profile meets, where I can work on getting my times down further. Throughout it all, I have to deal with this prejudiced myth that I possess an unfair advantage, that I'll somehow come into women's sports and dominate every race. But that, of course, isn't true. I lose plenty of races to other female athletes. And the aggressive hormone regimen I'm on to meet NCAA regulations actually places me at a disadvantage—I've experienced a loss of strength, endurance, and longer post-workout recovery times due to the effects of my HRT.

There is no scientific evidence, no clinical studies, nothing that conclusively states that trans women have an advantage over cis females.

I also worry for my safety at the meets I attend, but I push through. Mostly I stay out of the spotlight, train behind the scenes, at Franklin Pierce, though at times I'm worried for my safety even on my own campus. The stress is high. I'm scared that people might somehow figure out where I live. That one of the online threats could be made real. That someone might find my dorm. Attack me. I cry every day before practice. I cry every day after practice. Sometimes it feels like the only time I'm *not* crying is at practice itself.

Why don't you come stay with me, in our guest bedroom, for a little bit? Sasha-Lee asks one day, after I've vented to her about the crushing anxiety and fear that has come to dominate my days. Sasha-Lee is a friend who lives nearby, an older woman, a mother with a son and daughter in college, who volunteers frequently for the school. I met her during orientation, when she was helping with an LGBTQ event, and we hit it off. She's someone I trust, someone who is invested in my journey, someone I talk to regularly when I need support.

I think that could be a good idea, I say.

That night, I'm at Sasha-Lee's, chatting over a home-cooked meal, laughing with her husband and their kids, and sneaking the dogs bits of food under the table. Soon, I'm overcome with emotion. Despite all the unimaginable hate, despite the literal death threats that nearly every one of my supporters has received, no one has abandoned me. Not Sasha-Lee or her family, not my coaches, not my teammates. The NCAA has not wavered in their commitment to allow me to compete as myself. I've followed all their guidelines and rules, and they in turn have refused to bow to pressure from angry parents to ban me from the sport, they've refused to discriminate against me. They've stayed true to the integrity of their organization, and their commitment to allow *all* athletes to compete, regardless of gender, race, or sexual orientation. And as I sit here with Sasha-Lee and her family, lingering over the last bites of dessert, I feel such immense gratitude to know that no matter where I go, no matter what obstacles I face in life, I will always have a group of people who love me unconditionally, who support me even in the face of unimaginable hate. People who love the young woman I am, who will do anything to see her succeed.

CHAPTER THIRTY

I'm climbing the bleachers when I hear it. *Yo, that chick's a dude.* Then, an eruption of laughter. I don't look, not then. I don't want to give them the satisfaction. I ignore them, keep climbing. It's a group of athletes, and there are a few Jamaicans among them, going off in patois. A steady stream of hate follows me as I make my way to the section of the stands that's been designated for my school. They make crude jokes about my appearance, my anatomy, and I'm filled with anger. We're at the Northeast-10 Conference Championships, on the campus of Smith College. I've already qualified for nationals, so I don't feel as much pressure as some of my teammates at this regional competition. Still, I want to do well for my team, I want to score points, to help our whole track team place.

Hey, are you okay? Paola comes up to me, followed by Lillian. My track sisters.

Yeah, whatever. They're just irritating assholes.

Don't listen to them, Sasha-Lee comes up to our group in the stands. *The people who really matter are standing right here. Supporting you.*

And it's true. Sasha-Lee has become an important support system in my life. She comes to most of my meets and has taken on the

183

role of track mom, rounding out my track family, which of course includes Lillian and Paola, my devoted track sisters. I look at the rest of my team, and I'm suddenly overwhelmed by gratitude. Because no matter what happens in the stands, no matter what names people call me, no matter how much hate is aimed my way, I know that I will always be safe here, with my teammates and coaches and supporters.

I look back briefly, to see the same group of Jamaicans pointing and laughing.

They can say whatever they want in the bleachers. But they better watch out on the track. Because I'm a bad ass bitch. If you fuck with me, I'm gonna hand you your ass.

And I'll do it with a smile on my face.

It's Day One, the preliminaries. The athletes with the best times in their heats today will progress to the finals tomorrow. I'm competing in five events, so I'm prepared for an intense two days. A part of me is annoyed at my coach for putting me in so many events, but I know he's doing it because he believes in me. He knows I can score points for our team. So I'm feeling the pressure. But there's another reason my heart is pounding at the beginning of the day.

I'm singing the national anthem.

A week before the conference championships, I told my athletic director, Rachel Burleson, that if they needed someone to sing the national anthem at the meet, I would gladly volunteer. Of course, there were some safety concerns, but after talking it through, we decided this would be a beautiful opportunity to contribute to the day, to try and bring people together, especially after all the hate that has been aimed my way. Music has the power to bring people together, to help us set aside our differences. If people can see that I'm just a girl with a dream, with a passion, with a purpose, just like every other athlete at this meet, then maybe I can change hearts and minds. But after the incident with the Jamaican athletes, I'm not so sure. I'm worried that people will taunt me as I step up to the mic.

But it's too late to turn back now.

First, however, it's time to compete. I'm heading into the 60-meter dash. Warm-ups were solid. I'm feeling ready.

I dominate the competition.

I take first place in my heat. The other girl wasn't even close. My time is 7.69; she ran an 8.00. I watch the remaining three heats. See how the other girls stack up. In the end, I don't have the best time today. A girl from Stonehill got a 7.62, which puts me in second place for the prelims. Still, I feel confident in my performance, and ready to blow this girl out of the water tomorrow.

Next up, is the 60-meter hurdles. I've got this one in the bag, this is *my* event. Sure enough, I dominate my heat, and walk away with the best time of the day, an 8.54. Finals, here I come.

Then, it's time for the national anthem.

Rachel comes to get me. *Are you ready?* she asks.

Yes, I say, though I'm not sure I mean it.

She guides me onto the field, where a microphone stands, waiting for me. I take my place. The crowd settles. I stand alone, in front of everyone. I take a deep breath, attempting to quiet my nerves. I remind myself of why I'm doing this. I want to stand in my power, to say: *I exist, and I won't stop existing just because you hate me.* I want to show that I am an athlete who loves my sport, who loves this country—no matter how flawed and fucked up it may be at times—and who loves all her fellow humans—no matter how flawed and fucked up they may be at times. Yes, I remind myself, *love* is why I do all of this. *Love* is my motivating force.

I hear the opening chords of the anthem. I take a breath. My nerves dissipate. I open my mouth. My voice comes out, calm, confident, soaring on the winds of that familiar melody. My confidence grows as I look out into the audience, and see smiling faces, faces that earlier that day scowled at me, faces of prejudiced athletes, parents, and coaches. I know that one song won't be enough to solve all the hostility I face as a Black trans woman competing in the sport that I love. But today, that song brings us together. And as I sing the final notes, my heart fills with the hope that maybe, one day, I will be fully embraced.

The room fills with applause. I bask in it for as long as I can.

But not too long, because I've got two more events today.

First up, it's the high jump. Not my event—Coach Zem put me in this one to push me as an athlete. There're no prelims for the high jump. Today will determine the overall winner. I give it my best and come in seventh. But my Mexican sister, Paola, takes first place, and my heart fills with happiness for her. She's such a dedicated athlete, and she truly deserves this win.

Then, it's the 200 meters. I'm dragging at this point. Three events, plus the national anthem. But when that gun goes off, adrenaline kicks in, and I kill it, getting the best time in the prelims and securing a spot for myself in the finals.

Day One—done. I feel confident in my performance. I secured the bag. And I'm ready to do it all again tomorrow. Because I'm not done until I walk out of here a winner.

Day Two, the finals.

Lean, right as you cross the finish line. That's the only way you're gonna win this race. I hear Coach Zem's words echo in my mind as I get into the starting blocks for the 60-meter dash. This is not my event. Yes, I'm good at it, but not necessarily the best. It's not a guaranteed lock. And the girl from Stonehill who took first place in prelims is a fierce competitor. If I have any hope of winning, it's gonna be because I lean in the final seconds of this race, pushing my body over the finish line at the last minute.

On your marks!

I focus. Do a quick jump. Slap my legs all the way down, to get the blood flowing. Then I center myself. Go down on my mark. Visualize the race ahead.

Get set!

I'm in the zone. Ready to bolt.

Boom! The gun goes off. I'm the last girl out of the blocks. Damn. I'm at the back of the pack. I have to make up that time in the middle of the race. I push, push, push. Pass girl after girl, in pursuit of my competition. The girl from Stonehill. And this girl is fast. But I'm gaining on her. Catching up. Finally, we're neck and neck, side by side as we fly down the track.

I see the finish line.

I hear my supporters screaming for me. Hear my coach in my mind: *lean, lean, lean.* I'm almost there, almost at the end of the race, and I do what Coach Zem told me, I lean forward, and we pass the finish line at what feels like the exact same second.

I recover, doubling over, catching my breath.

As it turns out, we *did* cross the finish line at the exact same time, both getting a 7.63.

The officials disappear to deliberate. They're gone for ten minutes.

Finally, they return. It was so close, they had to break things down to one hundred thousandth of a second. And, finally, it was decided that I won. First place, by a lean. Just as Coach Zem had predicted. My teammates go wild, cheering. I just won my first Northeast-10 Conference title. But I don't have time to stay and celebrate. I head to my next event.

The 60-meter hurdles. I've got this in the bag. I know it.

I run it even faster than I did yesterday.

My time is 8.49. I take first place.

Now, I'm on a roll, I've hit my stride, I feel confident, like nothing can stop me. I'm ready to dominate the 200 meters. I'm ready to take home three gold medals. I'm ready to show everyone here that CeCé Telfer is a champion, that no amount of hate can stop her.

But then, as I'm walking back to where our team has set up camp, I hear someone yell at me. I guess not everyone was moved by my national anthem. He yells nasty things, degrading things. Despite how resilient I am, something about this man's words cut deep. Maybe it's because I'm exhausted from this intensive two-day event, maybe it's because I'm tired of being the center of attention, the center of controversy, maybe it's because I'm sick of feeling like everyone in this track facility is policing my body, but regardless, I am suddenly thrown. Knocked off my axis. I start to panic. I start to cry.

Are you okay? Sasha-Lee rushes up to me.

I don't know, I say. I look into her eyes. She is the closest thing I have to a mother at this moment in my life. I push thoughts of my own biological mother out of my mind. It's too painful to think of her now. A time when I need her the most. But I have Sasha-Lee, a woman who loves me. So I tell her everything. Tell her how lonely it feels, because no one here understands what it's like to live in a body like mine, how hard it is to wake up every single day and look in the mirror and be okay with what I see, how hard it is to walk out my door and deal with a world that doesn't understand me, that doesn't accept me, how hard it is to be okay with my body when everyone else is looking for ways to critique it, or make fun of it, or hate it.

Sasha-Lee comforts me, strokes my back. *Let's take a little break,* she says. *Let's get you to the bathroom, so you can collect yourself.*

She brings me to the bathroom. *I'll be right outside, okay? I'll make sure no one bothers you.*

Okay, I say and wipe my tears. *Thank you.*

Love you, CeCé, she says.

Love you too, I reply.

I walk into the bathroom. Dry my eyes. Reapply my makeup. Adjust my running gear. Get back in touch with my body. The dysphoria fades. I take a deep breath.

Suddenly, there's a gentle knock on the door. *CeCé?* Sasha-Lee says.

Yes?

It's time for the 200 meters.

* * *

On your marks!

I slap my legs, up and down, to get the blood flowing, yes, but also to get my head back in the game. *Pull it together*, I tell myself. *You have a race to run.*

Get set!

I get into the blocks. But I'm frustrated, furious that all the other athletes get to just focus on running and competing, but I have to deal with so much other bullshit—petitions to remove me from the NCAA, death threats, dirty looks, and stupid assholes yelling slurs at me.

Boom! The gun goes off.

My block shifts. I stumble. Fall to the ground. My knees hit the track. My hands slam against the rubber. *Fuck.* There's no hope. No coming back from this. I'm so embarrassed.

But then, a surge of adrenaline hits.

Fuck it—I don't care what people think. I'm still gonna run this fucking race.

My body springs up from the ground. I feel superhuman. Like I could do anything. The other girls are almost a hundred meters ahead. But I'm flying. Gaining on them. I pass girl after girl. Each time I do, the adrenaline surges even harder. I'm not gonna come in last. In fact, I might even win this thing. My teammates are screaming. Jumping in the stands. Calling my name. I throw my entire body into this race. I don't feel dysphoric, I don't feel at war with my body. Now, we are working as one. Me and my body.

And then I see it: the finish line.

I cross it. The crowd goes wild.

I did it. Against impossible odds, against the immense pressure that no one else on that track faced, I picked myself up off the ground, came from behind, and secured the motherfucking bag.

I won the race, and gold medal number three.

* * *

Can I see your nails? Yogi asks. We're sitting together on the infield of the Smith College track, waiting for the awards ceremony to begin. Yogi is one of the cutest kids I've ever met, he's about four years old, with a mop of dark brown hair, and the most adorable smile. I'm so glad he's here today. He's my athletic director Rachel's son, and I babysit him from time to time.

Yes, you can see them! I say, fanning out my pink stiletto nails.

His eyes go wide. *Wow. They're beautiful.*

I laugh. Yogi has always been obsessed with my nails, ever since I started babysitting him and his brother. One year, he begged his two moms to get him "nails like CeCé's" for Christmas. So they got him the most adorable tiny press-on nails you've ever seen. He wore them the next time I babysat, saying, *Look, I've got CeCé's nails!* The whole episode was so sweet, and it made me feel so close to Rachel and her family. It was so beautiful to see Rachel encourage her child in this way, creating such a loving atmosphere.

A meet official steps up in front of the crowd. Everyone quiets down. All the teams are here, each sitting in their own designated area on the infield. They announce the All-American award winners—which are for athletes with the best academic records—then move on to the most coveted category: Most Outstanding Track Performer.

And now, the official says, *the award for Most Outstanding Female Track Performer at the 2019 Northeast-10 Conference Championships goes to…CeCé Telfer.*

My team goes wild. I'm in shock. Not only did I win those three gold medals, but now I'm being honored as the most outstanding female athlete at this meet? After all I've been through to get here, this feels like real validation. I stand up and survey the field. Not everyone is happy about my award. Some other teams sit there silently, arms folded, or staring down at their phones, refusing to acknowledge my win. I feel a flutter of doubt as I walk up to accept the award. But then I look back and see Yogi running toward me, clapping and smiling. His mom follows in hot pursuit, laughing. I'm filled with such love, such gratitude. I swoop Yogi into my left arm, holding my plaque with the right. Rachel comes up and hugs me. Then a photographer walks up. *All right now, smile for the camera*, he says. And the three of us grin ear to ear, and pose for the picture, and I decide to ignore all the hate.

This is my moment. My victory. No one can take that away from me. I'll have this award, these medals, for life. While many people may object to my presence here today, may hate me, there are so many other people who love me. And *those* are the people I seek out in the crowd, the people with smiling, cheering faces. The people who know how hard I've worked to get here, how many obstacles I've overcome, to finally be able to compete as my true self.

I glance down at Yogi. He smiles up at me, and I think: *Look at this beautiful being I'm holding. He loves me. He sees me as CeCé, she/her, nothing else. No questions asked.*

As I walk back to my seat, I feel a new confidence build within my heart. I am loved. I am seen. I am accepted. And I am so profoundly grateful.

CHAPTER THIRTY-ONE

I'm off social media. There's a surge of hateful backlash in the wake of my performance at the conference championships. People are furious that I won three medals, that I was honored as the Most Outstanding Female Athlete. It seems like every time I experience a victory, there is a new horde of haters waiting in the wings, ready to tear me down. And this time, the outrage isn't limited to athletes and parents from other schools within our conference—it has spread to a national level. Conservative news sites have turned me into a villain, printing awful untruths, prejudiced things. They've turned me into a political cause, painted me as a threat to women's sports. People from all over the country are now calling to have me banned from the NCAA, to strip me of all my medals, all my awards. People are sliding into my DMs, saying I'm a horrible person, saying they know where I live, saying they're going to come and kill me.

But like I said, I'm trying to stay offline. Honestly, I was rarely on social media before, too absorbed in my training to invest much time on Instagram or Twitter. It wasn't until all this backlash that I started to pay attention, tempted to dive into the discourse and fight back. But I can't let the voices of the trolls get to me. I need to steer clear of Twitter. Keep my head down. Stay focused on training. The

National NCAA Indoor Track & Field Championships are coming up. I don't have time to get distracted.

CeCé we need to talk, Sasha-Lee says, as she bursts into the admissions office. There's an intensity in her eyes that scares me. *Can you step outside with me for a second?*

Um, I think so? Let me just get someone to cover for me.

I leave my desk in search of my manager, Braelin. I'm honestly grateful for the distraction of this job—it feels like a relief to be able to focus on anything other than all the building controversy. I work the front desk, scheduling appointments, and inputting student information into our database. Braelin agrees to cover the phones, while I step out to talk to Sasha-Lee. We find an abandoned conference room.

What's going on? I ask.

I'm going to need you to sit down, she says. *Because this is serious.*

What is it? I find a seat. She pulls up a chair next to me. My heart beats faster. My palms start to sweat. *You're scaring me.*

Have you been on Twitter today? she asks.

No, I'm staying off social media.

Right. Which is good. But I think it's important that you know what happened today.

What? My mind is now racing.

The Trump family is targeting you. Donald Trump Jr. tweeted a link to a conservative news article that attacks you. He tweeted that this was unfair to everyone in women's sports. Then, President Trump himself retweeted it.

I can't believe it.

I just want you to know that I'm here for you. We're all here for you. And we all will do whatever it takes to ensure that you're safe.

Sasha-Lee eventually leaves. I'm in shock. I have three hours left in my shift in the admissions office, but I can't focus. My mind is spiraling. It feels surreal. Terrifying. To be targeted by one of the most powerful men in the world. A man who knows that this will result in a huge outpouring of transphobia and death threats—all aimed at me. What a disgusting way to use your influence as president of the United States. To spread violence and hate and target a college student—a young woman simply trying to get through school, to excel in athletics and academics.

I get home. I hesitate. I'm not supposed to be on social media. Especially not now. But I can't resist. My finger hovers over the Twitter icon. I open the app. I pull up the president's account. But then, I throw down my phone. Because you know what? I don't have time for the president.

I'm too busy training to be a motherfucking champion.

CHAPTER THIRTY-TWO

*W*e've *been in contact with the NCAA,* Coach Zem says. I've been summoned to his office for a meeting, and we're also joined by my athletic director Rachel; the throwing coach, Coach Cir; and Sasha-Lee. *The NCAA has been worried about your safety at nationals,* Coach Zem continues. *And now, after the Trump tweets, they're even more concerned.*

So we've come up with a plan, Rachel says. *We're going to fly you out to the competition two days after all the other athletes. We'll also be flying into a different airport than everyone else, one that's a three-hour drive from the hotel.*

But that's so unfair, I say. Though the competition is obviously the main event at the NCAA Indoor National Championship, there are many events to celebrate the athletes in the days leading up to the competition. By flying out later than everyone else, I'll be missing the welcoming gala, where everyone dresses up, consumes delicious food and drinks, and the NCAA celebrates all the achievements of the assembled athletes. Which will be sad, of course, but I can live with missing out on a party. What's more concerning is that by arriving later than everyone else, I will have almost no time to adjust to the Kansas climate, no time to prepare mentally or physically, no

195

time to get into a pre-meet rhythm. I'll have to jump off a plane, endure a three-hour road trip, crash at my hotel, and wake up to prepare for the competition the following morning. *Why do I need to do this?*

Everyone in the room exchanges a series of nervous glances. *There have been threats to your safety, CeCé,* Coach Zem says. *I'm sure you've seen some yourself. We've also been getting them. We think it's best to take every precaution possible. The NCAA will hire two private security guards to trail you throughout the meet.*

But you have the ultimate say here, CeCé, Rachel insists. *We're only going through with this plan if you agree.*

I hesitate. I feel trapped between two conflicting emotions. On the one hand, I'm grateful that I have so many supporters who are concerned for my safety, who will even put themselves at risk to help me achieve my dream. But on the other hand, I'm frustrated. It feels so shitty, so unfair, so infuriating that I have to arrive late, miss out on the awards ceremony, and put myself at a competitive disadvantage because I do not have the same amount of time to settle and acclimate before I compete on the national stage. I just want to compete like everyone else. Do what every other athlete gets to do. Without a security detail trailing my every move.

But I know that would be unwise. I look around the room, at the nervous glances exchanged by everyone else. I get the sense that they know something I don't, that they're protecting me from the worst of the threats, trying not to alarm me.

What do you think? Coach Zem asks.

Okay, I reply. *Let's do it.*

The Princess Protection Program. That's how I think of it. My little nickname. A joke to make me feel better about an awful situation. I focus on getting into competition mode. The week of indoor nationals arrives. I push myself more every day. Keep track of how my body feels. On Monday I'm at 35 percent. On Tuesday it's 50 percent. On Wednesday, the day I fly out, it's 75 percent.

I pack my bags. Get ready for my flight. Sasha-Lee and Coach Cir are going to travel with me. I have two other teammates who are also competing at nationals—my best friend Paola, and Hugo, an international student from France who absolutely kills the 800 meters. They went ahead, two days earlier, participating in all the events leading up to competition day. As I fold my gear into my suitcase, I get a text from Paola. It's a picture of her in a beautiful gown, smiling brightly, holding an award with my name on it. At the dinner the night before, they acknowledged all conference champions who made it to nationals. My coach accepted my award on my behalf. Paola texts again, saying she wishes I could've been there, but she's excited to see me tomorrow.

I burst into tears.

It's just so unfair. I was robbed of the opportunity to celebrate my achievement. But it's not just that, it's so much bigger than that. I feel so alone. Even though I have so many supporters, no one else is going through what I'm going through. I'm surrounded by love, but still so isolated in my experience. I'm sick and tired of being the only one. I wish I could confide in someone who could validate my feelings, who could say, *Yes, I've been there, too, I've suffered that same loneliness, I know what it's like when you feel that the whole world doesn't understand your struggle.*

I collect myself. Take a deep breath. Then I realize: What if I'm not the only one? What if there are others out there just like me, and I just haven't taken the time to do my research? I pull out my phone. Start googling. And as it turns out, I'm not the only trans woman trying to navigate the world of elite athletics. There is a woman named Chloe Psyche Anderson, who recently competed in NCAA volleyball. There are the high school track athletes Andraya Yearwood and Terry Miller, two Black trans girls who became the targets of an anti-trans lawsuit in Connecticut, attempting to ban transgender students from competing in high school sports. I read these stories, and I start crying again, tears of relief. I'm not alone—there are other trans women out there fighting on the front lines. I feel so deeply for Andraya and Terry, these two beautiful young girls, just trying to do what they love, while facing so much hate. I feel a deep motivation stirring in my soul. I wonder how many young trans athletes out there are experiencing a fear of coming out, a fear of living their truth on the field, a fear that they will be banned from the sport they love if they express who they truly are.

I dry my eyes, zip up my suitcase, and walk out the door. I can't give up; I can't break down. Because there is a generation of young trans athletes waiting in the wings, ready to follow their passion, and fight for their right to compete as themselves.

I have to do this for them.

CHAPTER THIRTY-THREE

We speed along a darkened highway. One of the only cars traveling this late. I look out the window, straining to see our surroundings. The Kansas landscape is swallowed by night. We've been on the road for three hours, driving from the airport. Me, Sasha-Lee, and Coach Cir. All I want is to crash in our hotel room. I wish I could've flown into the closer airport, the same airport as everyone else. But this is part of the Princess Protection Program. I feel exhausted from traveling, yet also keyed up from that pre-competition adrenaline.

We arrive at the hotel. Our whole group is staying at a different hotel from most of the athletes. Again, to help protect me. To ensure that no one knows where I'm staying.

We're starving, but it's 10:00 p.m., and nothing is open except an Olive Garden. So we grab a table and order quickly. There are only a few other people eating at this hour, but I can feel their stares. They're clocking me, whispering. I feel a surge of anxiety. I'm beginning to realize that I might not be welcome in Pittsburg, Kansas, a small conservative city. My exhaustion dovetails with irritation. I don't even want to eat; I just want to go back to my hotel room and try to get to sleep. I have a big day tomorrow. We have our pre-meets, which is when all the athletes warm up and get used to the new facility on the day before the competition begins. Everyone else has already been here two days, settling in, adjusting to the time zone, to Kansas. But I have to launch right into competition mode. Right into pre-meets. And because of this, I feel like I'm at a disadvantage. I rush through dinner, and we hurry back to the hotel.

I try to sleep as best I can. But pre-competition jitters keep me tossing and turning. I wake up the following morning on edge. I feel rushed, like everything is unfolding too quickly. Like I'm barreling into the biggest competition of my life, but I haven't had time to prepare.

We head to the Pittsburg State University track facility for pre-meet, where I'll warm up and get in an abbreviated practice, just long enough to get accustomed to this new facility, but not so long that I deplete my energy. The competition starts tomorrow.

I step onto the field. I'm introduced to my private security guards, two intimidating older men who inform me that they'll be watching over me, to ensure that I'm not targeted. It feels surreal. Throughout the day, they follow me, lingering just out of sight, surveying the facility for potential threats. Every time I go to the bathroom, they station themselves outside, monitoring everyone who comes in and out. I'm grateful for the extra protection, but it also just makes me feel even more anxious. How have things really escalated to this point? Is all this necessary? Are there threats my coaches and the NCAA haven't told me about?

The security detail is there to stop any credible threats to my life, but unfortunately, they can't do anything about microaggressions. And I get them all day long. People go out of their way to avoid me; people taunt me with their stares.

I start warming up on the field, and a bunch of Jamaicans from another school start making fun of me. Here we go again, another group of Jamaicans, trying to make my life a living hell. But they're going off in patois, not realizing that I can understand everything they're saying. So I start shouting "16 Shots" by

Stefflon Don, singing in patois, to let them know that not only can I understand what they're saying, but that they're on notice: *No boy can diss me or my mother / Round here ain't safe, everybody need armour!*

That shuts them up.

But I feel on edge. During warm-ups, Coach Zem warns me that this track is different than most. The 200 meters usually starts on a curve, then you run into a straightaway. But this track is unusual; it starts on a straightaway, then runs into a curve, then ends in another straightaway. It feels backward. I run it a few times, trying to adjust. But I'm completely thrown.

That night, sleep is almost impossible.

I wake up in the morning. I eat my oatmeal. Drink my green tea. I spend time with Paola, Sasha-Lee, and Coach Cir. We're all chatting, trying to distract ourselves from our nerves. I'm doing my makeup, applying my lashes.

I want some CeCé lashes, Sasha-Lee says suddenly.

Me too, Coach Cir chimes in.

Me too, Paola says, laughing. *But I don't know how long they'll last on the high jump.*

Which is how I end up giving all the girls fake lashes. Our little femme army, all wearing lashes like they're armor. I feel so grateful for the solidarity. We laugh and chat and pass the morning together, and our joy feels healing. I feel so close to these women.

Then, it's time to compete.

The 200 meters is difficult. I psych myself out. The new track, the taunts from my competitors. It's all throwing me off my game. I place twelfth. I won't be progressing to Day Two. But then, it's time for the 60 meters. I feel more confident. I have this one in the bag. And I kill it—I come in second. I qualify for finals. Which means I still have a shot tomorrow.

A shot at taking home a medal at my first NCAA National Championship.

* * *

Day Two. I feel vulnerable. At risk. My security detail hovers over my every move. It doesn't help that Kansas is already such a conservative state, that I get clocked every time I leave my hotel room, that people point and stare. It doesn't help that it seems like just about everyone in the conference hates me, that I get mean looks from my competitors, their parents, even from some race officials. It's so hard to focus in this environment, where it feels like an entire stadium of people is rooting for you to fail. It's so hard to focus when you have death threats running through your head, when it feels like at any moment someone could come charging at you from the stands, or from the field, and attack.

The announcers call my event. I make my way to the starting blocks. I find my lane. The crowd settles.

On your marks!

I narrow my focus. Block out all the hate, all the fear.

Get set!

I can feel the energy from my competitors. We're all in the zone. The stadium is totally silent. Waiting for the gun to go off.

Suddenly, someone yells. I jump out of the blocks. Terrified. I realize this man is yelling at me. Calling me a man. Calling me derogatory terms. Is this the moment I'll be attacked?

Runners stand up, please. We are dealing with an issue in the stands.

This doesn't happen. I've never seen someone disrupt a race like this. My heart is racing. I feel exposed. Out on the track, for everyone to see. The person keeps yelling. An official walks up to him. Tells him to calm down. Tells him that if he disturbs the race again, he will be kicked out of the stadium, and never allowed back to an NCAA event again. The person settles, takes his seat. I can't believe he's allowed to stay. But there's nothing I can do.

All right everyone, take a minute to shake it off.

Everyone else is thrown off as well. We all do our best to do as the announcer says, to shake it off, to regain our focus. But now I'm in my head, distracted, fearful. *Come on, CeCé,* I tell myself. *Get it together. Get back in the zone.*

On your marks!
I back into the blocks.
Get set!
I remind myself that a championship is on the line. That I can still win this.
Boom! The gun goes off.
But my heart's not in the race. I can't regain my focus. Horrifying scenarios keep running through my mind. I worry that someone else will scream something from the stands, or threaten my life, or run onto the track, or even shoot me. We're deep in a Red State, and many people have been hostile to my presence so far. Danger feels imminent. I feel physically and mentally exhausted from dealing with the stress.

I take fifth place. Not bad, especially considering what happened. But ultimately, I'm glad I didn't win today. There's too much negativity tainting this event. My win would've been tainted too.

And this isn't my last shot.

There's still outdoor nationals. I still have one more chance to win an NCAA championship. I'll use this incident as fuel. Because people can threaten me, people can try to fuck up my game, but in the end, I refuse to let them get the better of me. I'm going to dominate every meet going forward.

I'm not going to stop until I'm a national champion.

CHAPTER THIRTY-FOUR

Once again, I feel so alone. I want to talk to someone about what I'm going through, but I don't know anyone who will truly understand. Yes, I have so many supportive cis people in my life, and that's wonderful. But I wish I knew other trans athletes. I wish I knew someone who's already been through what I'm going through now. I wish I had someone to guide me through those moments where I feel isolated, depressed, and unsure of my path moving forward.

I'm disappointed by my performance at indoor nationals. I'm frustrated that I had to deal with so much noise, so much hate, so much hype. I let it knock me off my game.

I'm back to training for the outdoor season. Trying to regain my focus. But those negative voices still swirl inside my thoughts, rob me of my confidence. I'm struggling with dysphoria. I find myself increasingly worried that if I train too aggressively, then people will still see me as a man. So I pull back. I limit myself. Try to make myself fit into other people's ideas of femininity. I tell myself that I need to be pretty, I need to be soft, I need to slow down, I can't be too strong. I need to "run like a girl." Not that I'm even sure what that means. I guess I'm just worried that people still think of me as "running like a guy." My times stop improving. My strength plateaus. All because I'm afraid that if I give it my all, if I push as hard as I can, there will be someone out there, waiting in the stands, ready to call me a man.

Then, one day, Rachel, my athletic director, comes up to me after practice. *I wanted you to be the first to know*, she says. *We have a special speaker coming to speak to all the athletes at Franklin Pierce. His name is Chris Mosier. He's an elite pro athlete, a member of Team USA. And he's a trans man.*

After all the darkness I've felt since indoor nationals, suddenly there's a burst of light.

All the athletes—including the football, basketball, and volleyball teams—assemble in the field house. Folding chairs have been set up on the basketball court. Paola, Lillian, and I all find seats together. I feel nervous, but excited. Suddenly, Chris Mosier walks out onto the court. He has short brown hair, an expertly barbered mustache, and the lean, muscular build of an elite athlete. He smiles and it lights up the whole room.

Damn, this man is handsome, Paola whispers to me and Lillian.

So fine, Lillian agrees, with a smile.

Hi everyone! he says. *I just want to thank you all for having me here today.*

Chris launches into his story. I'm riveted. I can tell all the other athletes are also engaged, so in tune with what he's saying. Chris shares his experience being trans in the world of elite athletics. The challenges he faced, the resistance, the prejudice, the joy he feels competing in the sport that he loves. He described what it took to become the first transgender athlete to represent the United States in international competition, and how he blazed a trail by pushing the International Olympic Committee to change their policy on transgender athletes.

I sit in the audience, tears streaming down my face.

It is so validating to hear his story. To know that I'm not alone. That he has been here before. That he has made it to the world of international competition, and he did it as an out trans man. It gives me such hope.

I've been told that there's a trans athlete competing at Franklin Pierce? he says at one point. *Is she here today?*

Yeah, that's CeCé! Paola says and points to me.

I wipe my tears away and wave. *Thank you for coming. It really means so much to me to hear your story.*

Stick around afterward, he says. *I'd love to catch up and chat.*

We dive right into conversation. The rest of the crowd disperses as we talk, until finally it's just the two of us, standing alone in the gym. I feel like I could talk to him forever. I share some of my story, my own struggles and triumphs. We bond over the similarities between us, but also discuss the differences. Chris acknowledges that he has certain privileges that I do not, because he walks through the world as a white man. He knows that I face additional prejudice as a Black trans woman, discrimination to which he'll never be subjected. He knows that within the world of professional sports, trans women face additional discrimination that trans men do not, due to the myth that trans women possess an unfair advantage. We discuss all this and more, and it feels so good to not have to *explain* myself, to have someone who just *knows* what I'm going through.

How are you doing now? he asks. *Right now. Today. How are you feeling?*

Honestly, I'm struggling, I say. I tell him how I've been holding back in practice. How I've internalized everyone else's prejudiced idea that I have some sort of advantage, and because of this, I don't train as hard as I could, I don't push myself as much as I could. I don't want to be seen as masculine. I'm afraid of what other people think. And I hate it. I hate feeling like I'm not living up to my true potential.

He considers what I say for a minute, then looks me straight in the eye. *Never limit your greatness to make other people feel more comfortable.*

Those words change my life forever.

CHAPTER THIRTY-FIVE

I come back with a vengeance. Dominate the outdoor season.

First up, Pepsi Florida Relays. One of the biggest, most important track meets in the nation, and my first pro meet. All divisions from the NCAA are present, along with pro athletes, members of Team USA, and even international competitors. I run the 400-meter hurdles, going head-to-head with some of track's top athletes. I take third place. Not number one. But I am proud of my performance. It's a very strong start to my season.

And my time qualifies me for NCAA Outdoor Nationals.

Now, there's a fire burning inside me. I'm determined to dominate. My momentum builds. The rest of the season is a blur of training, travel, hotels, track meets, and triumph after triumph. I kill it at meet after meet, tearing up the track, taking first place in every race I run. I'm racking up the gold. I'm firing on all cylinders. I ignore the hate. I focus on my game. I'm grateful for moments where I am respected, seen, and celebrated. I'm unstoppable. I'm hurtling toward that NCAA Championship, showing the entire country that I'm the girl to beat.

* * *

Graduation arrives. I'm going to walk again. I wasn't sure at first—I already did this last year. But last year was filled with so much turmoil and pain. It felt like I was ending my college experience on such a strange, sour note.

So I graduate again. I'm grateful I got a second chance to do my senior year my way, to embrace my truth and pursue my dream with the full support of my school. This year, I feel like I've truly come into myself as an athlete, as a woman, and as a human being. It feels incredibly satisfying to walk across this stage again on my own terms, as my true self. Franklin Pierce has given me such incredible space to bloom. Now I feel confident in who I am, and ready to conquer the world.

After commencement, the campus turns into a bustling hive of activity. The sun beats down on a parade of overheated parents, helping their children move out of the dorms. People pack every inch of their cars, shoving suitcases into trunks, stuffing small furniture into backseats, and students cram their bodies into what little space remains before driving off, into adulthood. Gradually, as the day progresses, the campus begins to quiet. By 5:00 p.m. everyone is gone. I'm the only one who remains. Of course, I have no family to come get me. I'm not speaking to my mother. My siblings are out of the picture as well. I have no family to fall back on, no one to support me in my first year out of college, no one to ease the transition into adulthood, to lend me cash, or connect me with a job, or offer me a place to live until I can figure out my own housing.

Which is why I've arranged to keep living on campus. I have an entire Lakeview apartment to myself. I'll stay here until the NCAA Outdoor National Championships. After that, I'm not sure where I'll go, what I'll do. But I can't worry about my impending adulthood right now. I have to pour everything into my training. I have one more shot at a national title, and this time, I'm not stopping until I win it.

* * *

Once again, the Princess Protection Program is in full effect. I fly into Texas two days later than the rest of the athletes, into a different airport, with Sasha-Lee and Coach Cir by my side. We drive hours to get to our hotel, just outside Kingsville, Texas. We arrive on Wednesday morning, quickly drop our things off, and then I'm on my way to Texas A&M University-Kingsville for our pre-meet, with Coach Zem and Paola and Hugo, the other athletes from Franklin Pierce who qualified for nationals. We enter Javelina Stadium together, a massive 15,000-seat sporting facility, bordered on either end by groves of gigantic palm trees. As we make our way to the field, I click into competition mode. My two events at nationals will be the 100-meter hurdles and the 400-meter hurdles. *Execute, execute, execute.* Those three words run through my head on a loop, as I attempt to visualize each race I'll be running. We dive into a pre-meet, pushing ourselves enough to become acclimated to this facility, but saving our energy for tomorrow. The first day of competition.

My pre-meet is solid. I'm feeling confident. I have one national competition under my belt, and I'm now more accustomed to the ins and outs of the Princess Protection Program. I won't let anything throw me this time around. I can't. Not if I want that national title.

Later that night, there's an event on the USS *Lexington*, an enormous World War II–era Navy ship, which has been turned into a museum and docked permanently in Corpus Christi. It's a dinner to honor all the athletes, and I'm happy that this time around, I'm able to attend at least some of the special festivities the NCAA has planned for us.

We walk on board the ship, and the air is electric. Athletes and coaches are dressed in their finest, mingling on the deck, in the Texas heat, as the sun sinks into the Corpus Christi Bay. I make my way through the crowd, flanked by our little crew, looking cute, turning heads, wearing my tight red off-the-shoulder top, and an olive green skirt that hugs my curves in exactly the right places.

210

After all, if people are going to stare, you might as well give them something gorgeous to look at.

And people do stare.

Their eyes are filled with the same scorn and ignorance that I've come to expect at these events, though it doesn't make it hurt any less. We walk through, and though many people smile and say hello, there are plenty of other athletes who misgender me, or make jokes under their breath as I pass, or shake their heads and frown. But you know what? I look too cute to be mad. So I let them talk; I don't let them bother me.

I focus on the love of the people who surround me.

We make our way to the bow of the ship. The bay stretches infinitely. The sun bathes us all in golden light. The wind whips at our hair, tugs at our clothing. For a moment, we settle into silence, taking in the incredible view. I can't believe I'm here, with one more shot at becoming an NCAA Champion, one more opportunity to compete as my authentic female self. I close my eyes, let the breeze caress my face, and visualize myself winning.

CeCé! I hear Paola's voice and open my eyes. *Let's take a picture.*

Yes! Let's do it, I say.

We should do the Titanic *pose. On the bow of the ship.*

I laugh and agree. It's the perfect opportunity to re-create the iconic moment from *Titanic*. All we're missing is Celine Dion. We decide that I'm going to be Rose and Paolo will be Jack. Hugo, Coach Zem, Sasha-Lee, and Coach Cir cheer us on. I step to the tip of the bow and spread my arms wide. Paola comes up from behind, but before she can wrap her arms around me, a massive gust of wind blows my skirt *all* the way up. I scream, and laugh, and push my skirt back down. Paolo is bent over, giggling uncontrollably. Our whole group breaks down into hysterics, and as our waves of laughter echo across the deck, I feel so lucky to be here, with people I love, on the eve of the most important competition of my life.

* * *

Day One.

I wipe my brow. Take a deep breath. Thick, hot Texas air fills my lungs. The tall palm trees cast long shadows over the field where I stand. Prelims were okay. I came in fifth in the 100-meter hurdles. Enough to qualify me for finals. But I need to push harder if I want to take home first. I go and sit in the competition tent, to get out of the sun and preserve my energy.

Suddenly, a man walks up to the tent, right up to where I'm sitting, and he takes a picture of me. I'm shocked. I feel violated, unsafe. An NCAA official hurries up to him. *Sir, you need to delete whatever picture you just took. You can't be in this area. This area is for athletes only.*

I just took a picture of my son, the man says, and points to a boy standing far behind me. *I can't take a picture of my son?*

But there is no way this man was taking a photo of his son. I felt his gaze on me. I saw him point his lens directly at me, and not anyone else. The man continues to argue with the official, until finally the official forces him out of the tent. The official smiles and nods at me, as if to say: *Don't worry, I got you.* Adrenaline rushes through my system. I take a breath, try to calm myself, and regain my focus.

Then, it's time for the event. The announcer calls the finals for the women's 100-meter hurdles. Our names echo across the stadium as all the athletes walk toward their lanes. But something happens when my name is called. A pocket of people in the stands burst into boos. A race official quiets them down, but the damage is done. My adrenaline spikes again. I feel a lump rise in my throat. But then I look to my right. Brianna Burke, one of my competitors from Southern Connecticut State University, is standing in the lane next to me, applauding for me. Smiling. She reaches out, takes my hand.

For a moment, the world stops spinning. And it's just me and Brianna here, holding hands, two talented athletes, competitors but sisters in sport, rooting for each other. Ignoring the hate from the crowd. A beautiful moment. There's a warmth and tenderness to her gaze, as if she's saying: *You deserve to be here. I've got your back.*

Then, it's time to compete.

I run my race, fight as hard as I can. But this isn't my strongest event. I come in fifth place. Brianna comes in right behind me, at sixth. But I don't feel sadness, I don't feel regret. I only feel an incredible sense of belonging, of gratitude, because Brianna stood by my side, in front of the whole nation, and proudly held my hand. A signal to everyone that I belong on that track, just as much as any other female athlete. A simple gesture, but a powerful one. I don't care that I didn't win the race; this feeling of belonging is more valuable than any title.

Besides, I still have the 400-meter hurdles. That's *my* event. And I plan on dominating it.

Day Two.

I'm on the field, waiting in the competition tent with Paola. Her event is the high jump. Her family is flying in from Mexico to see her compete, but they're not at the stadium yet. Suddenly, Paola gets a call on her cell phone. She answers. I see her face fall. She begins to cry.

There's an emergency. It's Paola's grandmother. Her *abuelita*. She was supposed to attend nationals with Paola's mother. But instead she's being sent to the hospital, for emergency surgery related to a complication from her diabetes. Her leg will have to be amputated. Paola's whole family is deeply concerned. There's a chance she won't survive.

I comfort Paola. I take her into my arms. Rub her back. She is so close to her grandmother. I can't imagine what she's feeling right now.

Then, it's time for the high jump.

Paola doesn't pull out. She's made it this far. She's not going to stop now. Her *abuelita* wants her to compete, wants her to follow her dream. Even at this moment. But I can tell Paola is thrown. Her head isn't in the game. She places fifth. Not enough to secure a title.

But I am so proud of her. She's a warrior. She got it done, even under unimaginable circumstances. I love that girl so much.

Hugo is next from our team to compete. He attacks the prelims for the 800 meters. But he doesn't make it to the finals.

Which means that I'm our team's only hope of securing a national title.

I feel immense pressure as I head into prelims for the 400-meter hurdles. Coach Zem pulls me into a huddle, right before the event. He tells me to take it easy. To not go too hard. I just have to get into the finals. I don't have to give this everything I've got. Because if I do, if I run this race like I'm going to run it in the finals, then I'll give my competitors an advantage over me. They'll know what to expect. They can strategize, based on what they learned from my performance. That's why he wants me to hold back. So we can surprise them in finals.

Just take it easy, he says.

But I don't know how to do that. I don't know how to take it easy at nationals, when the stakes have never been higher, when I'm running the most important race of my life.

No, I'm gonna run this race the only way I know how: With everything I've got. With all the fire that burns inside me. I'm gonna run it so hard, these girls aren't going to know what hit them. Because I need to know what it will feel like on that final day. I need to know what it will feel like when my muscles are burning harder than they've ever burned, when I'm pushing harder than I've ever pushed, when it feels like my whole body might burst from the pressure.

I need to know what it feels like to win.

And I do. I win. I take first in the prelims. And right then, I vow that I'll do the same tomorrow. I won't leave this stadium until I have that gold plaque in my hands.

Day Three.

The day I take first place in the 400-meter hurdles.

The day I make history.

The day I become the first openly transgender woman to win an NCAA title.

By the time I cross the finish line, no one is even close to me. I finish the race with a 57.53, over two seconds ahead of the next competitor.

This is it. This moment has been a lifetime in the making. All the pain, all the joy, every single challenge I've had to overcome has led me to this victory. And I did it *my* way, I did it as myself, I refused to hide who I was to get here. It wasn't the easy choice, but it was the right choice. Because I can stand on this track, as the woman that I am, and show the world that I'm a champion. I deserve the same respect and love as any other female athlete in this competition. *Be the change you want to see in the world.* That's been my motto. And today, I *was* the change. Today, I transformed the world of sports, and made more space for people like me. It's confirmation that I am on the right path, that track is my destiny.

Soon, it's time to take the podium. I walk up to the highest plat-form and take my place as the first-place champion. I shake hands with the other girls as they take their spots, congratulating each one on a great race. Once all my competitors are in place, Coach Zem hands out the awards. He comes to me last. I bend over, and Coach Zem pulls me into a hug, as he hands me the gold plaque.

You did it, kid, he whispers. *Let's go all the way to the top.*

He means the Olympics. *Yes, let's fucking do this*, I reply.

All the winners pose with their plaques for a photographer. A smile spreads across my face. I feel pure joy. I scan the crowd, see my crew cheering for me: Sasha-Lee, Coach Cir, Hugo, Paola. All these people invested in me, believed in me. I know they would have cheered me no matter how I placed, but I have to say it feels incredi-ble to come in first. I made everyone so proud—my school, my team-mates, my coaches, and friends. I lock eyes with Paola in the crowd. Tears come to my eyes. Thankfully, her *abuelita* made it through sur-gery okay. But I still feel for Paola—she's my family, my sister. A part of this win belongs to her, because I never would've made it up to the top of this podium if it wasn't for the love she gave me.

I smile, and smile, and smile some more. Cameras flash. And I think bigger. I think of my community. I think of all the young transgender and non-binary kids out there, struggling to find themselves in a world that is not welcoming. I hope they see this photo of a beautiful Black trans woman, standing in her power, with joy in her eyes, and a smile on her face.

I hope it brings them hope.

Eventually, we make our way off the podium. My supporters swarm me; we share celebratory hugs and make our way out of the stadium. But as we're leaving, I hear a group of Jamaican athletes making fun of me in patois. Then, they take a picture of me as I walk by. And I can't handle it, *not again*, not *another* group of Jamaicans. So I turn around, look one of them right in the eye and say, in perfect patois: *Wah yu say?*

He looks shocked. *Oh, you're Jamaican?*

Ya man, mi Jamaican. Mi hear everything yuh sey, so wah yu say?

Oh, no man. No, no, no. Big respect. Big respect for you. Come take a picture with us.

I know they're just taking the picture to make fun of me, but you know what? I don't give a fuck. At the end of the day, I look good, feel good, and I did conquer. Period. Let them take a picture. It'll give them something to remember. And I hope they *do* remember this day, because when they remember it, they'll also remember that I'm a champion. They can say whatever they want, but nothing will change what it says in the history books: CeCé Telfer—NCAA title winner.

So, I take the picture. I can see they're momentarily humbled by my kindness, by my unwillingness to take the low road and meet them at their level. But before I can say goodbye, another one of them steps forward. *Congratulations, man*, he says, then hesitates. *But I just think it's a shame that you're running on the girls' team. How can you give into this type of American culture? What about your background?*

And when he says this, I'm instantly transported back to my childhood. The smell of a ripe black mango. The taste of a hot Jamaican patty as it burns my mouth. The sensation of running on dirt tracks in the humid St. Thomas heat. The mornings I spent cooking with my mother.

My mother.

The way she broke my heart. The way she still breaks my heart. It's similar to the way my homeland breaks my heart. I see so much beauty in both, I love both with all my being, and I wish more than anything that I could feel that love reciprocated. But worry I never will. You don't get to choose who you love or where you're born, so this love is the burden I carry, a weight that brings me both joy and pain. It's a bittersweet conflict that plays out in my heart every day.

Something these Jamaican boys don't know shit about.

The boy continues, a sad look in his eyes. *How can you give up your Jamaican heritage?*

I didn't give up shit, I say, calmly and to the point. *And I'm never gonna give up shit. I've always been true to myself, even as a young child in Jamaica. I've always known I was female. And it's just unfortunate that so many people in my own country don't recognize my truth. But I love Jamaica, and I always will. So, with that being said, have a great day.*

And I walk off, into the Texas sunset, with a smile on my face.

No one can take away my joy. Not now, not ever.

CHAPTER THIRTY-SIX

The future feels uncertain. The structure of the school year is gone. I'm back on campus, but I know that my time here is limited. Franklin Pierce will only let me stay until the end of the summer. Then, I'm on my own. Now that the track season is over, I need to focus on finding a job, I need to start saving money. I have nothing to fall back on, no one to support me, to lend me extra cash until I get on my feet. So, I've got to hustle hard.

But I also can't stop training. My next goal: the Olympics.

So I meet with Coach Zem. I tell him I want to keep training at Franklin Pierce. With him. I want to go all the way to the top, like he said we would.

We'll need to figure out how to make that work, now that you're no longer a student here.

Okay, I reply.

I think I could bring you onto the team in a sort of assistant coach role. You'd need to work hard to support the team. You'd need to be the first person here. The last person to leave. You need to push these athletes to be their best.

I agree to his pitch, though it does feel strange to me. I'm not asking to coach; I'm asking to *be* coached. I need someone who can guide me on a pro level. Who can provide me with intensive, one-on-one training. I need someone to help me navigate the world of international competition. All the complex rules, and requirements. I need an ally, someone who will fight alongside me, as I travel the road to the Olympic Trials.

And as the summer progresses, I start to wonder if Coach Zem can really be that person. It seems like his focus is primarily with his college team, keeping them in shape over the summer. Of course, I understand he needs to do his job, which is to work for Franklin Pierce as the head track coach. But I rarely get that individual attention I need. I begin to doubt. Does Coach Zem really have the time I need from him? He's never guided a female athlete to the Olympics before. And, based on how he's acting, it seems like maybe he doesn't want to.

Maybe we're just drifting apart.

I realize: I need to find a pro coach. Someone who is singularly invested.

Someone who has been to the Olympics before.

But first, I need to find an apartment.

I reconnect with Sonja. I need my "sister" again. I need her support. We've long since apologized to each other and have slowly rebuilt our relationship. She lives in the area, and now that many of my college friends have moved away, I'm eager for a friend. It feels good to be reunited, even if some of our old issues bubble to the surface occasionally. It's worth it to feel that familial connection again. Sisters fight, after all, but they also make up. And it feels like there is some sort of undeniable connection that will always keep us together.

I tell Sonja I need a job. I need to save up for my own place. Sonja is working as a licensed nursing assistant at a local nursing home, and she says they need more help. I'll have to complete coursework to get certified as an LNA, but the good news is that I'll be paid to complete the course, and I can start working at the nursing home as part of my training.

So, I begin school. My schedule is intense. I'm working around the clock, seven days a week. I'm still working part-time in the admissions office at Franklin Pierce, in addition to taking my LNA course, working out, training with the Franklin Pierce team, and working as an assistant coach. But it soon becomes clear that Coach Zem will not be my coach moving forward, after this summer is over.

So, in addition to everything else, I start researching coaches. Elite coaches. Coaches who can take me all the way to the top. It shouldn't be too hard, not with my NCAA title. Most girls in my position have no trouble finding a coach. My time at nationals has qualified me for the Olympic Trials. I'm in the top thirty women in the country for my event. There is a very clear path to Team USA. But soon, I learn that my road will not be so simple.

I reach out to coach after coach. They all reject me. Some just say "no" right away. That's fine—I don't expect every coach in the world to want to coach me. But many say "yes," initially, and these are the coaches that break my heart. It's always the same—they're excited by my talent, they see the potential in me. But then, there's always a follow-up call or email, where they say they did more research into my story, and they don't feel comfortable coaching "someone like me." No one wants to deal with the controversy that I will bring to the world stage, no coach is willing to fight alongside me if it comes to that, no coach wants to risk their own career by aligning themselves with a female trans athlete, when it is such a lightning rod in the culture wars.

But I just want to run. I *need* to run. I know I have what it takes to become an Olympian.

I get my LNA license. I start working full time at the nursing home. Many days, I enjoy what I do. I love caring for other people. I inspire many of my coworkers, they tell me to keep that smile on my face, to keep that positive attitude, because burnout can be a real issue. I soon see why. I work in the Alzheimer's dementia unit. One of the most intense units at the facility. With dementia patients, there are no filters. They can be openly rude, even hateful. Patients misgender me, call me slurs, some patients tell me that they don't want me to touch them because I'm Black. Some refuse to work with me because I'm trans. The job takes a toll on my body; I lift patients from their beds, help them to the bathroom, help them bathe, feed them, change their linens, and clean up after them. Because my coworkers know I'm an athlete, they lean on me for the more intense physical work. I'll spend an eight-hour shift straining my body, then hit the track for a four-hour training session. I don't know where I get the energy. I don't know where I get the drive. I'm exhausted, but I keep pushing. I keep saving up money.

And I keep reaching out to coaches. I've reached out to easily over a hundred coaches at this point. All rejections. But I refuse to quit.

My testosterone levels have been hovering right below 5 nanomoles. If my levels go over 5 nanomoles, I will be disqualified from competing, based on the World Athletics guidelines for transgender female athletes. So I ask my doctors to up my dosage and get me on a more aggressive HRT regimen. My doctors advise against it; they say it's not healthy for my body, that it places me at greater risk for a stroke or a blood clot. But I don't have a choice, this is what World Athletics demands that I do to my body to qualify for the Olympics. So my doctors increase my dosage. But this new regimen makes me sick. Makes me weak. I get dizzy whenever I stand up. I get vertigo during track practice. I faint a few times.

My body has never felt more exhausted, but I don't know what else to do. I can't give up on my dream. I remind myself that I am a Black woman, and Black women are the strongest beings on this earth. I pull my strength from that knowledge, from that deep sense of history.

I pray that it's enough.

* * *

How does three hundred dollars a month sound? Maria asks me. She sits on her plush couch, with Paco, her adorable dog, in her lap. Her living room is immaculate, just like the rest of her charming, four-bedroom, New England Colonial home. Little candy dishes dot almost every end table and credenza, popping up like little sweet surprises throughout her meticulously kept house.

Sounds great to me, I reply. Larry Leach connected me to Maria, a kind Greek Canadian woman who lives here in Peterborough, New Hampshire. We've bonded over our shared Canadian backgrounds, reminisced over our respective time there. She lives in this large house by herself—she's divorced from her husband, and their son spends much of his time at his dad's house—and I can tell it's a lot of space for one person. She seems genuinely happy to offer me a place to stay, at a rate that is significantly lower than the other rooms available in the area. By paying just three hundred dollars a month, I'll be able to keep working at the nursing home, saving up money so I can move into my own apartment eventually.

I think this will work out perfectly, she says. And it does. I'm happy at Maria's. We make good roommates. For the most part, I keep to myself, and try not to impose too much on her space. Yes, I'm renting a room, but she's also giving me a deal, so I don't want to get in her way. Besides, I'm busy, and rarely home. With my schedule of track practice and the nursing home, I rarely have free time. When I do, I'll often hang out with Sonja or my friend Chari. Other times I spend the evening with Maria and we'll watch a movie together, or have a wine night, where we laugh late into the evening.

Fall turns to winter. I settle into a regular routine. I feel like I'm getting my adult life on track, like I've landed on my feet. I'm grateful to have the time and space to save up for an apartment of my own. I help Maria when I can, cooking the occasional meal, shoveling out the driveway whenever there's a snowstorm. I'm tired but optimistic about the future. I'm still training, still reaching out to coaches every day. Still getting rejected. But I refuse to give up: 2019 is ending, and 2020 is on the horizon.

Which means one thing: the Summer Olympics are just around the corner.

CHAPTER THIRTY-SEVEN

February 2020. Maria is worried. More worried with every passing day. She's not alone, of course. I feel anxious too. The whole world does. COVID-19 is starting to spread across the globe. Italy has become a hot spot. The death toll is rising. The first US cases have been reported, which means that many more are likely to follow. There is so much uncertainty. So much fear.

March 2020. Cases in the US are starting to rise. Soon, the whole country is in lockdown. As an LNA, I'm on the front lines. Working at the nursing home. Going through intense new COVID protocols, dressing head to toe in PPE (personal protective equipment), fearing for my own safety, knowing that I am more likely to be exposed because of my proximity to the sick and the elderly. Other people have the ability to work from home, but I don't have that option. I put myself in danger every day for my job.

And then, one day, Maria says she needs to talk to me.

I'm so, so sorry, she says regretfully. *But I'm just worried that with your job and all the people you come into contact with, that you're at a much greater risk for this virus. I have an elderly mother I need to see. And I'm just not comfortable with you continuing to stay with me.*

Oh, I say, as panic sets in. *Okay.*

I really am sorry, she says. *I just don't know what else to do.*

I understand, I say. *When do you need me out?*

I guess as soon as possible.

I need a new place. Right away. I call Sonja. I explain my situation. I ask if I can spend the night at her place. She agrees. She knows I don't have any other options. So I drive all the way to Massachusetts, where she lives, and spend the night there. The next day, I drive all the way back to New Hampshire for work. Then, that night, not wanting to overstay my welcome at Sonja's, I ask my other friend, Chari, if I can stay with her, on her couch. She agrees, though I can tell it makes her anxious. So, after work, I drive all the way to Vermont, where Chari lives.

This becomes my pattern. Driving between Massachusetts and New Hampshire and Vermont, spending hours and hours on the road every day, exhausted after draining shifts at the nursing home covered in head-to-toe PPE, sliding on ice and slush because I can't afford snow tires, because I need to keep saving for an apartment, an apartment that just refuses to materialize, an apartment I keep hunting for whenever I can, whenever I'm not working or driving, which seems to consume almost all of my time. And the apartments I do find either reject my application, or the landlord simply isn't interested in taking on new tenants during these highly stressful and uncertain times, especially tenants who work in a nursing home and have a higher risk of being exposed to the virus. So I keep working. Keep couch hopping. People start to quit at the nursing home. Which means I have to work longer shifts. I start doing double shifts, sixteen-hour days. I can tell Sonja and Chari are getting tired of the couch hopping, especially during the pandemic. Sometimes I'll crash on a coworker's couch after a shift. Franklin Pierce has closed its campus to outsiders because of the pandemic, so I can no longer use their facilities. No one is training indoors anywhere, because of the pandemic. I start training outside, in parks, or running on snowy streets. It's not ideal from a health and safety perspective: running in the freezing cold, on slippery streets, at risk for injury. But I don't have a choice. And gradually, I have less and less time to train.

Eventually, I stop running altogether.

I'm driving through a blizzard. Up a hill. I'm absolutely exhausted, but the panic pumping through my system ensures that I'm wide awake. I climb the incline slowly, carefully. Suddenly, my tires spin out beneath me. *Fuck.* But then, they gain traction. Thank God.

I reach the crest of the hill. The snow is falling so hard, I can barely see one foot in front of me. But then I'm up and over, safe. The road flattens out. I accelerate just a little bit, eager to bring this hellish ride to an end. But as soon as I hit the gas, I feel the wheels spin out again. Only this time, they don't gain traction. My car spins. I lose all control. There's nothing I can do. I hurtle toward the shoulder. Beyond it, I can see a steep drop into the forest. I'm headed straight for it. There's nothing left to do but pray. So, I do. I pray to God to let me live.

SLAM!

My car hits a snowbank. My body lurches forward from the force of the impact.

But I'm alive. Safe. Just feet away from the drop that could have ended my life.

No more. I can't keep living like this. I can't keep working these brutally long shifts, and drive for hours each way to and from the nursing home. Especially not in this snow. I *need* a place to live. A place that's closer to work. But I still can't find an apartment. So I decide to check into an Extended Stay America. Supposedly, according to their website, Extended Stay America is a hospitality chain specializing in "affordable" long-term hotel rooms. But I've agreed to pay five hundred dollars a week, which doesn't seem so "affordable" to me. Still, it's a relief. The place is clean, efficient. There's laundry, and my own kitchen where I can make meals. The price is so high, I'm putting almost my entire salary into rent every week. I can't save up, I'm working harder than I've worked in my entire life, on the front lines of the pandemic, but still living paycheck to paycheck.

But I don't have a choice. Besides sleeping in my car.

So I rent the room. And I finish out the winter in Extended Stay America.

Then, they hike their rates for spring. My room is now seven hundred dollars a week.

A price I can't afford.

But I catch a lucky break. A unit becomes available in an apartment building in Keen, New Hampshire, that is now being used as housing for traveling nurses who work at our nursing home. So I snap it up.

Finally, a space of my own. I feel so independent. So free. Stability, at last. I have a big, beautiful room, with giant windows that flood the space with light. And, most importantly, the space is *mine*, all mine and no one else's.

After a bitter and uncertain winter, spring has finally come.

CHAPTER THIRTY-EIGHT

He pulls up in a Jeep. The giant, hulking vehicle glistens in the August sun. The grille is splattered with mud, probably from off-roading. Its massive wheels come to a stop, as he finds a space on the edge of the road. The door opens, and out steps Jeremiah, handsome and tall, with wavy brown hair. He spots me, waiting by a bench, and waves. My heart beats just a little faster. He has a sweet smile, and I'm immediately relieved. He looks like his photos.

We met through an online dating app. After all the turmoil and uncertainty of the winter, I finally feel like I'm in a stable, safe place. I've settled into a routine, living in my apartment, working at the nursing home, and training. But even though I'm grateful for this stability, lockdown is lonely. Sonja and Chari both have boyfriends, and they seem content to live in their quarantine bubbles with their significant others. I talk with people at work, but it's so busy, the job is so demanding, and there's not much time to bond with my coworkers. Now that summer is here, training outside is much easier, and I run in public parks or on the side of the road. But I feel such a deep longing when I come home every day, exhausted from work or training or both, and I have no one to talk to, no one to snuggle with, no boy to hold me tight and listen to the details of my day.

Maybe Jeremiah can be that boy.

Hey, I'm Jeremiah, he says, as he approaches with a nervous smile.

I'm CeCé, I say. *Nice to meet you.*

You wanna go Jeeping?

Which is how we end up speeding along a mountain trail in his Jeep. This was *not* the date I planned for—I'm wearing pumps, serving legs from here to China—but I go with it, and it's actually a lot of fun. Soon, he brings the car to a stop, in a patch of dirt where a fleet of other Jeeps have parked.

At first, I'm terrified. It's like something out of a horror movie. Is this man gonna murder me on our first date?

But then I realize these people are his friends. He introduces me to everyone, and they're all very sweet. I feel immediately welcomed into their little group.

Jeremiah looks in my eyes. Offers a kind smile. And then, he takes my hand. I feel the warmth of his palm in mine, and I'm filled with happiness. It's such a small moment, but such a significant one. As a trans woman, I constantly deal with men who are attracted to me, but want to keep that a secret, who want to keep *me* a secret, who want to fetishize me in private but refuse to acknowledge me in public. I hate having to worry about my safety when it comes to men. It's why I rarely go on dating apps—after being burned so many times over the years, sometimes it feels almost impossible to find someone who is willing to treat me like a human being, instead of just some sexual object. But here's Jeremiah. Holding my hand. In public. Unashamed. In full view of all his friends. I feel seen, supported, validated. I feel like this could be the end of my loneliness, and the beginning of something real.

From that one date, we speed into a passionate late summer fling, spending all our spare time together. It's cuddly, it's cute, and it feels so good to finally have someone, after being alone for so long. Soon, the temperatures cool, and the trees change colors, and Jeremiah asks if I'll be his girlfriend.

I say yes.

How's it going with your man? Tessa, one of my friends at work, asks me one day.

It's cute, I reply. *He asked me to be his girlfriend.*

Oh my god! Tessa squeals. *Well, you have to bring him to my party! It's gonna be cute. Sonja will be there too.*

We're there, girl.

Excitement sets in. I can't wait to introduce everyone to Jeremiah.

The day of the party arrives. Jeremiah picks me up in his truck. I give him a quick peck as I climb inside. *Did you remember the tent?* I ask. *And the sleeping bags?*

Yup, he says and smiles. *They're in the back.* The party is a sleepover. Tessa told people to bring tents, so they can sleep outside, in her backyard, under the starry New England sky.

We get to Tessa's house; we can hear the music pumping and people laughing even as we pull into the driveway. Soon, we're in the middle of the party, dancing and drinking. Jeremiah seems a little nervous, and I get it—it can be intimidating to meet your partner's friends. He's filling up his cup a little too frequently, and soon it's clear that he's drunk, drunker than he should be, especially at a party where he's meeting my friends for the first time.

I'm gonna get another drink, he says, slurring his words.

Are you sure you really need one? I ask.

I'm fine, he snaps. *Don't look at me like that.*

Okay, I say, and throw up my hands. *Go for it.*

I don't love this new side of Jeremiah. The drunk, mean Jeremiah. He stumbles toward the bar, and I decide to give him some space. I hope he'll cool off. I try to distract myself. I find Tessa on the dance floor. But soon, I hear Jeremiah's voice. He's shouting. I walk toward the sound of his voice and realize that he's yelling at Tessa's boyfriend. I'm confused, embarrassed.

You think you're so fucking tough because you're an ex-marine? You're just a fucking meathead, bro.

Dude, chill, Tessa's boyfriend says. He's calm, he's not taking the bait, but I can tell that he's pissed.

You're a fucking idiot. Jeremiah keeps antagonizing him. Keeps trying to pick a fight. *You don't have shit on me.*

Jeremiah stop, I say, and pull him away from the crowd, out into the backyard. *What are you doing?*

He's a fucking ex-marine. I hate marines. He's swaying back and forth now, even drunker, having a hard time keeping his eyes open. *They're all these alpha male assholes.*

He's not an asshole. He's nice. And he's Tessa's boyfriend. You can't pick fights with my friend's boyfriend. You're just starting drama for no reason.

Whatever, he slurs.

You're mean when you're drunk, I say. *It's not a good look.*

I'm not mean.

I think you need to go to bed, I say, upset, because he's ruined the night. I grab the tent from the back of the truck, and we start setting it up in silence. He's not much help, because he's wasted. Finally, the tent is standing. *There you go,* I say.

Where are you going? he asks, suddenly upset.

I'm going back to the party.

No, you're not, he says. *Stay here with me. Come lay with me. Come on.*

I try to protest, but he won't take no for an answer. Soon, it's clear that if I want to keep him calm, I'll just need to go to bed with him. So, into the tent we go. Jeremiah is passed out and snoring within seconds. I lay in my sleeping bag, fuming, but eventually I drift to sleep.

A little later, I'm woken up by the sound of Tessa calling my name. *CeCé? Are you out here? Are you coming back in?*

I stay silent. I don't want to get up, and risk upsetting Jeremiah. But then I think: *fuck it.* Why am I hiding in this tent, scared of the man sleeping next to me, when I could be back inside the house,

231

enjoying a party with my best friends? This night is supposed to be *fun*. And I'm not going to let Jeremiah ruin that. So, I unzip my sleeping bag, careful not to wake him, and get my ass back to that party.

And I'm so glad I do. Because we have such a good time.

The hours pass, and things start to wind down. Everyone says good night. Those of us who are camping out, make our way to the backyard.

But as I walk through the grass, I stop dead in my tracks, shocked.

Our tent is gone. And so is Jeremiah.

I run around to the front of the house. And there he is, throwing the tent into his truck.

What are you doing?

I'm leaving, he says.

You can't just leave.

Yes, I can. He pushes past me, stumbling drunkenly.

You're way too drunk to drive.

No, I'm not.

And I also need a place to sleep. You packed up our tent.

Because you left me there! I wanted you to lay next to me and you just abandoned me to go back to the party!

You were asleep! What difference does it make? I just wanted to hang out with my friends a little longer. I don't think that's too much to ask.

No, it was shitty, he yells. *I'm done.*

He jumps into the truck, slams the door, and drives off, swerving drunkenly down the road.

I stand in the driveway, stunned. Alone. On a cold, October night. My shock gives way to hurt, then anger, then fear. I don't know where to go. Where I'll sleep.

Then, in the distance, I see his truck round the corner. He's coming back. My heart beats faster. I'm afraid of what mood he'll be in when he's back. I'm afraid of what he might do. He pulls into the driveway. He opens his door. The look on his face is so sad. He apologizes. Says he's so sorry for causing a scene, for leaving me the way he did. He says he'll never do it again.

I want to believe him, but I'm not sure I do.

I have an idea, Jeremiah says to me. We're getting ready for bed; he's sleeping over at my place, like he's been doing more and more recently, because his living situation is so crowded; he's staying with a friend, the friend's girlfriend, and their two kids. *What if we move in together?*

My heart leaps. My first instinct is to say yes. To live with my partner, to create a home that fills with love and happiness—that seems like a dream. But I hesitate. The episode at Tessa's party has been worrying me. He's been on his best behavior since then, he's apologized again and again for how he acted, he insists it was just a case of getting too drunk at a party. He's been so attentive, so loving, and we've settled into such a cozy routine as a couple. And we're already basically living together, so it wouldn't be that much of a change from our current situation. *I'd like that*, I tell him.

He kisses me, a little celebratory peck. *Think about it. We'll have a place of our own. I've been saving up, so we can split the rent. It'll be cheaper for us both. And we can find somewhere closer to your work, so you don't have to deal with such a long commute after your shifts.*

I think that sounds great, I say. *Let's do it.*

He looks so happy. I'm filled with excitement. My first time living with a boyfriend. I'm moving into the next chapter of my life, this time with the man I love by my side.

I break my lease at the end of November.

We move into our new place at the top of December.

* * *

The coach search continues. The Tokyo Olympics have been post-poned to 2021 due to the pandemic. But that's no reason to stop training. I have to keep my body in top shape, so that when the time comes, I'll be ready to fight for my spot on Team USA. At this point, I've reached out to over two hundred coaches. I feel so frustrated, so rejected, so dispirited. One day, I call my friend Nikki Zeigler to vent; she's a fellow Franklin Pierce track team alum, and she's always been so supportive of my journey. *No other female athlete in my position would have this trouble. Other girls, girls who don't have my track record, they don't have trouble finding a coach. And not only that, but they're also getting sponsored by major brands. So they can focus one hundred percent on making it to Team USA. They don't have to take a day job. But because I'm a trans woman, no one wants to give me the support I need—no coach, no sponsor, no one.*

I'm so sorry, Nikki says, then pauses for a minute. *But I have an idea.*

Okay, I say.

What if I try to help? I'm not an Olympic coach. But I could be your manager. I don't really have any experience. But I do believe in you. And I promise I'll do everything I can to help you fight your way to the top. What do you think?

I think that sounds great.

We hit the ground running. It feels wonderful to have someone by my side, hustling with me, when for so long I've been on my own, fighting this battle by myself. As winter starts, we gain momentum. She helps me navigate the nitty-gritty of eligibility rules for compet-ing on an international level. I have a green card, but as it turns out, I need full US citizenship to officially join Team USA. At first, we look into alternatives—I'm a Jamaican citizen, so I could technically compete on Team Jamaica, but when we reach out to them, it's made very clear that they will not let me compete as my true gender. So Nikki helps me with the application process for becoming a full US citizen.

She also sets up a website for me. She reaches out to colleges to see if they want to book me as a speaker, so I can make a little extra money on the side. She starts managing my social media, bolstering my profile, filtering out the hate, and helping me get my story out there, in hopes that someone will come across it and be inspired to coach me. She also seeks out sponsorships, trying to find a brand that will support me financially. When no brands bite, we think of other ways to fund my training. She suggests we start a GoFundMe page. She creates the page, which features a picture of me, a short description of my story, and the title: Support CeCé Telfer's Journey to Gold.

By the time December rolls around, we've earned seven thousand dollars. Not a massive sum, but enough to make a difference. Nikki puts the money into a business account, setting it aside for the future. Because we're still hoping for a coach. And if I need to travel to train, I want to have that money waiting so I can afford the plane ticket to wherever I need to go.

Finally, some momentum. Some hope. And as we approach the New Year, I'm more determined than ever: 2021 will be the year I go to the Olympics.

I can't believe you just let that guy check you out like that, Jeremiah says, fuming, sitting in the driver's seat of his truck.

What guy? I ask. *I don't even know what you're talking about.*

Don't lie to me.

I'm not lying, I insist.

That guy at the bar. He was checking you out and you were just like, looking at him, encouraging him.

Jeremiah, stop—I didn't even see a guy.

Don't fucking lie to me! he shouts. *That guy was checking you out and you liked it!*

We speed down the highway. Miserable. This has become our recurring fight. A new side of Jeremiah has emerged since we started living together. He's paranoid, jealous, angry. Everywhere we go, he seems to think men are checking me out, and that this is somehow *my* fault. That I'm doing it to piss him off. Or that I'm planning to cheat on him. I feel crazy, like we're living in two separate realities. I constantly have to defend myself when I've done nothing to betray his trust. If anything, it's been Jeremiah who's betrayed *my* trust.

He's been going through my phone. I caught him with it one day, after I'd come back from a run. I never gave him permission to do this, and I was angry—it felt like a violation of my privacy. But somehow he took this anger as a sign of guilt, that I was hiding something from him. Now he goes through my phone all the time. Overanalyzing every text message, every DM, purposely misinterpreting them, to try and find proof that his paranoia is justified. But I'm *not* hiding anything. It feels like he's constantly looking over my shoulder, monitoring my every move, picking fights out of thin air.

Still, I'm afraid to leave him. Afraid of how he'll react if I try. Afraid to be alone again. I'm worried I won't find another partner. Also, we're on this new lease together. We've just moved, which was expensive. I can't afford to move again. Not so soon. And there's a deeper part of me that *wants* this to work out. I want to believe that this is just a rocky patch. I want to believe that there's still hope for us.

I need a way out. The days pass. Jeremiah's paranoia gets worse, the fights get worse. I can't take the emotional abuse anymore. The gaslighting. He's constantly yelling at me, berating me for things that never happened, finding fault in everything I do. I'm worried about my safety, and exhausted from dealing with his outbursts, along with all my other responsibilities.

I call Paola. I'm missing my Mexican sister. Missing the girl who had my back at every track meet. Who supported me no matter what. Unlike the man I'm sharing an apartment with.

Hey girl, I say, when she picks up the phone.

CeCé! she cries. *It's so good to hear your voice.*

We dive into conversation, and it's like no time has passed. It's like we're right back at Franklin Pierce, competing on the track team together. She asks me how I'm doing—and I'm honest. I tell her how hard it's been with Jeremiah. How I'm searching for coaches non-stop, how no one will take me on. How bad it feels to face constant discrimination, in the sport I love.

I have an idea, Paola says. *What if you come train with me? In Mexico?* Paola has moved back to her hometown of Querétaro to train with a coach there, in hopes of making her way to the Olympics.

I would love that, I say, suddenly filled with adrenaline—this could be the answer to everything.

I have to ask my coach. To see if he'd be willing to take you on.

Of course, I reply, and a familiar fear fills my heart. Chances are, he'll reject me like the rest once he learns my story. But something tells me to trust the excitement I hear in Paola's voice. *Just let me know.*

I'll ask him, she promises. *And I think you could stay at our house, with my family. But I'd also have to ask my parents.*

Okay, I say.

You're really serious about this? she asks. *Like, if everyone says "yes," you'll really fly out here?*

Bitch, I'll be on a plane tomorrow, I say, and Paola laughs, and I hope, with every ounce of my being, that Mexico will work out. It's my escape plan—a way to solve all my problems at once, a way out of my emotionally abusive relationship, a way to reignite my life-long dream of becoming an Olympian. I know that if I can just get there, Mexico will be my salvation. Still, there are so many pieces that need to fall into place before that can happen. So much that is out of my control.

All I can do is pray.

CHAPTER THIRTY-NINE

I wasn't expecting to work a double shift. But someone at work called out, and they needed me. I can always use extra money, so I agreed. Also, if I stayed at work, there was a chance that Jeremiah would be asleep by the time I got home, and I wouldn't have to deal with another pointless fight.

But now, driving home in the dark, I'm regretting it. A sixteen-hour shift is always brutal. I feel exhausted, but also wired from all the stress. I see a liquor store. Pull in. Buy a bottle of cheap champagne, something to take the edge off, then get back on the road. It's getting late, it's so cold, and I know the roads are starting to freeze over. My car slides over a few patches of ice. Adrenaline overpowers my exhaustion. I'm now wide awake, going as slow as possible, just trying to get home so I can pop this bottle and relax.

Finally, I pull into our driveway. I get out, relieved to be off the road. It's past midnight, so I gently open the door, careful not to make a sound, in case Jeremiah is sleeping.

The lights are off, the apartment is dead quiet. I tiptoe into the bedroom. Jeremiah is passed out, on his side of the bed. *Jeremiah?* I whisper. He doesn't respond. I walk over to his side of the bed, kiss him on the forehead, then leave the bedroom and close the door behind me.

I walk into the kitchen, grab a glass from the cupboard, and pour myself some champagne. Then, I head to the couch, to find something to watch on TV, to help me wind down from the day. I don't work tomorrow—thank God—so I can sleep in. I grab the remote, start flipping through the channel guide.

Suddenly, the bedroom door bursts open. It's Jeremiah. He's wide awake, eyes filled with fury. I jump in surprise. *Jeremiah—I thought you were asleep.*

What the fuck, CeCé? he yells. *Where the fuck have you been?*

I...I was at work.

Why are you home so late?

I picked up an extra shift. They needed me.

Don't fucking lie to me! he shouts. *You were with someone else! Just admit it. You were with another dude.*

What are you talking about? I plead with him. *I swear, I was at work.*

You didn't call me. You didn't text. And you are fucking lying! He keeps screaming, louder and louder, but it's almost like I stop hearing what he's saying, because my mind is overwhelmed with panic, with fear, with the feeling that I am in danger. I want to run out of this apartment, but I'm afraid to get up. Afraid he'll hit me if I do. I stay frozen on the couch in fear.

I swear to you, I plead, exhausted, trying not to break down. *I was just at work.*

Finally, he eases up. He considers me quietly. *Okay,* he says. *Okay. But I still don't understand why you didn't lay in bed with me when you got home. I missed you. I wanted you by my side.*

You were asleep. I didn't want to wake you up.

All I wanted was for you to come to bed.

Are you serious? If that's what you wanted, why couldn't you just come out here like a normal person, and calmly ask me to come to bed?

Because I shouldn't have to ask! You're so fucking selfish.

Selfish? I just had the shittiest day at work. Sixteen hours on my feet. And all I wanted to do was have a glass of wine and a moment to myself. I don't see how that's selfish.

Well, I think it is.

Well, I guess we disagree.

Just come to bed!

I think I should sleep on the couch tonight, I say.

He storms back into the bedroom and slams the door.

I can't sleep. I spend the whole night wide awake. My adrenaline surges with every sound. Afraid it's him. I'm afraid he'll wake up. I'm afraid he'll come back into the living room. Start yelling again. Start beating on me. I dread the moment he wakes up. I don't want to talk to him. I don't want to see him. Ever again.

His alarm goes off at 5:00 a.m. I hear it through the bedroom door. I'm terrified. I hear him get out of bed. I hear him rustling in the bedroom, getting ready for work.

The door bursts open.

I shut my eyes. Pretend to be asleep.

He walks into the kitchen. Starts opening cupboards and drawers. Slamming them shut. Loudly. I know he's trying to wake me up. Provoke me. I just keep my eyes closed. Breathe.

Finally, I hear the front door slam behind him. Hear the engine of his truck starting up. Hear him pull it out of the driveway. Listen as the sound of his car slowly fades into the distance.

I wait. For just a moment.

Then, a switch flips inside me. I get up, rush into the bedroom, and start stuffing a suitcase with clothes. I do this all without thinking. Like my body is running on autopilot. Like I'm a robot. I zip up my bag. I run out to my car. Throw the suitcase in the backseat. Jump behind the wheel. My hands shake as I insert my key into the ignition. I pull out of the driveway. And it isn't until I'm speeding down the highway, that it hits me: *This is it.*

I'm done. I just packed all my shit. I'm leaving him. And I'm never coming back.

Girl, get your ass over here, Sonja says, in protective sister mode, after I finish telling her the story, sitting in traffic, tears streaming down my face. *We got you. Whatever you do, do not go back to that man.*

It starts snowing. The roads get wet, then icy. My pulse races for the entire drive. I pass an accident site. Traffic is awful. Finally, after over an hour of driving through the snow, I arrive.

Sonja sweeps me into a hug and welcomes me inside. She's staying with her boyfriend, Steve, and technically this is his place. But he also welcomes me, says that they're just glad I'm safe. That I should absolutely spend the night.

The day passes. I'm on edge. I tell them the whole story. They listen and comfort me. Eventually, we sit down to dinner.

Which is when we hear someone pounding on the front door.

CeCé! It's Jeremiah. He keeps pounding. *Come out and talk to me!*

We stay silent. All three of us. Of course, he followed me here. We've been to Steve's place before, he knows where it is, and he knows that Sonja is my best friend. He knows that she would be the first person I'd run to.

I know you're in there, CeCé! he yells. *Your car's in the driveway. Just open the door!* Suddenly, my phone vibrates. It's him. He's calling. I press decline. He calls again. I decline again. He calls again, and again, and again. *Pick up your phone! I know you're in there.*

But I ignore him. We all do. We sit there in tense silence. Eventually, he gets tired, stops pounding, and leaves. Sonja looks at me, grasps my hand. *You okay, girl?*

Yeah, I say. *I'm okay.*

A part of me feels guilty for pulling Sonja and Steve into this mess. I know it's not my fault, but I hated when Jeremiah showed up, pounding on the door. I hate bringing my drama to their doorstep. And it feels like I'm starting to outstay my welcome, like they were happy to have me sleep on the couch a couple of nights, but they're starting to wonder where I'm headed after this. I wonder the same thing. I can't go back to my apartment, obviously. Jeremiah's there. I don't have enough saved up to get a whole new place by myself. There's the GoFundMe money, but that's for my training. I can't dip into that. I'm saving that for my dream. In case things work out with Mexico and I need to buy a plane ticket. Oh god, I'm *praying* that Mexico works out. But there's no word from Paola. And I need somewhere to stay, now.

I'm gonna go to Chari's place for a while, I say to Sonja one morning.

Okay, great, Sonja says. I can tell she's relieved that I've figured out another situation.

But I haven't. I lied. I haven't reached out to Chari. I don't want to burden another friend with this drama. I don't want Jeremiah to show up on Chari's doorstep too, yelling and screaming. I know this isn't my fault, I know I shouldn't feel ashamed about my situation, but I can't help it. Also, Chari's roommate doesn't like people spending the night. I've crashed on her couch before, and it turned into an issue. I can't go there. I can't stay here.

Keep me updated, Sonja says, later, as we say goodbye in her driveway. *And stay safe.*

I will, I promise. Then, I drive off. The sun starts to set. I don't know where to go.

So I find a park, pull into a spot that looks safe, and spend the night sleeping in my car.

Homeless. It's a word that I can't quite grasp. A word I never thought would apply to me. I feel so embarrassed. I know I shouldn't feel this way, I know I should tell people what I'm dealing with. Ask for help. But the shame is too great. I don't want to show weakness. I don't want to admit that it's come to this.

Sleep is almost impossible. I park at truck stops or gas stations. It's freezing at night. I wear as many layers as I can. Sweatshirts on top of sweaters. Sweatpants on top of leggings. I turn on the heat in my car, let it get as hot as possible, then try to fall asleep. I sleep as long as I can, until eventually the cold seeps inside, and I wake up freezing. Groggy, I turn on the heat for ten minutes. Go back to sleep. Wake up again when I start freezing. And I repeat this cycle through the entire night.

Then, it's time to go to work. I drive to the nursing home, trying to keep my eyes open. I head into each shift exhausted, running on barely any sleep. I don't have a way to shower. I feel unclean, uncomfortable. As the days stretch on, I sink deeper and deeper into depression. I eat one meal a day. Rotisserie chicken from the grocery store. Not ideal for my nutrition, especially while training. But I have to save money. I know I should try to take on more shifts at the nursing home, to earn more cash, but I'm already so exhausted, so depressed, I feel like if I take on any more work, I might collapse.

I feel so hopeless, so lost.

And then, after two weeks of living in my car, I get a call from Paola.

I talked to my coach, she says. My pulse is racing. *And he says he wants to train you.*

CHAPTER FORTY

I feel a hunger in my gut as I board the plane. I haven't eaten this morning. I don't want to buy food. I need to save my money. I'm now living off what little savings I have from the nursing home, and the seven thousand we earned from the GoFundMe campaign. I need to make this money last as long as possible. It needs to last the three months that I'll be training in Querétaro, Mexico, and beyond that as well. I need it to fund my move back to the US at the end of April. I need it to carry me to the Olympic Trials in June.

I find my seat, slide in, and burst into tears.

Just in time, I think. *I boarded this plane just in time.*

I don't know how much longer I could've endured the hell of being homeless in New Hampshire in the dead of winter. I'm so relieved to be on this plane, speeding through the air, soaring out of the awful nightmare I've been living, and into my dream of becoming an Olympian. I won't be working a day job for the next three months, and even though that scares me from a financial perspective, I'm ecstatic that I'll *finally* be able to train full time. Not only that, but I'll be getting *professional* training, like most other girls pushing for a spot on Team USA. No more running on the side of the road, dodging cars, trekking through snow. Finally, it feels like the playing field is level. This has been all I've wanted for so long: to find a coach, and train around the clock until I'm ready to dominate Olympic Trials.

This is it, girl, I tell myself, as the plane lands in Mexico, after my eight-hour journey. *Every struggle you've endured has been worth it. Because you're gonna be an Olympian.*

CeCé! Paola screams as she runs out of her car and tackles me into a big hug. *I can't believe you're here!*

Yes, girl! I squeeze her tight. *I can't believe it either.*

We hold each other on the concrete walkway of the Arrivals area, standing at the base of a massive palm tree, illuminated by bright streetlights. The night air in Querétaro is temperate, cool, and dry. Slightly chilly, but nothing like the bitter cold of New Hampshire in the winter. We'll be training at an outdoor facility, and Paola says the days will be sunny and warm. I take a deep breath and notice that the air is thinner, that it takes more effort to fill my lungs. It's because Querétaro is in the Central Highlands of Mexico, so the elevation is higher. This is something else I'm looking forward to—altitude training. It's gonna hurt at first, getting used to the thinner air, but ultimately it will increase my endurance and aerobic capacity.

You ready? Paola asks.

She has no idea how ready I am.

We load my suitcases into her car, then I jump into the backseat. She introduces me to Puga, one of her best friends, who's offered to drive us back to Paola's family home. *How are you feeling?* Paola asks once we speed off.

Hungry, I say. Paola and Puga laugh.

Well, not to worry, Paola says. *We've got something waiting for you at home.*

Home. It feels so good to have one again.

We depart the airport, driving through beautiful hills. The moon illuminates vast scrublands, dotted with large cactuses, gnarled acacia trees, and bursts of desert grass and wildflowers. Soon, the landscape gives way to the cobblestone streets of the city. Stunning colonial buildings rise at every corner, painted in vibrant colors— burnt oranges, faded pinks, dark greens. The architecture is a mix of Spanish and indigenous influences, featuring intricate balconies and beautiful stonework.

Finally, we pull up to Paola's house.

As we make our way inside, the first thing I notice is the incredible aroma—garlic, onions, coriander. We head into the kitchen, where Paola's mother greets me with a warm hug. *CeCé*, she cries, throwing her arms around me. *We're so happy to have you here.* Paola's father also hugs me, followed by her little brother. We all sit around a large kitchen table, as Paola's mother brings out rice, beans, a delicious-looking chicken, and fresh homemade tortillas.

My stomach growls. I haven't eaten all day.

And so, I dig in, grateful for this food, and this family that has folded me into their ranks so effortlessly. We laugh and chat. Paola helps translate. Finally, after an hour around the dinner table, I feel full, satisfied, and ready for bed.

Paola takes me up to her room, where her parents have put in an extra bed. Just for me. It's neatly made, with fresh sheets and pillows. I slide into bed, and my exhaustion immediately sets in. I say good night to Paola, and drift to sleep. It's been a long day. But a wonderful one.

I can't wait to start training tomorrow.

I wake up, and Paola is already gone. Practice starts early every morning, but because I landed late last night, we decided it would be best to let me recover from my trip, and head into the training facility in the afternoon.

Paola's mother makes breakfast, complete with fresh-squeezed orange juice. Her husband joins us. Communication is a little tricky without Paola there to translate, but we stumble through an early-morning conversation, with plenty of smiling and gesturing. Paola's mother is more proficient at English than her husband, and she teases him about it over our breakfast tortillas.

CeCé's going to teach me English, she says to her husband. *And take me to visit Toronto, where she grew up.*

I'll come too, he replies.

No, you don't come to Toronto, she says with a mischievous glint in her eyes. *Your English is not good enough. Just me and CeCé.*

Everyone bursts into laughter, and we finish our meal. There is something so simple and tender about breakfast. It makes me think, for a moment, about my own mother. How I wish it was her sitting across from me at the breakfast table, making sure I was fed before heading out to my first day of real Olympic training. How I wish she could support me as I pass through yet another milestone.

Soon, we clean up and Paola's mother drives me to practice. Querétaro is even more stunning in the daylight; the sun's rays cast a golden hue across the historical buildings, caressing terra-cotta roofs, and intricate wrought ironwork. Cobblestones rumble beneath our tires as we pass through a beautiful square, complete with a stone fountain and lush greenery.

Eventually, we arrive at the entrance to a park. Green fields stretch in every direction; trees bursting with blossoms loom over the road. We pass a yoga class assembled on the lawn, stretching beneath the hot midday sun. Soccer players sprint across a sprawling field. A gym, complete with a massive indoor swimming pool, comes up on our right. The entire park is nestled in a mountainside; I spot a dirt trail that leads up the slope, offering hikers a view of the city below. Finally, we arrive at our destination: the track. The first thing I notice: the color. The rubber is a bright, electric blue—deep and vibrant. An army of athletes cover the field—sprinters running drills, pole vaulters flying, coaches yelling encouragement, parents overlooking the scene from stands. Top athletes come from all over Mexico, all over the world, to train here at Parque Querétaro 2000, and prepare for international competition.

Now, I'm one of them.

I say goodbye to Paola's mother and get out of the car. I walk toward the high jump, where I find Paola cooling down from her morning practice. She runs up to me and gives me a hug. *Want to meet Coach Andres?* she asks.

Let's do it, I reply.

Minutes later, we're talking with Coach Andres. He introduces himself and welcomes me to Querétaro. *Are you ready to train?* he asks.

Yes, I say. *When do we start?*

A smile spreads across his face. *Right now*, he replies.

I'm dying. Altitude training is no fucking joke. No matter how hard I push, it seems like I can't get enough air in my lungs. Add the blazing sun to the equation, and I feel like I might pass out at any minute. My makeup is running off my face. I missed the morning practice, but I've joined the girls for an afternoon weight lifting session. I hear another girl whisper: *Is she okay?* And the answer is no. But I'm gonna push through. I'm gonna get stronger.

The weeks pass, and I train harder than I've ever trained in my life. I'm not wasting this opportunity. And I do get stronger, faster— I can feel my endurance building. Coach Andres puts me through the most aggressive sprinting and hurdling drills. It's brutal, but I love it. Other athletes tap out when they're too exhausted. But I never do. I do everything my coach demands of me. He can see my champion mentality and keeps pushing me. I feel totally depleted at the end of practice. I'm taking my body to the limit and beyond. The pain is excruciating at times, but it's worth it. Because I know I'm on the right path. The plan is to stay here for three months, then go back to the States, kill it in the Olympic Trials, then make Team USA.

All my teammates are so supportive. No one questions my gender. They help me with my Spanish, and I help them with English. There's a group of professional male athletes from Oaxaca who've traveled here to train, and it seems like the Oaxacan boys like me most of all. They'll chat with me after practice, maybe even flirt a little; sometimes they'll bring me bags of candy. It's just so wonderful to live in my truth and purpose, to surround myself with athletes who are equally dedicated. I can feel myself elevating my performance with every passing day.

Eat, sleep, train. That's my regimen. I'm so grateful to be staying with Paola's family; it almost feels like I'm their adopted daughter. They're looking out for me, making sure I get to practice safely, making sure I get fed, that I'm getting the nourishment I need to build my strength. Paola's mother is an incredible cook; I always look forward to her delicious Mexican feasts. One night, I insist on giving her a break from cooking, so I make jerk chicken and rice for the whole family, bringing a little Jamaica to Querétaro. On Sundays, Paola and I have the day off from training, and sometimes we take day trips to nearby destinations, like the beautiful historic city of San Miguel, or to La Peña de Bernal, a massive stone monolith that is one of the tallest in the world.

I feel so happy. So filled with life and purpose. Which is why I'm so devastated when, after being in Querétaro for just one month, I'm forced to return to the United States.

I get a call from the US Citizenship and Immigration Services. I feel a pang of dread as I pick up. They tell me that it's time for me to come into their New Hampshire offices for my citizenship interview. I'll have to return on March 1 and then, due to COVID restrictions on international travel, quarantine for twenty days before going in. There is no option to reschedule. I am completely at the mercy of government bureaucracy. And I must complete this interview, because I need to become a US citizen to qualify for Team USA.

I knew that this would be a possibility. When Nikki and I first applied for my citizenship, we were informed that it may take up to three months for the USCIS to process my application, before they called me in for an interview. I was counting on those three months. Those were the three months I was going to train in Mexico, getting in the best shape of my life. I wasn't going to pass up this incredible opportunity, just to stay in New Hampshire, live out of my car, and wait for Immigration to call.

But now, my time will be cut short.

Paola's family is so sad to see me go. I feel frustrated that the elite training I'm *finally* receiving will end abruptly all due to a stupid technicality. This was not my plan.

Now, I'm heading back to New Hampshire. Back to uncertainty. Instability.

I wish I could say I was traveling home, but I don't have one.

Back to living in my car. Back to cold sleepless nights. Back to one meal a day. Back to brutal shifts at the nursing home. Back to depression, to darkness. Back to running on the side of the road, desperately trying to hold on to the strength I gained in Mexico. But it's hard with no coach, no guidance, and no regular training schedule or facility. I need to take as many shifts at the nursing home as I can—I need the cash—but I also need to train as much as possible, to stay in shape for the Olympic Trials. I also have to keep current with my doctors, go in for my hormone tests, to stay in compliance with the requirements that World Athletics maintains for female trans athletes. I never get a break. Never get enough rest. After experiencing the beautiful expansiveness of Mexico, my life suddenly feels small and constricted again. My body is depleted, but no longer in a way that feels satisfying. Now I just feel drained, like I'm *losing* strength instead of gaining it.

March turns into April. I become a US citizen. I am so relieved—this is one of the requirements to join Team USA for the Olympics. But I am still unhoused. I still haven't told a single person that I'm homeless. The embarrassment is too deep. I don't feel comfortable sharing this fact with friends, because I don't want to be a burden on anyone. So I isolate myself. I live with this secret. A secret that's killing me. I slide further into depression.

It seems like there's no way out.

CHAPTER FORTY-ONE

Sasha-Lee walks toward me in the darkness. A small cluster of candles illuminates her face. She sets a cake in front of me. *Happy birthday, dear CeCé*, she trills, and her family sings along, assembled around the dinner table. I do my best to fake a smile, to pretend like this is just another birthday dinner, that I don't feel unbearable pressure weighing on my mind. But Sasha-Lee can tell something is wrong. The conversation tonight has been a delicate dance. She's subtly hinted around the topic of where I'm living, but I've avoided it every time.

...Happy birthday to you!

I blow out the candles. Someone turns on the lights. Sasha-Lee cuts a slice for me, then distributes cake to the rest of her family. We all begin eating, as an awkward silence descends on the table. I can tell by the way Sasha-Lee looks at me that there's something on her mind, something she wants to say.

So, she says gently. *Where are you living these days, CeCé?*

I burst into tears. The way she finally just asked the question outright—it takes me off guard. I haven't told anyone where I'm living. I haven't spoken the truth out loud. Sasha-Lee comes over, rubs my back, comforts me.

Are you homeless? she whispers.

I'm...I'm living in my car, I say between sobs.

Well, that ends today, Sasha-Lee says, a fierce affection in her voice. *You're sleeping here tonight.*

I...I don't want to be a burden.

You're never a burden, she says. *And you can stay here as long as you need. You're a part of the family, CeCé.*

I stay with Sasha-Lee's family. Life improves. The stress of being unhoused fades. I get into a regular routine. I keep working at the nursing home three days a week. I'm saving money so eventually I can get a place of my own. Sasha-Lee refuses to take any money from me for rent, even a small amount. I'm so grateful to have a roof over my head again, so grateful for her generosity.

Olympic Trials are from June 18 to June 27, 2021. I keep training as best I can, though I don't have an official training facility. And once again, despite the near daily emails I send, I have no coach. I train on the side of the road, and this becomes my makeshift gym. I sprint up the tree-lined incline, pushing my body as hard as I can. Some days I'll head to the local high school and use their track, though due to COVID restrictions I can't be on the track if there are students present. If I'm lucky, they'll leave out the hurdles, so I can run drills for my event. This makeshift regimen is far from ideal, far from the Olympic-quality coaching I received in Mexico, but it's all I have. So I persevere.

Soon, it's May. I start taking less shifts at the nursing home, so I can train as close to full time as possible. I continue my quest to find a coach. My search leads me to the New Hampshire chapter of PFLAG, the national organization devoted to advocating for LGBTQ+ individuals and their families. The president of the New Hampshire chapter, Erica Allen, is familiar with my story, is also a trans woman, and is able to connect me with a man named David McFarland. David is not a coach, but he is a manager for elite professional LGBTQ+ athletes, as well as a TV/film producer, social impact advisor, and the former CEO of another legendary LGBTQ+ advocacy organization: The Trevor Project. David's connections in the worlds of sports, entertainment, and political activism run deep, and from our first phone call, I can tell that this man sees my potential. He believes in me and knows that my story has the power to change the course of history for trans athletes. Though I truly appreciate everything Nikki has done for me as a manager, it's clear that David simply has much greater reach in terms of his connections; this is a man who can take my career to the next level. So, after a difficult discussion with Nikki, in which I thank her for all the help she's given me, I make the decision to move on, and hire David as my manager. I'm so excited—this feels like a lucky break. I have someone high-powered and well-connected on my side. Even if he's not a coach, he is at least someone who is fighting for me, and who has the connections and knowledge to advocate for me on an international level.

Soon we get confirmation that I'm officially seated in the 400-meter hurdles at the US Olympic Team Trials in Eugene, Oregon. David immediately secures a short-term corporate sponsorship that infuses my bank account with some cash, so I can focus solely on training. I'm able to stop working at the nursing home temporarily. I devote myself solely to training and competing in a few high-profile races, just to get my legs going and get into competition mode.

It feels incredible to be back on the track, thrust into competition with other elite athletes, operating at the top of my game. I'm gaining momentum. The Olympic Trials in Eugene are just around the corner. Then, it's Team USA. I feel unstoppable. Which is why it is so shocking when my entire dream grinds to a halt, before I ever step foot on the plane to Oregon.

Something is wrong. I can feel it.

I've submitted all my bloodwork to USATF—USA Track & Field, the national governing body for track and field events. At this point, this is a normal procedure for me. Ever since I first started competing within the NCAA, I've been working with my doctors to ensure that my testosterone levels are less than 5 nanomoles per liter for a period of twelve months prior to any competition. The rules are the same for events governed by the USATF. In college I submitted my bloodwork documentation to the NCAA, but now I submit to USATF. It does feel unfair that I am the only female athlete subjected to this medical monitoring of my body, but I have complied, stayed current with all testing—even when I was homeless—to ensure I would be eligible to compete. I often wonder why cis female athletes are not tested in the same way, because if they were, it is very likely that some, if not many, would fail to "qualify" as a woman as defined by USATF. Furthermore, the "science" behind the idea that a certain hormone level should be the determining factor for womanhood is bad, widely discredited, and transphobic.

When someone tells you what their gender is, you should believe them. Period.

That, in my opinion, should be the sole "qualifying" factor in terms of determining whether someone is "really" a woman.

But we do not live in an ideal world, and I know that I need to make concessions, especially because I am at the forefront of changing ideas of gender in the world of sports. So I have always complied with their rules. I have never complained. And I have always met the requirements. Which is why I feel like it is so odd that I've submitted this information to USATF as usual but received no confirmation from the organization. No official word, telling me that I've been approved to compete. Just absolute silence.

The days pass. I become increasingly worried. I send follow-up email after follow-up email. No response. I begin calling their headquarters, leaving messages for anyone I can. No response. I beg the assistants who answer the phones for information, asking if they can just confirm that my tests were received. Each assistant tells me that they are unable to offer me any information. Time is running out, and I have no idea if I'm confirmed to compete.

Finally, with just one week left, we receive word back from USATF. They tell us that the Olympic Trials are different, and that we actually need to submit documentation to World Athletics, the governing body for international competition in track and field. (Many people don't realize this, but there are separate international governing bodies for each sport at the Olympics, which is why certain sports have different regulations than others.) I ask USATF if they can supply me with a copy of the World Athletics Regulations for trans athletes to ensure I submit everything they need. USATF says they do not have a copy, but that I can go to the World Athletics website and search for it.

So I go to the website and search for it. It is nowhere to be found. I ask other people to help search for these documents. David searches and cannot find them. I even call up Coach Zem—he searches and cannot find them. I am the first female athlete that I am aware of to go through this, so I have no one who has been in my position before, no other athlete I can turn to for guidance. I also have no coach to advocate for me, so I must advocate for myself. I feel so alone.

I reach out to USATF again, saying I cannot find the regulations anywhere on the World Athletics website. Finally, USATF provides me with a copy of the regulations. USATF says that the deadline has technically passed to provide my documentation to World Athletics, but that I will be granted an extension because the World Athletics Regulations were inaccessible. However, the twenty-one-page document containing the regulations for transgender athletes does not have a comprehensive list of materials that trans athletes must supply World Athletics. Rather, it specifies "The athlete must also provide the appropriate consents and waivers (in a form satisfactory to the Medical Manager) to enable her physician(s) to disclose to the Medical Manager and the Expert Panel *any information that the Expert Panel deems necessary to its assessment.*" This means that the Expert Panel at World Athletics can ask for whatever medical and therapeutic records they want, until they are satisfied. It feels to me like they have unlimited access to my body and mind. It feels like if I wish to qualify for Olympic Trials, I have no right to privacy. As a trans woman, I am used to my body being under constant scrutiny. That does not make it right, that does not make it feel good, but I soldier on. I will do anything it takes to get to the Olympic Trials.

I am connected with Dr. Stéphane Bermon, the medical director of World Athletics, who is based in France. He details the documentation that he believes will be sufficient to "prove" that I am female. He asks for a letter from my primary care physician confirming my gender, a year's worth of hormone testing, and a letter from my therapist confirming my gender.

We supply him with everything. We wait. It is agonizing to just sit there, powerless, standing by for a decision that will change the trajectory of my entire life. There is so much at stake.

Finally, we hear back on the day before I'm supposed to fly to Eugene, Oregon, to compete in the Olympic Trials. Dr. Berman says we have not supplied sufficient documentation. He wants a record of every therapy session I've had with my therapist, including a detailed description of exactly what was talked about in these therapy sessions. I am shocked. According to the rules of patient confidentiality, everything I shared with my therapist is supposed to be confidential. But I consent to sharing these records—I don't have a choice if I wish to compete. Additionally, my doctors have only submitted six months of hormone testing, but World Athletics needs twelve. World Athletics also want the blood tests in a European format—we've supplied them with the standard American format that I've used in the past. I promise to supply them with everything they need. Of course, it will take time to collect these documents from my physicians, and World Athletics will need time to review all additional documentation.

But thankfully, World Athletics says they will not prevent me from competing in the Olympic Trials. So far, everything I have submitted is satisfactory, and nothing has ruled me ineligible for competition. World Athletics says they are willing to accept the additional documentation later, that I will simply be disqualified after the race if any documents I supply fail to meet eligibility standards. However, because this is technically a domestic competition (and not a global one), World Athletics says they will leave the final decision in the hands of USATF.

A wave of relief washes over me. After all the bureaucratic back-and-forth, after all the stress, after everything I have put my body and mind through to comply with World Athletic regulations, it looks like I will be able to compete at Olympic Trials.

But then, in the final hour, late in the night on the evening before I fly to Eugene, we receive an email from USATF. They are choosing to bar me from the Olympic Trials, even though World Athletics said they would not prevent me from competing. USATF *can* let me run, but they simply *won't*. I'm devastated. We pushed so hard in the weeks leading up to their decision, especially in the final hour. But it was all for nothing. My dream is destroyed in an instant.

I learn a very hard lesson: when you're blazing a new trail, sometimes you get burned.

The media blitz begins in the morning. The USATF sends out a press release. It reads, in part: "Following notification from World Athletics on June 17 that the conditions had not yet been met, USATF provided CeCé with the eligibility requirements and, along with World Athletics, the opportunity to demonstrate her eligibility so that she could compete at the US Olympic Team Trials—Track & Field… According to subsequent notification to CeCé from World Athletics on June 22, she has not been able to demonstrate her eligibility."

David releases a short, diplomatic statement, saying we will respect the decision: "CeCé has turned her focus towards the future and is continuing to train. She will compete on the national and world stage again soon."

Privately, I am furious. Why did it feel like USATF failed to return my calls for so long? Why did it feel like I was stonewalled? If they'd simply let me know from the start that I needed to be in contact with World Athletics, I could've submitted everything on time. Regardless, I'm disqualified over minor bureaucratic details. And it's even more painful to know that, if the decision were up to World Athletics, they would've let me compete.

The story is first picked up by Reuters, then circulated by multiple international news outlets. It quickly gains momentum in the press. Nowhere in their statement does the USATF say that I was not allowed to compete due to my testosterone levels, yet this is what Reuters prints, and soon this becomes the story. The truth is lost. David issues a correction to the Reuters story, to clarify that I was not barred from competing because of my testosterone levels. Reuters corrects their story online, but at this point it's too late; the false story has already gained traction, and every major news outlet has already published the incorrect information. It hurts so much to see a falsehood printed over and over again, especially when I worked so hard to ensure that I *did* meet the requirements for testosterone levels. When David pushes Reuters for the reason they incorrectly printed that I was disqualified for my testosterone levels, the journalist says that this information was given to him by USATF. If true, USATF seemingly spread a false story about me in the press. A fact that makes me so angry. Especially because I have been working tirelessly to monitor my own body, doing everything USATF asked of me, going through an overly aggressive HRT regimen that my doctors believe to be detrimental to my health, all to meet their regulatory standards. I want to scream the truth, tell the world that I met all the hormone requirements, that it was simply a bureaucratic issue of supplying additional documents to World Athletics, that World Athletics said I *could* compete because, so far, I *did* meet eligibility standards, but USATF made the decision to rule me ineligible.

But I stay silent. I take the high road. Put on a brave face for the public. I know that I can't show emotion. I'm afraid to be labeled the angry Black woman, because I know that will only lead to more discrimination. I must stay in "good standing" with World Athletics and USATF. If I publicly speak out against their decision, they have the right to bar me from their organizations. So I hold my composure. Stay poised. Turn the other cheek. Pretend like nothing happened. But behind closed doors, it's a different story. Soon, the anger fades into sadness, into depression. Soon, all I'm left with is my tears.

I'm bedbound. Too depressed to move. I don't see anyone. Barely talk to anyone. Friends text me from the Olympic Trials, asking me what happened, asking me why I'm not there competing alongside them. I don't answer. I can't. It's simply too painful.

I lock myself in my room. For two weeks.

Soon, I get the sense that I've become a burden to Sasha-Lee and her family. That they were happy to host CeCé the Track Champion in their house, but Depressed CeCé is a different story. It seems to me like their demeanor has shifted; they seem less warm, less welcoming. In the past, Sasha-Lee has told me how she views me as a daughter, has told me that I am a member of the family, but it doesn't feel like that now. It feels to me like she is pulling away when I need her the most. It feels like my situation has become too stressful for this family, that they are beginning to doubt me, and that I've outstayed my welcome. Which is fine—I'm grateful to Sasha-Lee for housing me when I was homeless, and I understand that she can't keep me under her roof forever. But in that case, don't go around telling people that I'm your Black adopted daughter. Because ultimately, what I begin to realize is that we're not family. That's okay. But why raise my expectations to believe that we are, especially when you know my history, when you know how much I long for a love my mother never supplied?

Sasha-Lee pushes me to go to track meets, any track meets, just to get back out there. But the last thing I want to do is run in a track meet, especially a track meet that is not an elite-level competition. That would be a waste of my time on a good day. But now, after the whole fiasco with USATF, I don't want to be anywhere near a track meet. Period. It's too painful. I get the sense that she is pushing me because she wants to see me fulfill some sort of idealized sports story, like "CeCé went through hell and still prevailed, still came out on top." But fuck the story. What about my mental health? Right now, I can't even think about another track meet, I just need a break. And I can sense that Sasha-Lee is disappointed by this.

I start to feel uncomfortable around the house. I spend as little time there as possible. I make sure that I'm on an opposite schedule from the rest of the family. I'm out of the house whenever they're home. I stay on top of my chores. I clean my room. I clean the house. I watch the dogs, feed them, take them on walks. I occasionally cook for everyone. I try to make my presence as small and contained as possible. I feel sad, alone, like they want me out of their home. But I have nowhere else to go.

Summer drags on. David books me to appear at a few Pride events and though I'm grateful for an opportunity to connect with the LGBTQ+ community, my heart simply isn't in it this year. Everywhere I go, people ask me what happened at the Olympic Trials. I answer their questions as best I can, but I hate reliving one of the most painful moments of my life.

After about a month, I start training again. Every day. I've made another agreement with Franklin Pierce: if I work again as a sort of assistant coach they'll let me keep training there. But they know that I'm still looking for a coach and professional training facility. One of the coaches suggests that I reach out to Greater Boston Track Club, that maybe I could compete on their team, and I would at least no longer have to compete unattached. So, I connect with Greater Boston Track Club, and they agree to take me on. Still, I train more regularly at Franklin Pierce, because it's only a twenty-minute drive from Sasha-Lee's house, as opposed to a two-hour drive to Boston. Gradually, I push through the pain. I tell myself that I've come too far, that I can't give up now, that all I've achieved and all I've overcome can't be for nothing. I set my sights on my next goal: the World Athletics Championships in 2022.

* * *

What happened at Olympic Trials can never happen again. David and I are determined to ensure that all my documentation is in order, well before the World Championships rolls around. We've now been through the eligibility process with World Athletics once already, so we know what to expect. It is vital for my doctor to be briefed on exactly what is expected, so we can avoid a similar situation in the future. So we schedule a conference call with Dr. Mark Rodriguez at the New England medical center where I've been receiving care.

He apologizes to me for failing to submit the full year of testing needed; he says that it was simply an issue of the time, an error that happened at the last minute. There's no point in litigating the past or pointing fingers, so we simply move on and explain what is needed moving forward. We remind him that I will need a full year of testosterone tests to be deemed eligible for World Championships. We also remind him that it is essential that the tests are submitted in the correct format, using the European format for this type of bloodwork, and *not* the American format I've been using so far throughout my career. Together, we go through the important clauses in the World Athletics Eligibility Regulations for Transgender Athletes. He agrees to it all, and I do feel some relief.

I keep training. Soon fall arrives, then winter. I start competing again in January of 2022. I feel like I'm getting back into that competition mindset. I head to meet after meet, regaining my confidence and determination. I attend my monthly doctor's appointments religiously, ensuring that I am not a minute late for a single hormone test. Eventually, the weather turns warmer, and it's time for the outdoor season. I keep competing, keep killing it. National Trials for World Championships are just around the corner. And this time, there will be no fuckups. This time, I will not be disqualified over a technicality. This time, I'm going all the way to the top.

CHAPTER FORTY-TWO

June 7, 2022. I'm in Washington, DC, for my final track meet before I head to National Trials at the end of June. Though the competition is almost a month away, I want to make sure we have all my documentation sent to World Athletics well in advance. So I call my doctor's office. I am sent to Dr. Rodriguez's voice mail. I leave a message. He doesn't call me back that day. Or the next.

I compete in my event. I run the 200-meter open. I come in second place. A solid time. I'm happy with the meet, but honestly, I'm much more concerned with getting in touch with my doctor, to ensure that he submits all the proper paperwork so I can compete at National Trials.

So I call again. And again. He never returns my call. I talk to a receptionist at my doctor's office and ask if she can help me. I simply need someone to send all my records to World Athletics. She says she is not able to do that—I need to talk to my doctor. I say I can't get in touch with my doctor. She suggests I come into the office when I return. I say I want these documents sent now. She says there is nothing she can do.

Finally, I return home on the fourteenth. The first thing I do is head straight into my doctor's office. I walk up to the reception desk, filled with anxiety, and tell her that I need to speak with Dr. Rodriguez.

I'm sorry, the receptionist says. *But Dr. Rodriguez no longer works here.*

That's not possible. He's the one who's been handling my case. He would've told me if he was leaving. What do you mean he doesn't work here anymore?

I'm afraid I'm unable to give you any further information.

Well, who's going to handle my case now? I need to talk to someone as soon as possible.

The receptionist looks at my file. *You've been assigned to Farrah, a nurse practitioner. Shall I set up an appointment?*

Yes, I say. *And I need it to be today.*

They set up a Zoom appointment with Farrah. I don't understand why I've been assigned a nurse practitioner instead of a new doctor, but I don't have time to fight with the facility. I need my full year of records submitted to World Athletics as soon as possible. Then I'll also need one final test, administered by this new nurse practitioner, to show my testosterone levels for the month of June.

I sign onto the video chat. After brief introductions, we dive right into the issue at hand.

I'm assuming Dr. Rodriguez briefed you on my case? I ask.

No, actually, she says. *I'm coming in fresh.*

I'm shocked. I don't even know where to begin. She doesn't know my medical history? She's not familiar with all the intricacies of the World Athletics regulations? No one has told her about the very specific care that I need in order to ensure that I will be eligible to compete?

Okay, I say, as patiently as possible. *I'll start from the beginning.*

I tell her that Dr. Rodriguez has been testing my hormone levels monthly, and that she needs to find these records, and submit them to the medical director at World Athletics in France. I tell her that she needs to order a hormone test for this month, which is the final test World Athletics needs to see in order for me to compete at nationals. I tell her that the bloodwork needs to be in the European format and *not* the American format. I tell her what my HRT dosage levels need to be, to ensure that my hormone levels remain low enough to compete. I provide her with the Medical Consent form that she needs to sign, as well as a copy of the World Athletics Eligibility Regulations for Transgender Athletes.

All right, she says, once I've finished. *I'm gonna get right on this.* But she seems overwhelmed. Unprepared for this meeting. Still, I don't have a choice. I have to work with her.

The next day, I go into the doctor's office. Farrah administers my hormones, then draws my blood. I remind her of all the protocols she must follow. She assures me that she's reviewed all the regulations, and that her test will be in line with World Athletics mandates. As I leave the office, she promises to send everything. And sure enough, she sends an email to Dr. Bermon later that day. He says he'll take the weekend to review all the documents, to ensure everything is in order.

On Monday, they come back with their decision.

Once again, I've been barred from competition.

As it turns out, Dr. Rodriguez ordered the wrong blood tests for the entire year.

Despite that meeting we had with him where we outlined exactly what was needed, despite having a copy of the World Athletics Eligibility Regulations for Transgender Athletes, despite the fact that we reminded him over and over again that the bloodwork needed to be in the European format and *not* the American format, despite all of this, he still ordered the wrong tests every single month.

Farrah's blood test was the only one in the correct format.

I'm devastated that we're here again. Despite my vigilance. Despite how hard I advocated for myself with my own doctor. I am furious that my health care facility failed me in this way. That once again I am barred from competition over a stupid technicality. Over my doctor's stupid mistake. Something out of my hands.

But I also experience a deeper frustration. I am angry that I am the only elite female track athlete who has to jump through all these extra hoops, that there is a twenty-one-page regulatory document that applies only to me, that I am the only person whose body is surveilled in this way. I'm angry that there are probably some cis female athletes who will compete at World Championships this year who have *higher* levels of testosterone than I do, who would technically be disqualified due to their hormone levels if they were forced to do the same blood tests that I am. But we will never know, because I am the only female athlete forced to do this type of testing. I am angry that they can single me out in whatever way they wish, I am angry that they have carte blanche to ask for whatever private medical information they see fit, I am angry that they can police my body in whatever way they want, all because I am trans.

There's a term for what I'm forced to endure: discrimination.

CHAPTER FORTY-THREE

It's so hard for me to sit here and watch you self-destruct, Sasha-Lee says to me one day, hanging in the door of my bedroom, where I'm hiding, once again, desperate to be left alone, to be out of the public eye, to nurse my wounds in private.

Well, then don't just sit there is what I want to say. *Help me. Fight my battles alongside me. You've seen everything I've gone through with USATF and World Athletics, you've seen how I've scrambled and fought against discrimination. But it feels to me like you've chosen to sit on the sidelines, in the moments it matters most.*

But I stay silent. Because I feel like she won't help. A strange dynamic has developed between us. Throughout all my issues with my doctors, with USATF, and with World Athletics, Sasha-Lee has seen me struggle, knows that I need extra support right now, but she hasn't helped me. She constantly asks me to drop my guard, to let her in, because she says she loves me like a daughter. But would a loving mother just "sit here and watch" her daughter self-destruct? Would a mother not step in and intervene when her daughter is dealing with the most difficult professional obstacles in her entire life? Would she not get on the phone with World Athletics, or USATF, and advocate for her daughter? She would. She would do whatever it took to protect her child. But what I'm realizing, of course, is that Sasha-Lee is not my mother. She is a very kind and caring woman who put a roof over my head when I was unhoused. But because she has set up this expectation of motherhood, of family, I feel increasingly disappointed by her. It feels like she demands a deep level of intimacy from me but fails to provide the type of support that usually accompanies this familial intimacy.

Are you really training that hard? Sasha-Lee's husband asks me one day, when I come home from practice. *Or are you just pretending? Just going through the motions?*

I tell him that of course I'm training hard. I'm back out there, after the most painful chapter in my running career, and I'm putting in the work. I can tell he doesn't believe me. I can tell Sasha-Lee shares his suspicions. They think I've given up on my dream. But I'm pushing harder than I've ever pushed, pushing through my devastation, pushing through intense depression, to go to that track every day and *hold on to* my dream. I don't understand why they can't see this. It's like they expect me to have a higher threshold for pain, that my depression signals some sort of weakness, and that weakness is an indication that *I* am somehow to blame for everything that has happened with World Athletics and USATF.

I don't want to seem ungrateful. Sasha-Lee is a good person with a kind soul; she was a great friend for a while, and only wanted to help me. I am so profoundly thankful that her family took me in when I was homeless. But it seems like this relationship has reached its expiration date. It would be healthier for everyone if we all moved on.

I'm on a plane to Los Angeles. Everything I own is packed in a suitcase, sitting in the cargo hold. I'm leaving New Hampshire. Yes, things have become uncomfortable at Sasha-Lee's, but that's just one small part of the equation. The bigger issue? I need my independence. I could've moved somewhere else in New Hampshire, kept working at the nursing home. Let my dreams fall by the wayside. Get used to small town New England life. So many people I know are settling down, getting married, and having kids. And that's a beautiful life for some people.

But not for me. Not yet.

I still have so much to conquer, so many goals I've yet to achieve. I feel like God put track in my life for a reason. I feel like this sport is a mission that was given to me, and I'm not done with it yet. Because this mission isn't just about me. There is still so much change that needs to happen in this world, so that the next generation of trans athletes have an easier path than me. So I need a city that will match my ambitions. A place that will challenge, inspire, and offer opportunity.

Which is why I'm moving to Los Angeles.

I have a little saved up from the nursing home, enough to rent an Airbnb while I'm hunting for apartments. David lives out in LA, and he's already setting up some meetings for potential media opportunities and brand partnerships. I'll also have to hunt for a job, so I can continue to pay rent on my own place. I'll need to get set up with new doctors as soon as possible—which I wanted to do anyway after the fiasco with my health care facility (they've at least acknowledged the serious mistake they made with my documents for National Trials, though no one can tell me *why* this happened). It's a big move, a huge leap. It will be uncomfortable at first, I'm sure. But part of what I'm realizing is that I'll need to be comfortable with being uncomfortable. This discomfort is just a part of growth. If I risk nothing, I gain nothing, I achieve nothing. And I still have so much I want to achieve.

I still want to become an Olympian.

My number one goal when I get to Los Angeles: find a coach.

At this point, I've easily reached out to over five hundred coaches as a part of my ongoing email campaign. Still, each attempt is met with rejection or silence. Despite all my efforts to change the public narrative around trans athletes, despite my stellar track record, rock-solid work ethic, and national title, I still cannot find a coach willing to work with a female trans athlete. I've become used to living with this frustration. I'm accustomed to acting as my own coach, monitoring my own progress, coming up with my own workouts, my own strategies for competition, advocating for myself with World Athletics and USATF. But it's just not the same as having an elite coach, like every other Team USA hopeful.

So, I have a new strategy. No more emails. I'm going to find one in person.

Another reason I moved to LA is because I knew that many elite athletes train here. And where there are elite athletes, there are elite coaches. So I go to UCLA—a track where I might be seen and scouted.

My first practice. I walk into Drake Stadium, one of the best training facilities in the country. A blue track, as bright as the Los Angeles sky, stretches around an immaculate infield. A place where champions are made. I feel inspired, driven, affirmed in my decision to move to Los Angeles. I'm in the right place.

I warm up, find a lane, and start running my drills. I scan the field periodically, hoping to catch a coach watching me, assessing my performance, waiting to approach and ask me to join his team. But I'm alone in the stadium, not a coach in sight.

I don't give up hope. I return the next day, and the next. Still no coach. I return for a third practice, a fourth, a fifth, and finally, a sixth. I power through my drills, frustration building. As I cool down, doubt starts to creep in. I wonder if my dream of being scouted was naive, as delusional as an aspiring starlet hoping to be discovered by walking down Hollywood Boulevard.

After practice, I start packing up my spikes. Suddenly, I hear a man's voice behind me.

Excuse me, he says. *Do you have a minute to talk?*

I turn around and recognize him immediately. He's a well-known Olympian who now works as an elite coach.

My heart beats faster. *Sure*, I say. *What's up?*

I saw you training out there. What are your events?

The hurdles, I reply. *The 100 and 400.*

Do you have a team you train with?

No. I don't.

Do you have a coach?

No, I don't have a coach either.

You know, when I started out, I was just like you. I didn't have a coach and it was hard. I was training on my own.

Really? I ask.

Yeah, he says. *Then, eventually, I found a coach. A man who took me under his wing. And I became an Olympian.*

That's...that's incredible.

I guess what I wanna know is: Would you want to train with me?

I want to scream. I want to jump up and down and hug this man and cry and tell him that this is what I've been looking for, a real elite coach with Olympic experience, someone who can push me to new heights. But I don't do any of that. I don't want to scare the poor man. I want him to train me. So I simply say: *Yes. When can we start?*

How about tomorrow?

That night, I pray. I kneel on the floor, in my new Hollywood apartment. I thank God for leading me here, to Los Angeles. All the hardship I've endured has been worth it. I found my coach. There's nothing that can stop me now.

CHAPTER FORTY-FOUR

I'm up before the sun rises. Practice is at 5:30. It's so early, but I don't feel tired. I'm energized, ready to pour everything I have into training. I get to the track and I introduce myself to the other girls on my coach's team; I recognize some of them—he's got an incredible roster of athletes, some of the top talent in the country. I feel at home in their company. Finally, I'm in the right place. Training alongside other elite female athletes.

I pour everything I've got into this first practice. I go hard. The coach tells me that I'm ahead of the other girls, that I'm almost ready for competition, but I need to pace myself because it's still fall, we're still in preseason. He says I need to slow down and build with the team. I agree, happy for the guidance. I can tell he's impressed with my performance. I feel exhilarated.

After we're done on the field, we head to the gym for strength training. I'm at the leg press, resting between sets, when a small commotion breaks out on the floor. In the distance, just out of earshot, I see one of my new teammates in a heated exchange with our coach. He gestures for her to follow him out of the gym. Together, they leave the room.

I stare at the door. Imagine the conversation they're having behind it. I try to tell myself they're not talking about me, that she probably just had a bad day and needed to blow off some steam. It happens, even to the best athletes.

But it's hard to ignore the dread building within me. It's hard to ignore the voice inside my head that says: *It's all over, CeCé. This is your last day with this team.*

I head home after practice. I say goodbye to my coach. He doesn't seem to treat me differently, which I take as a good sign.

Later that night, my phone buzzes. I see his name pop up on my caller ID. Anxiety invades my thoughts. I pick up. He tells me how well I did in practice today. I thank him. But I can tell by the tone in his voice that this isn't the reason he called.

CeCé, he says finally. *It's been brought to my attention that you're transgender.*

Yes, I say. *I am.*

And you competed on the men's team at Franklin Pierce?

I did. But I've always been a female. Even when I was running with the men. I didn't realize it was a possibility for me to run on the women's team until my final year. Which is when I won my NCAA title. A familiar exhaustion sets in. It is exhausting to constantly explain yourself to others, to educate them about what it means to be transgender, while also defending your right to exist in the sport you love more than anything else. But I don't have a choice.

Right, he says, then hesitates. *I just want you to know that I don't have a problem with you. I think you're a talented athlete, with so much potential. But some of the other women on the team know who you are. And the fact that you're trans is an issue to them.*

I knew it. I feel so hurt, so angry that once again I have to contend with such intense prejudice. But I bite my tongue. *Okay* is all I say. *So are you kicking me off the team?*

No, he says. *But we are going to have to figure out a Plan B.*

* * *

273

The other women refuse to train alongside me. His solution: he'll coach me privately. I show up to practice after all the other athletes are gone, and we have a one-on-one training session. I am so grateful to him; he's pushing himself harder than most other coaches push themselves, he's giving extra time, extra energy, all because he believes in me. I know how hard it must be for him to lead back-to-back practices. So I'm not gonna let this man down. I'm going to work my fucking ass off, and when it's time to compete, I'm going to deliver.

The weeks pass, and I feel myself getting stronger, faster.

Then he tells me we need to have another conversation. His other athletes don't like that he's still training me, that now I'm receiving one-on-one sessions. He's worried that people may walk off his team. He's worried that being associated with me, with all the controversy surrounding trans athletes, could ruin his career as a coach. He wants to stop training me.

I am absolutely devastated. I try not to show it. I try to remain strong.

But I don't want to drop you completely, he says. *I really do believe in you.*

So what can we do? I ask.

We come up with a new plan. I'll train on my own. By myself. But he'll assign me workouts, he'll hammer out a training regimen. And I'll send him videos, pictures, and detailed reports of my workouts. He'll text me back with an analysis of my form, new workouts, and words of encouragement. We won't meet in person, but we'll do as much as we can virtually.

I stick with this routine throughout the winter. I send him updates every single day. He texts back. It's not anywhere close to having real, in-person, sessions with a coach. But at least it's something. Still, it depresses me. Every time I text him another update, I'm always reminded of *why* I have to do this, that there is someone out there who hates that I'm trans, who doesn't believe I have the right to compete as my true self in the sport that I love. And this begins to wear on my psyche. It affects my training. Depletes my morale. Leaves me increasingly depressed. So, in February of 2023, I decide that it's best for us to part ways.

I'm used to training alone. I've done it before. I can do it again.

It's not ideal, but it doesn't matter. It's my only option.

CHAPTER FORTY-FIVE

David calls with good news.

CNN wants to do a story about me. About my journey. The challenges I've faced as a transgender athlete. My Olympic goals.

And my search for a coach.

At first, I worry that this interview will just distract from my training. I don't want to be at the center of a media blitz again. But then I remember that my story is bigger than me, that I'm also fighting for the rights of my community.

The journalist is a woman named Amanda Davies, a correspondent for CNN International based out of the network's London bureau. David has been in ongoing discussions with CNN for a while now, lining up this opportunity. His hope is that this can be a longer feature, a ten-minute documentary that will air internationally on CNN. The goal: To present the public with the human being behind the headlines. To show the person on the receiving end of the targeted political rhetoric. To remind the world that this issue impacts the lives of real trans people everywhere.

Now, CNN is ready to start shooting. But before I sit down for my on-camera interview with Amanda, she wants to do a pre-interview, to get a greater understanding of who I am.

My heart fills with hope. I'm happy that I'll get to tell my story on a global platform. I hope that this can help to change hearts and minds. I hope people will begin to realize that we are all part of the same human family, and we need to learn how to better love our trans sisters, trans brothers, trans children, trans parents. And I also hope that my story reaches the trans kids out there, young athletes who've been too afraid to compete on the team of their true gender. I hope this gives them courage.

But before any of that happens, I need to meet with Amanda Davies.

So, we set up a time to talk.

David calls with bad news.

He's heard from sources with inside knowledge that World Athletics is reevaluating their regulations concerning female transgender athletes. They are considering lowering their requirements for testosterone levels from less than 5 nanomoles per liter to less than 2.5 nanomoles. This would require an even more aggressive HRT regimen for trans female athletes, a change that would put them at even greater (and unnecessary) risk for blood clotting, which can lead to deep venous thromboses, pulmonary embolism, or stroke. Additionally, this hormone regimen lowers your blood oxygen levels dramatically, leading to deterioration of muscle and bone, which leaves trans female athletes at greater risk for injury, and makes it extraordinarily difficult to gain strength and endurance. The commonly held yet misinformed belief is that trans female athletes have an advantage over cis females; this is not true, and these new testosterone requirements would ensure that trans female athletes are at an even greater *dis*advantage than they were before. This is bad enough, but there's another concern. In the end, World Athletics may not change the requirements for testosterone levels.

They may ban trans women from track and field entirely.

*   *   *

David calls with good news.

We have a date for our CNN sit-down with Amanda Davies.

The pre-interview went well. It was clear that she's informed on transgender issues within the world of elite athletics. I feel like I can trust her.

We'll tape the interview at CNN's Los Angeles bureau. Coincidentally, it's on the bus route I take home every day. I never imagined that I would one day walk inside to be interviewed, as part of a documentary about my life. Now, whenever I pass, I feel a nervous thrill.

During the pre-interview, we discussed the impending ruling from World Athletics. We talked about how much is at stake for me. How, in just one week's time, I could be banned from competing in the Olympics, bringing my lifelong dream to an abrupt and premature end. Amanda told us that she will now be reporting on the World Athletics ruling, that she will speak with representatives from both World Athletics and USATF to get their official stance.

David says this is a good thing. We're shining an international spotlight on these organizations. They can't sweep this under the rug, hoping no one will notice. They know that whatever decision they make, will now be global news.

We're applying pressure. We're hoping that pressure encourages them to do the right thing. Even still, I can hardly sleep at night. I feel like I'm on a precipice. I don't want to believe that I'll be banned from the sport that I love. But I know there's a chance that I will be.

David calls me.

I'm outside your place, he says. *Are you ready to go?*

I leave my apartment. Head down to the car. Get in. We're headed to CNN for my interview with Amanda. We go through all my talking points. We don't know what Amanda will ask. But

David and I have prepped for every possible question. There is so much at stake. I hope this documentary can be the key to preventing a ban, that if we bring attention to this issue, we can save my Olympic dream, and the Olympic dreams of all the trans female track and field athletes that come after me.

We get to the studio. A producer greets us at the reception area. She is friendly, funny, and sweet. She guides us to a green room. Asks if we need anything. Any food or coffee. But I'm not hungry. I just want to get into that studio and get into this interview.

Then, it's time.

I sit down in a small room. Right in front of a camera. Amanda will be patched in from London. I'm told to direct all my answers straight into the camera lens. I get mic'ed up. David gives me some final words of encouragement, and then leaves the room. I'm so nervous.

We start the interview.

It's immediately clear that Amanda is such a professional. She's so prepared. She dives into my story, dives into all the controversy, doesn't shy away from the tough questions. And I'm prepared for every single one. I tell her about my journey, my fight, my hopes, and how this ruling will directly impact my life. I feel seen. I feel heard.

After the interview, David greets me with cheers in the green room.

That was incredible, he says. *Perfect.*

The producer says that she wants to schedule a time to shoot some B-Roll with me. They'll want to get footage of my training at UCLA. We promise to be in touch, then leave the studio. I feel high, I feel that post-adrenaline rush. I knocked it out of the park.

I just hope it's enough.

I call David.

World Athletics could be making their decision any day now. I can't stand the anticipation. I hate having this loom over my head.

I tell him that I want to meet with World Athletics. I want to talk to Dr. Bermon, their medical director, who will be advising the organization on their decision. This ruling will affect me directly. I am the only female trans athlete currently trying to compete at a global level. So far, my interactions with Dr. Bermon have been limited to discussions about regulations and medical records. I want him to get to know me on a human level. I wonder if anyone at World Athletics even knows a trans woman in their personal lives. Based on the decisions they're making, I doubt it. I hope that hearing from me personally might help them open their hearts and gain a greater understanding of what it means to be trans.

So David sets up a Zoom with Dr. Bermon.

The time comes for our meeting. I feel a jolt of adrenaline seeing Dr. Bermon's face. This man could alter the trajectory of my life. I take a deep breath. I thank him for meeting with me. He asks me what I want to talk about. I tell him that I want to share a little of my story, so I can shed some light on my experiences as a transgender woman and athlete. I start with my childhood in Jamaica. I tell him that from my earliest memories, I've always known that I was a girl. I tell him how I've been estranged from my family; I tell him about all the discrimination and hate I've faced. I tell him about how much I love this sport, and how hard I fought to compete with my fellow female athletes. And throughout, I communicate that I've been living this life forever, this life was not something I chose. I was born this way.

Most of all, I want to remind Dr. Bermon that I am a human being. That I am more than just a set of medical records that he must review. I want to touch his heart.

Eventually, our conversation comes to a close. He tells me that ultimately this decision doesn't rest in his hands, but that he will convey everything we spoke about to the powers that be. He says he's thankful that I shared my story. He seems moved. He seems optimistic that there will not be a ban. He thanks me for my time. He signs off.

I feel like there's still hope.

*   *   *

I call David.

Immediately after our Zoom.

I think that went well, I say.

David hesitates. *I wouldn't be so sure.*

Why? I say, caught off guard.

Well, he said that ultimately the decision isn't in his hands. But he's the medical director of World Athletics. I believe the organization may be looking to him for guidance on this.

Why would he say it's not in his hands then?

Maybe he's trying to avoid taking responsibility for whatever ruling they make.

Why would he do that?

I don't know, David replies. *But it makes me nervous.*

David calls at 6:00 a.m.

I wake up to the sound of my phone buzzing. I see his name on the caller ID. My adrenaline spikes. I know this is it. We were told that the decision was coming today. I just didn't realize it would be this early. I pick up the phone. I'm shaking.

They released the ruling, he says. *And it's not good.*

I break down. Start sobbing.

I've been banned from the Olympics.

CHAPTER FORTY-SIX

CNN wants another interview. As soon as possible. The piece will now feature news of the World Athletics ruling, and my reaction to it. I'm not in a good headspace. I've been crying for three days straight, never leaving my apartment. It doesn't seem real. It doesn't seem possible. And yet, it has happened. World Athletics has banned any athletes that have experienced what they call "male puberty" from competing in the female category in global competition. Not only that, but they announced their decision on International Transgender Day of Visibility, which feels like a wild "fuck you" to trans people everywhere. I am devastated, but I have to show up for this interview. I don't know if I'll have the strength.

Just speak from your heart, David advises me. *That's all you have to do.*

So I go back to the CNN studios. I sit in the same dark room. I feel emotionally raw. Like I might break down at any minute. And then, Amanda is patched in. We begin the interview. She asks for my take on the ruling. I push down the feelings of devastation and focus on my words. I've been given a platform to speak my truth, and I want my message to ring loud and clear. I want the world to know that this is discrimination, that this decision goes against everything that the Olympic Games are supposed to stand for.

At one point, Amanda asks me what my message to World Athletics would be. I take a breath and consider my response. *You cannot exclude a group of female athletes that exist and will continue to exist in sports and all levels and areas of society,* I say. *We matter and we continue to matter. Every person has the right to compete and to practice sport. Without discrimination for age, gender, race, sexual orientation. That is what the Olympic Charter is all about. And in order to be a part of the Olympics, you have to follow these things.*

What did it do to your Olympic dream? Amanda asks. *The hopes of representing Team USA?*

This decision has completely shattered my dreams of being a medalist in the Olympics and being a part of Team USA. But it has not... Tears come to my eyes. I take a beat. Fight against the emotion bubbling in my throat. Then, I press on. *It's not going to keep me back. And it's not going to cause me to hang up my spikes.*

So what will you do?

I will continue to fight, I reply. *I will continue to show up and show out. I'll continue to compete wherever, however I can. And I will stand up for what is right.*

The piece airs on CNN. I watch it and I'm relieved. Amanda did an incredible job. Her investigation is thorough, and it is validating to see my story so accurately portrayed on international television. I am happy that we shined a massive spotlight on World Athletics, that they were not able to do this discreetly, behind closed doors. We ensured that the world was watching, as they made one of the most discriminatory decisions in Olympic history.

But they haven't reversed their ruling.

So I am still in the same spot. Still struggling to pull myself out of the worst depression of my life. Still crying myself to sleep at night. The pain is unbearable. I want to hide. To disappear. To give up on my lifelong dream.

People send me messages, telling me that they found the video so inspiring, that they are so proud of me for sharing my story. They say I showed incredible poise in the face of such awful discrimination. I thank everyone who reaches out. But there's another part of me that thinks: *Fuck poise. Fuck being well-spoken. Fuck playing the game by their fucked-up rules. I just want to run.*

But then it occurs to me: I *can* run. Not in international competition. But they haven't banned me from competing domestically. The USATF has not issued any official ban of trans athletes. So I will keep running in America. I will train harder than ever. I will compete harder than ever. I will break records and take names. I will make it all the way to the World Championships. Which is when World Athletics will tell me I can't compete. They will remind me that I am banned. And that's when I will start making noise. I will let the world know that I will not stand for this discrimination. And then, we will take them to court.

Mark my words, I'll be in Paris for the 2024 Olympic Games.

It will be hard as fuck to get there, yet I have no choice but to try. I won't let them destroy my dream. Not without a fight.

CHAPTER FORTY-SEVEN

My car is waiting.

I take one last look in the mirror. My face shimmers in the light, beat for the gods. The lashes are lashing. I've got a fresh set of nails—pink, stiletto sharp. A sexy, strappy heel. And don't forget the pedicure—a dazzling summer white. I turn, take in the view. She's an athlete by day, princess by night. I look cute in a black Nike two piece. It's giving red carpet, with a sporty twist. A fitted crop top hugs my curves, showing just the cutest hint of skin at my midriff. The skirt stretches down to my knee, with a slit that runs up my thigh. Though it's a proper length, make no mistake—you *know* my ass is popping. You can take the girl out of Dairy Twirl, but you can't take the Dairy Twirl out of the girl. Put me behind any ice cream counter, and I'd be racking up those tips. But I'm not heading to Dairy Twirl tonight. I've got something much more important.

I take one final spin. A deep breath. Smile.

There she is: CeCé Telfer. Athlete. Activist. Fighter.

I step in my car. Greet the driver. *You ready?* he asks.

Let's go, I say.

Soon we pull up to the Los Angeles LGBT Center, the iconic institution that has provided care and community to queer and trans people since 1969. As one of the largest LGBTQ organizations in the world, its impact extends far beyond LA, reaching individuals and communities across the globe. It also has personally impacted my life; I've used their health care services, attended workshops, and participated in various community building events here. Today, I'm here for the opening night party of Trans Pride Los Angeles, where I'll be speaking at an event called Trans Town Hall, a series of panels featuring some of the most prominent trans figures in the country, including Raquel Willis, Miss Peppermint, Laith Ashley, Isis King, Trace Lysette, and Representative Zooey Zephyr, the first openly trans person to be elected to the state legislature in Montana.

But of all the faces I'm excited to see, there is only one person who makes my heart beat faster when I spot him from across the green room: Chris Mosier. I haven't seen him since he came to speak at Franklin Pierce, and he offered mentorship that pulled me out of one of the darkest chapters of my life. We make eye contact. His face lights up, and his bright smile beams at me from across the room. He runs over and swoops me into a warm hug. It's a wonderful, full circle moment, to be reunited with Chris in this way.

I'm so happy to see you again, he says.

Me too, I reply.

You ready to do this?

Moments later we're backstage, listening to panel after panel, amazed by all the brilliant speakers, impressed by the depth and power of their stories. My pulse races just a bit faster, as we near the section of the program devoted to Chris and myself, where we'll be talking about our experiences as elite trans athletes. Soon, I hear Raquel Willis, the MC for the event, announce our names. I step onto the stage and see hundreds of smiling faces staring back at me. The theater is packed—standing room only. I feel so grateful for the opportunity to connect with my community in this way.

Chris and I sit opposite each other on the stage. I look into his eyes and all my nervousness melts away. I feel safe and secure, because I know Chris is on my side, I know he understands what

I've been through. Not only that, but we're also speaking to an audience full of trans people. The love I feel from the crowd is incredible, so validating. So often, when doing interviews or panels or media opportunities, I find myself in a position where I have to educate people on what it means to be trans, and fight to change hearts and minds. And though I am happy to do this work, and think it's necessary to change society, it can also be exhausting to feel like you are constantly defending your right to simply exist.

But tonight, I'm here to speak to trans people, and with trans people. There is a baseline understanding. No one in this room has to explain or justify their transness. We can just celebrate and love one another, free of judgment and fear.

Chris and I launch into our discussion, and the dialogue flows so effortlessly. We share the story of when we first met, when he came and spoke at my college, offering those words of solidarity and encouragement that changed my life forever: *Never limit your greatness to make other people feel more comfortable.* We discuss all the commonalities between our journeys, and the challenges we face to compete as our true selves in the sport that we love. We also discuss our differences, and he acknowledges that I must face obstacles as a Black trans woman that he will never face as a white trans man. And when it reaches this point in the discussion, I feel the emotion rise within me.

You just show up at a starting line and it is global news, he says. *And so, we have such a different experience in that. You know, for any trans man in sports, the myth is "There's no way you could be competitive because you were assigned female at birth and it's just not possible." Right? These stereotypes, myths, misconceptions. And you on the flip side, are just trying to fight for your place at the starting line, just to participate like your peers.*

Absolutely, I reply, willing myself to stay strong in this moment. *And that came into play with World Athletics. They've banned trans women from international and elite sports.* The audience bursts into spontaneous "boos." It feels so good to be with my people in this moment because they *get* it. Their support moves me deeply. I look out to the audience, acknowledging their frustrations. *Yeah. Ridiculous, right?*

We talk about the importance of welcoming trans people into sport because it can be a place of affirmation and growth. I talk about how, when I was allowed to run with the women's team, it gave me a profound sense of belonging and acceptance. We discuss the unique pressure trans athletes face, not only to excel in their sports, but also to endure hatred and prejudice.

There's also the pressure of feeling like, I'm doing this for my people, right? he says. *What do you feel your presence in these elite athletic events means for those folks that you're representing?*

For other athletes like me, it's life changing to see that there is somebody else that looks like you, that's been through the same struggles, the same journey, I reply. *I'm doing this for myself but I'm also doing this to pave the way for other people like me, so it's a little bit easier and they don't have to go through all this hate later on down the road, because it's going to be normal for people to see us on these stages and in these corners.*

The crowd bursts into applause. I stare out into the audience, feeling so grateful. I hope that my words can bring us all a bit closer together, that we can continue to build community in this space.

Chris and I walk offstage. He gives me a hug.

I feel safe. I feel seen. I feel loved.

And now, it's time to party.

The plaza is alive with people. Trans people, non-binary people, queer people, and our allies. The entire crowd is buzzing, filled with inspiration after hearing so many wonderful people share their truth. Cheers and laughter erupt from joyous groups scattered throughout the after party. There is abundant food, all free of charge, just like this event was free of charge, to ensure that everyone had access to this safe space, regardless of their income.

Truly everyone is welcome.

So many people come up to me, to thank me for coming here

tonight. Some are friends I know from the Center. Some I'm just meeting for the first time. I stop and talk to everyone, listen as they share their own stories, thankful for the chance to connect with my community.

I feel a brightness within me. I haven't felt this happy in a long time. I've been in such unbelievable pain, ever since I was banned from my sport. The past months have been some of the darkest in my life, filled with agony and anger. But now I feel something shift within me. I feel my resolve return, I feel my passion renew.

I feel hope again.

Together, with my community here tonight, we are living out the change we wish to see in the world. I want to take all my sorrow and depression and turn it into fuel. I want to be a part of a revolution. I'm going to fight harder than I've ever fought before. I want to show people that you can stand in your power, you have a right to be seen, to matter, to claim your motherfucking place in this world. I want to show people what it looks like to never back down. I was banned from my athletic body, and I am still determined to make it to the Olympics. I want to empower others, to show that yes, you can be your authentic self *and* pursue your passions fiercely. No matter what other people may say, no matter how much they may hate you, don't let them take away your passion.

Even if they ban you from your dream, pursue that shit.

Pursue it harder than you've ever pursued it before. Defy their hate, and fight for love.

I'm thinking all this as I'm standing here in the glow of the after party, and I realize that I also need to listen to my own words. Because there have been so many times recently where I've wanted to give up on myself. To give up on life. But I didn't. And it's because of this community here. That's why I've stayed for the after party. Because I want to connect with my people. I *need* to connect with my people. I'm not here for the attention or the accolades or an Instagram post. I'm here because this community saves lives. This community has saved my life. And that's real. This is a safe space.

This is *our* space. So we are gonna stay and connect and show up for each other.

And we're gonna have a good fucking time while we do it.

The night passes, and the party is *lit*. And you *know* that your girl is looking cute on the dance floor. We dance and laugh and ride the wave of euphoria that pulses through the beautiful crowd. Soon, the event begins to wind down, and I convene with my friends to come up with a plan for where to go next. It's decided that we'll head to some queer bars in West Hollywood, where we can keep dancing the night away.

I take one last look around the crowd, the sea of blissful faces. I feel overwhelmed by emotion. Because I realize that this is our true power. People can try to take away our rights, people can try to rob us of our humanity. But they can never take our joy.

Are you ready to go? my friend asks.

Not yet, I say, as my heart fills with love. *Let's stay just a little longer.*

EPILOGUE

My fight is not over.

I am determined to become an Olympian. But I am still banned from the sport that I love. This awful act of discrimination still weighs so heavy on my heart. Because it's not just me who's been banned, it's every trans female track athlete with an Olympic dream. Some days I have trouble getting out of bed. Some days the darkness overwhelms my thoughts. Some days the pain is too great.

But whenever I feel hopeless, I always check in with myself, and tap into the deep well of love inside me. The love I have for God, for this sport, for all my supporters, and most importantly, the love I feel for every trans athlete who's come before me, every trans athlete who will come after, and every trans person out there fighting to live freely and openly. I hope that equality can arrive soon, that we can emerge from this awful era filled with anti-trans discrimination, hate, and violence. I believe in our community, and I know that we have the strength to fight, that we are brilliant, beautiful, and brave.

This book is different from most sports memoirs. Yes, I've had my triumphs. Yes, I achieved a historic win as the first openly trans person to win an NCAA Championship. But then my story was cut short. Because of the discrimination I face, I have been robbed of the opportunity to finish my story with the climactic victory, that moment my Olympian dream comes true, when I step on that podium, in front of the entire world, and collect my gold medal.

Sports narratives inspire, ignite, evoke emotions, and most importantly, transcend cultural boundaries and unite people from across the globe under a common passion. They should be about bringing people together, not tearing them apart. Allowing every human being to engage in sports fosters a more equitable world, where talents can flourish, stereotypes can be shattered, and dreams can be realized irrespective of one's race, sexuality, or gender.

No, this isn't your traditional sports story. But that's because the story of sport needs to change. It needs to make space for people like me. The story gets bigger, and more beautiful, when we allow everyone to compete. Which is why I'll keep training, keep fighting, and keep creating community with the people I love.

My story isn't over yet.

ACKNOWLEDGMENTS

I would like to thank Suzanne O'Neill, Jacqueline Young, and everyone at Grand Central Publishing who did such an incredible job in helping to bring this book to life. I would also like to thank Jonathan Parks-Ramage, Michael Signorelli, and David McFarland for supporting me during the journey to publication and beyond. I'm so grateful to the many people and organizations that have supported me throughout my life, including Lilian Baah, R. K. Russell, Kat Doughtery, Chari Robbins, president of Franklin Pierce University Kim Mooney, Paola Breña and her family, Lin Hill and her family, the Unique Woman's Coalition, the Los Angeles LGBT Center, PFLAG national headquarters, and Erica Allen and the New Hampshire chapter of PFLAG. And finally, to the Castor Newells, with love.

ABOUT THE AUTHOR

CeCé Telfer is a Jamaican American athlete who, in June 2019, became the first openly transgender woman to win a NCAA title. Telfer became an NCAA National Champion in the 400-meter hurdles event, which put her on the trajectory of becoming a US Olympic hopeful for the Tokyo Olympics 2021.

In June 2021, Telfer qualified for the 2021 US Olympic Team Trials—Track & Field in the 100-meter and 400-meter hurdles. Following her victory in the 400-meter hurdles, Telfer appeared on ESPN's *Outside the Lines* on June 13, 2019. Telfer has appeared on multiple national media outlets, including the *New York Times*, CNN International, ESPN, *Women's Health*, *People* magazine, the *Advocate*, and more, capturing global attention for her incredible story.